WOOD

IDENTIFICATION & USE

WOOD

IDENTIFICATION & USE
REVISED & EXPANDED

Terry Porter

GUILD OF
MASTER CRAFTSMAN
PUBLICATIONS

This edition published 2006 by
Guild of Master Craftsman Publications Ltd
Castle Place, 166 High Street, Lewes,
East Sussex BN7 1XU

First edition published 2004
Reprinted 2004, 2006

Text © Terry Porter 2004, 2006
© in the work GMC Publications 2006

ISBN-13: 978-1-86108-436-1
ISBN-10: 1-86108-436-6
(First edition: 1-86108-377-7)

To my late father, Don Porter, who introduced me to woody matters at a very early age, and whose tools I still use

684

Production Manager Hilary MacCallum
Managing Editor Gerrie Purcell
Project Editor Stephen Haynes
Chief Photographer Anthony Bailey
Managing Art Editor Gilda Pacitti
Designer Rebecca Mothersole

Set in Garamond and Glasgow

Colour origination by Altaimage
Printed and bound by Kyodo Printing (Singapore)

CONTENTS

INTRODUCTION

PREFACE

Building on the success of the first edition of *Wood: Identification & Use*, GMC Publications Ltd and I felt that there was scope for a substantially revised and expanded edition. This new edition presents a further 17 wood species described in full, and the introductory section provides an illustrated survey of wood figure and defects, together with updated information on the health hazards of working with certain woods. We have added some background information on several of the most important genera, and have taken the opportunity to review the text of every entry. There are many more photographs than before of artefacts made from wood. A particularly attractive addition is the new watercolour illustrations, prepared specially for this edition by Ann Biggs, which show the tree, leaf, flower and fruit of most of the species described.

We trust that woodworkers will continue to find the book a useful source of reference, and, in addition to that, an interesting read in itself.

Terry Porter
Cambridge, 2006

WOOD DIRECTORY

WHAT IS WOOD?

This may seem a very obvious question, but I suspect few people who use wood as a material in their trade or profession – or just eat their meals from a wooden table – stop to wonder about its composition. How is wood formed?

Like all green plants, trees make the materials for their growth in their leaves by the process of photosynthesis. This is a complex chemical reaction, obtaining its energy from sunlight, in which carbon dioxide from the air combines with water from the ground to form sugars. The reaction happens in the presence of chlorophyll, the green substance that gives leaves their colour. Tiny openings in the leaves, called stomata, allow carbon dioxide to pass directly into them.

Water has a long journey up from the roots into the leaves for the chemical reaction to take place. It is drawn in via root hairs, by the process of osmosis. Osmosis is the flow of one constituent of a solution through a membrane, while other constituents are blocked and unable to pass through. The water carries in solution salts and elements essential for life, including nitrogen, potassium and phosphorus, and smaller amounts of iron, magnesium, calcium, sodium, sulphur and other trace elements. The sap then flows under pressure through the **sapwood**, or **xylem**, to the tree's crown.

In addition to conducting sap to the crown of the tree, wood provides the mechanical strength needed to support the crown, and stores the food created by the leaves. This food is moved in solution from the leaves to all parts of the tree through the inner bark, or **phloem**, and is used to generate new growth.

New wood is produced by the **cambium**, a specialized cell layer situated between the xylem and the phloem. The cambium completely encloses the living parts of the tree, and during times of active growth the cambial cells divide to produce new wood cells on the inside and phloem cells on the outside. Consequently, new wood is laid down on the existing core of wood. If this growth is seasonal, as in more temperate regions or during periods of drought, then the familiar annual growth rings will form. If growth is continuous, which is generally the case in tropical regions, then usually no distinct growth rings are produced.

Two key functions – sap flow and food storage – take place in the most recently formed wood, the sapwood. However, as the tree continues to grow, the innermost layer of sapwood becomes so far removed from the active growth area that the tissue ceases to function and the cells undergo a chemical change, becoming **heartwood**. The new substances produced by this change may give the heartwood its distinctive colour and form.

Cell structure

Wood can be described as a natural material of a compound structure composed of cellulose fibres bonded together by lignin, a natural plastic. Without lignin, wood is a loose bundle of fibres; without cellulose, it is a porous sponge of lignin. In addition to the core constituents of cellulose and lignin, there is the water that is contained within the cells of the wood, and many trace elements and minerals.

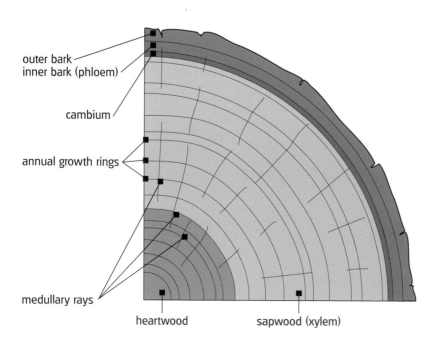

Section of a tree trunk, showing the various layers

outer bark
inner bark (phloem)

cambium

annual growth rings

medullary rays

heartwood

sapwood (xylem)

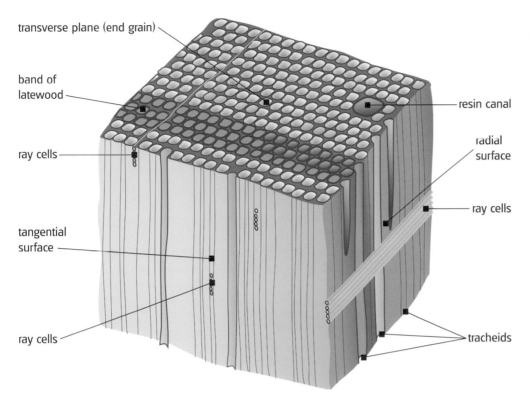

transverse plane (end grain)

Schematic diagram of the structure of a typical softwood

band of latewood

resin canal

radial surface

ray cells

ray cells

tangential surface

ray cells

tracheids

An outline understanding of the cell structure of wood helps the woodworker interpret the different properties of various woods and how they will work, bend, crush, and act in service. Unlike many other materials that are used for construction and furniture making, wood is hygroscopic – that is, it absorbs and releases moisture. The seasoning of wood is a drying process of which any woodworker should be aware (see pages 12–13); but it must always be borne in mind, when working wood and when planning a project, that wood can continue to absorb moisture at any time, especially if it is left unsealed. This will cause it to swell. The exterior wooden door that sticks in damp weather, but opens freely in dry weather, is a familiar example of this.

It is the cell structure of the wood that really determines the nature and extent of this movement. Softwoods have less complicated cell structures than hardwoods, so the two need to be discussed separately.

Softwood cell structure

Softwood has two basic types of cell. About 95% of them are the long fibres known as longitudinal **tracheids**, which are like tubes, but taper to a close at either end. However, there are small holes or 'pits' in each cell wall, which allow fluid to pass through the fibres. It is the size, and in particular the diameter, of these cells that determines the texture of the wood, and consequently its finishing qualities and smoothness. The other 5% are the **ray cells** that radiate outwards from the heart and serve to convey the sap horizontally.

Some softwoods, such as larch, Douglas fir and spruce (*Larix* spp., *Pseudotsuga menziesii*, *Picea* spp.), may also have resin canals, which can be an irritation to the woodworker, but serve as a protective system in the living tree, because they transport resin to injured or damaged parts of the tree.

Hardwood cell structure

Hardwood cell structure is much more complex than that of softwoods. There are more types of cells in hardwood, namely: vessel elements, wood fibres, parenchyma or storage cells, and rays, which are formed by parenchyma cells. The proportion of the different cells varies widely from wood to wood. The fibres in hardwoods tend to be shorter than those in softwoods.

Vessel elements are unique to hardwoods. They form a type of continuous pipeline in an end-to-end arrangement, which is used for transporting sap. They have relatively thin walls, and are fairly large in diameter. Their layout determines the nature of the wood, affecting its strength, drying, working qualities and appearance.

Fibres have closed ends and are the smallest in diameter of all the cells. They have thick walls and contribute to the strength of the wood.

The **parenchyma** or storage cells can be described as a hybrid of vessel and fibre cells, and their primary role is food storage. They form the medullary rays running radially to the tree's vertical axis. The rays can be very pronounced in some hardwoods, as in the broad medullary rays of European oak (*Quercus robur*), which give quartersawn wood its magnificent appearance. Depending on the wood, rays can be from one to 40 cells wide. Rays can also be the weak points in a wood: they can chip out in machining, suffer checks in drying, and aid the woodchopper when splitting logs.

Earlywood and latewood

As the names imply, **earlywood** is formed early in the growing season and **latewood** later in the season. Earlywood is less dense in structure, with large, thin-walled cells for good sap transportation, whereas latewood has smaller cells with thicker walls that serve to add strength to the tree. This pattern is characteristic of trees growing in temperate regions with distinct seasons, and produces the familiar annual rings of different densities.

Porous and nonporous woods

These terms can be a little confusing at first. They refer to the disposition of the vessel elements when cut transversely, as in cutting across the grain. The open end of the vessel is called a **pore**. Since softwoods do not have vessel elements, they are referred to as **nonporous**, whereas hardwoods are sometimes called **porous**. The uniformity of hardness in a wood depends on the distribution of vessels and fibres, and on their size and number. In some woods, such as ash, chestnut and oak (*Fraxinus*, *Castanea*, *Quercus* spp.), this varies, with the largest pores mostly in the earlywood, which results in uneven grain and often distinct patterns and figure. Such woods are referred to as **ring-porous**. In contrast, woods such as beech, birch and European sycamore (*Fagus* spp., *Betula* spp., *Acer pseudoplatanus*), in which the pores are distributed pretty evenly, are known as **diffuse-porous**. There is a further category, **semi-ring-porous**, which refers to woods where there is a difference in density between early and late growths, but it is not so pronounced and there is no clear zoning. American black walnut and butternut (*Juglans nigra*, *J. cinerea*) are good examples.

Growth rings and age

The life history of a tree is documented in the structure of its wood. Particularly if growth is seasonal, this can be seen clearly in the pattern of the growth rings. Slow-growing trees such as boxwood and yew (*Buxus sempervirens*, *Taxus baccata*) generally have very narrow rings, whereas trees that grow vigorously and rapidly, such as some pines and poplars (*Pinus*, *Populus* spp.), have much wider rings of up to ½in (13mm) a year. Environmental conditions are very important for tree growth. Trees that grow in parkland

Schematic diagram of the structure of a typical ring-porous hardwood

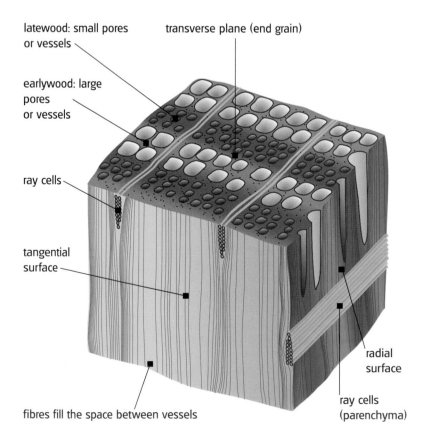

latewood: small pores or vessels

earlywood: large pores or vessels

ray cells

tangential surface

fibres fill the space between vessels

transverse plane (end grain)

radial surface

ray cells (parenchyma)

rather than in a forest tend to put on more growth, because there is less competition for water and nutrients; and soil fertility also plays an important role. In areas with short growing seasons, such as the Arctic or near the snow line, trees tend to have finer rings. Naturally, in periods of drought there will be less growth than in wet years. The rings are unlikely to be absolutely concentric and of even thickness. The prevailing wind and the slope of the ground can affect ring size and shape. The rings will show the experienced professional if and when the tree has been subject to fungal attack, or whether it has suffered fire damage. They will also indicate periods of vigorous or poor growth, and will show whether certain parts of the tree have ever been under tension.

In temperate regions, where growth is seasonal, the growth rings are usually clear; so a layer of less dense early growth and a layer of more dense late growth will add up to a year's total growth. The combination of these two layers makes up the **annual growth ring**, and from these a tree's age can be calculated, using the science of dendrochronology.

The botanical naming of wood

In the timberyard and workshop, woods are normally referred to by common or commercial names, such as Norway maple, brown oak or redwood. This is fine for everyday usage, but common names can vary from place to place, and confusion can occur. What is known as Sitka spruce in England can also be called silver spruce, tideland spruce and Menzies spruce in North America. Consequently, for absolute precision in identification, botanical classification is used. Every tree type has a botanical classification, which enables anyone, regardless of his or her mother tongue, to use the same mostly Latin- and Greek-based terminology for accurate identification. This system was

Conspicuous growth rings in a stump of leylandii (x *Cupressocyparis leylandii*)

developed by the Swedish botanist Carl Linnaeus, in his *Species Plantarum* of 1758. Linnaeus is regarded as the founder of modern taxonomy – the science of classifying animals and plants into related groups within a larger system.

The highest taxonomic division is the kingdom: living organisms are placed in either the animal or plant kingdoms. Then follows further classification into: division, subdivision, order, class, family, genus and species. (Garden plants may be further divided into subspecies and varieties, but this is only rarely of interest to woodworkers.) As an example, the full classification of European ash is set out at the foot of the page.

For general purposes the last three categories – family, genus and species – are all the woodworker needs to know. Taking the example of European ash, the family is Oleaceae, the genus is *Fraxinus* and the species is *excelsior*. So, European ash is termed *Fraxinus excelsior*, whereas American ash, which is of the same genus but a different species, is known as

The full classification of European ash is:

Kingdom	Division	Subdivision	Order	Family	Genus	Species
Plant	Spermatophyta	Angiospermae	Dicotyledonae	Oleaceae	*Fraxinus*	*excelsior*

Fraxinus americana. Only the genus and species are used in normal nomenclature, but it is sometimes useful also to know the family. In the alphabetical entries in this book, the family is given in brackets (parentheses) after the genus and species.

In scientific usage the genus and species are always given in italics, the genus with a capital letter, the species without. The genus name may be abbreviated to save space, provided it is given in full the first time it is mentioned. '*Fraxinus* sp.' stands for 'an unidentified species of the genus *Fraxinus*'; '*Fraxinus* spp.' means 'various species of the genus *Fraxinus*'.

Unfortunately, for one reason or another, botanical names are occasionally revised, with the result that some species may be known by more than one scientific name. The abbreviation 'syn.' (for 'synonym') is used to denote a name that is no longer current in scientific use, but may still be found in older or less scholarly sources.

Typical needle-like leaves of a softwood tree: European larch (*Larix decidua*)

By way of example, Alaska yellow cedar was originally classified as *Cupressus nootkatensis*, but its generic name was soon changed to *Chamaecyparis*, which remained the accepted name until very recently. In 2002, however, it was changed to *Xanthocyparis*, and in 2004 to *Callitropsis*. As far as we know, this is the accepted name at the time of going to press, but as there is no official clearing-house for name changes it is difficult to be sure.

We have tried to list species by their currently accepted names, but this is not always practicable: recently proposed names may take some time to be adopted by the scientific community, and may subsequently be declared invalid. In a few cases, therefore, we have thought it more helpful to list a species under its most widely used name, giving the newer name in brackets (parentheses). These entries will be reviewed in future editions.

Spermatophytes

Spermatophytes are all the plants that have seeds, and there are three main types that produce material of a woody consistency: the Gymnospermae (basically the conifers), that have naked seeds and produce softwoods, such as larch and hemlock (*Larix* spp., *Tsuga heterophylla*); and the two orders of Angiospermae, with encased seeds: Monocotyledonae and Dicotyledonae. The Monocotyledonae have one initial seed leaf, and include plants such as bamboo, palm and rattan, of tangential interest to the woodworker. The Dicotyledonae have two initial seed leaves and include the broad-leaved hardwoods, such as elm and mahogany (*Ulmus*, *Swietenia* spp.).

Hardwood and softwood

Although woods classified as softwoods are generally softer than those classified as hardwoods, this is only a partial guide and can mislead the unwary. The terms **softwood** and **hardwood** refer to a tree's botanical classification – Gymnospermae or Angiospermae, respectively – rather than the actual density of the wood. For this reason, the lightest of the commercial timbers – balsa (*Ochroma pyramidale*) – is classified as a hardwood, while a dense wood like yew (*Taxus baccata*) is classed as a softwood.

Typical broad, veined leaves of a hardwood tree: European beech (*Fagus sylvatica*) in early autumn colouring

FOREST TYPES

Timber used commercially is extracted from three basic forest types: coniferous, temperate broad-leaved and tropical broad-leaved. However, these three types do not always occur in isolation; some areas may have a mixture of forest types.

The softwoods come in great part from the coniferous forests of the arctic and subarctic zones of the northern hemisphere, and also from mountainous regions at lower latitudes.

Temperate hardwoods, which include both deciduous and evergreen species, are widespread in the northern hemisphere and often merge with the softwoods in more northerly areas. In the southern hemisphere the temperate hardwoods are found in Chile, New Zealand and Australia.

The bulk of the world's tropical hardwoods, which are largely evergreen, come from the rainforests of South and Central America, sub-Saharan Africa and South-East Asia.

Although there is continuing concern about deforestation in tropical areas, much more timber today is obtained from sustainable sources. Many countries, such as Britain, the United States, Canada and Sweden, have greatly increased the amount of forested land and timber reserves. Sweden now has twice the volume of standing timber compared with 1900. The Swedish forests produce 119 million cubic yards (91 million cubic metres) of timber each year, but only 76 million cubic yards (58 million cubic metres) are harvested, giving a net increase of more than 30% of timber stocks annually. The story is similar in Canada, with the volume of timber produced increasing by 77 million cubic yards (59 million cubic metres) a year after harvesting.

World distribution of forest types

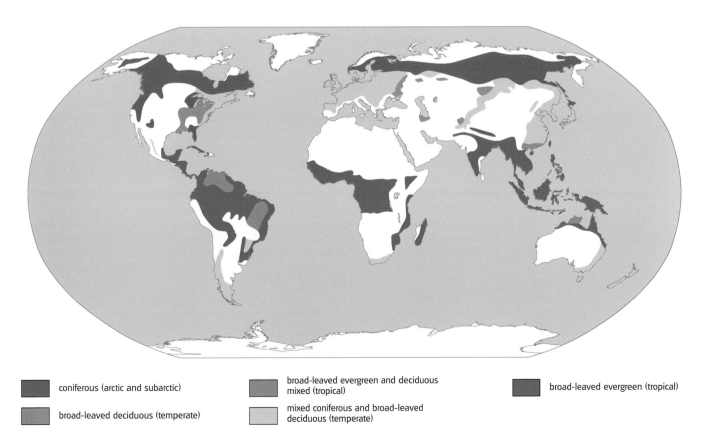

coniferous (arctic and subarctic)

broad-leaved deciduous (temperate)

broad-leaved evergreen and deciduous mixed (tropical)

mixed coniferous and broad-leaved deciduous (temperate)

broad-leaved evergreen (tropical)

SEASONING AND SAWING

The seasoning or drying of wood is a complex process, and varies according to the wood being dried, and its intended use. The dimensions of the stock, how it is stacked, and the local climate and humidity all have a bearing on the process. Wood is either air- or kiln-dried, or quite often a combination of both. Depending on the species and the size of the tree, it may be dried 'in the round' (as whole logs), or converted (sawn into boards) prior to drying.

Why do we season wood?

Most wood is worked in the dry state, for a variety of reasons. When wood is dry its dimensional stability is greatly increased. Also, its weight may be considerably reduced with the loss of water, which makes it more convenient to handle. Moreover, dry wood is not normally susceptible to sap stain and decay. Wood greatly increases in strength when dry: its stiffness, hardness and overall strength can increase by 50% compared to its green state.

How dry is dry?

Though we talk of wood being 'seasoned' or 'dry', it will still contain moisture, and also have the ability to absorb moisture. The quantity of moisture in a piece of wood, expressed as a percentage of the weight of the wood when completely dry, is known as its **moisture content (MC)**. This can range from 40% to as much as 200% in newly felled timber, and normally needs reducing to relatively stable levels before the wood can be worked. However, a piece of wood kiln-dried to 12% moisture content will not necessarily stay that way. It could dry out further if used in a dry, centrally heated office, or it could gain moisture if used in a humid or damp environment. So, how dry the wood needs to be depends largely on where it is finally going to be used. If a piece of furniture made from wood with a 15% moisture content is placed in a warm, dry office, it will probably split, whereas if the water content were 10% it would be fine. Surface treatments can also affect the movement of wood, by resisting or slowing the transfer of moisture between the wood and its surroundings.

Sawn boards stacked for air-drying

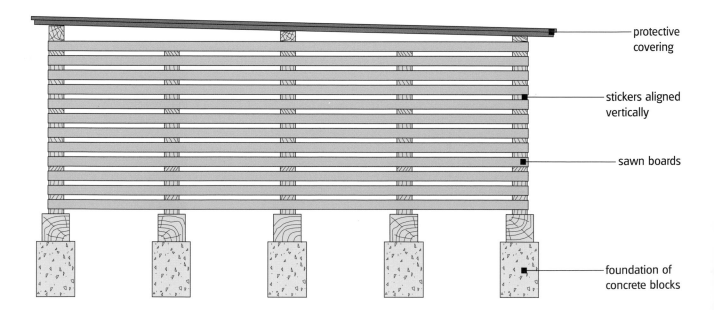

protective covering

stickers aligned vertically

sawn boards

foundation of concrete blocks

Air-drying

Normally, air-drying will only reduce the moisture content of wood – the normal equilibrium moisture content – to between 15 and 20%, but that can vary with climate and humidity. A basic rule of thumb is that hardwood needs one year of seasoning for every inch (25mm) of thickness, and softwood half that time.

Converted wood needs to be stacked very carefully and separated by stickers – battens of a neutral, non-staining wood – to allow the air to circulate between the boards. It is important that the stickers are kept in line vertically, because the boards must be prevented from warping or twisting as they dry. The thickness of the stickers can vary, depending on the optimum drying time for a particular species. Drying wood too quickly can often cause degrade such as checking and end splitting, but for some species slow drying will invite the development of decay and staining.

The top of the drying stack is normally protected with some form of sheeting to keep out rainwater and intense sunlight, and weighted down to prevent the top boards from warping. The sawyer will also consider the prevailing wind direction to allow a better airflow between the boards.

For amateurs or hobbyists who want to season their own timber in small quantities, all that is really required is a covered area with open or semi-open sides, that allows air circulation but protects the wood from rain and harsh, strong sunlight. My own wood is seasoned in a small barn with a pantile roof that lets in air freely, but protects the wood from the elements.

Kiln-drying

Drying wood in a heated chamber is very effective, but the subject is complex. Particular drying schedules have been devised for different woods, and the moisture content can be controlled very precisely. Heat is blown around the kiln chamber with fans, or simply circulates by convection. If care is not taken, the wood can dry too quickly with severe degrade; sometimes steam is added to the air in the kiln to slow down the drying rate. It is common for wood to be air-dried first down to about 20% moisture content, and then kiln-dried. If the moisture content is reduced to as little as 10%, then after kilning the wood must be kept in a dry environment; otherwise it will acquire moisture again (this is known as 'moisture pick-up'), and revert to the normal equilibrium for the location, giving a 15–20% moisture content.

A simple shelter for drying billets in the open air

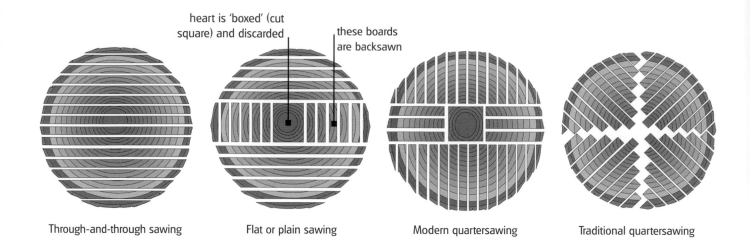

heart is 'boxed' (cut square) and discarded

these boards are backsawn

Through-and-through sawing

Flat or plain sawing

Modern quartersawing

Traditional quartersawing

Conversion

A log can be sawn or 'converted' in several different ways to make the best use of the wood – both to reduce waste as much as possible, and to obtain the best pieces for a particular purpose.

Through and through When a log is sawn 'through and through' or 'slab-sawn', it is simply sliced from end to end in line with the grain. Wastage is minimized, but the boards may be prone to warping.

Flat or plain sawing In this process the logs are predominantly cut through and through, except that the central part is cut at a tangent to the grain (riftsawn or backsawn) so as to avoid including the unstable heart of the tree.

Quartersawing In traditional quartersawing the log was cut like the spokes of a wheel radiating from the heart; this resulted in very stable boards but a considerable amount of wastage. Modern quartersawing uses a compromise method to reduce waste.

Radial, tangential and transverse surfaces

The appearance of the grain in the finished wood surface depends on how that surface was oriented in the tree before conversion. It is customary to distinguish between **radial** surfaces, cut at right angles to the annual rings; **tangential** surfaces, cut at a tangent to the rings; and **transverse** or **end-grain** surfaces, produced by sawing across the fibres.

Radial, tangential and transverse surfaces

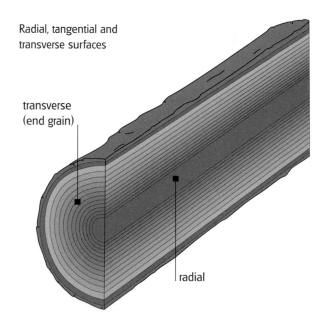

transverse (end grain)

radial

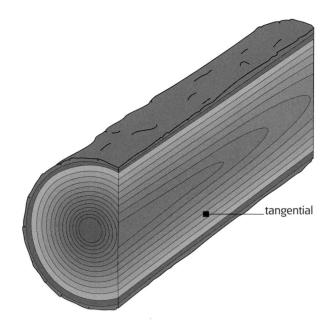

tangential

Veneer cuts

The art of cutting veneer involves making carefully judged cuts through the appropriate plane in order to expose the surface that has the most interesting characteristics and figure. Consequently, the cut chosen depends on the finished surface pattern required. There are six principal cuts used by veneer manufacturers:

Rotary or peeling cut The log is mounted centrally on a lathe and turned against a very sharp blade. It is rather like unwinding a roll of paper. As the cut follows the annual growth rings, strong variegated markings are produced. The veneer sheets can be very wide.

Flat or plain slicing The veneer is cut parallel to a line through the centre of the log. This can produce patterns such as cathedral figure (see page 17).

Quarter-slicing The wood is cut so that the growth rings strike the knife approximately at right angles, producing a series of stripes, which may be varied or straight depending on the wood.

Rift-cutting The rift-grain effect is brought about by cutting at an angle of around 15° off the quartered position. This cut is particularly favoured for oak (*Quercus* spp.), to take the best advantage of the medullary rays.

Half-round slicing A variation of rotary cutting in which segments of a log are mounted off-centre on a lathe, giving an interesting cut across the annual rings. This will reveal characteristics of both plain- and rotary-sliced veneers.

Lengthways slicing A board of flatsawn wood is passed over a stationary knife, which slices a sheet of veneer from the underside of the board. A variegated figure can be revealed in this way.

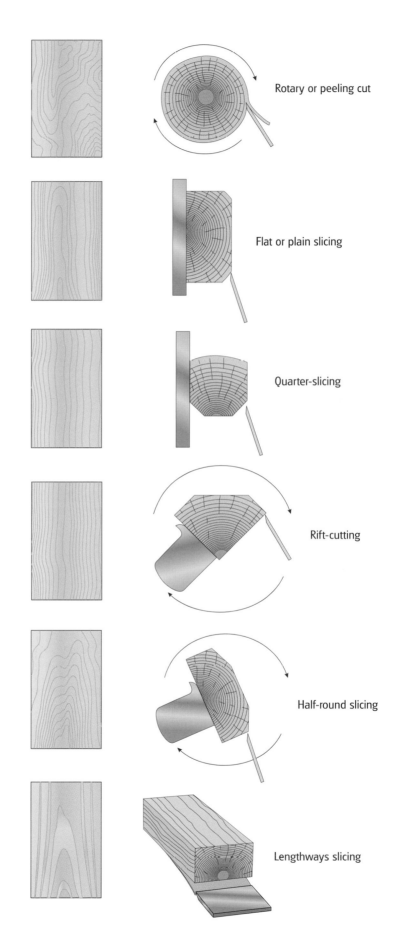

Rotary or peeling cut

Flat or plain slicing

Quarter-slicing

Rift-cutting

Half-round slicing

Lengthways slicing

FIGURE IN WOOD

The term 'figure' refers to characteristic, special or unusual markings that may be found on the surface of wood, typically on side-grain surfaces. Interesting figure comprises a combination of colour, grain, lustre and texture, and can be brought about by various features of that particular wood, from the peculiarities of its normal growth structure through to defects, abnormalities and extractives which may be present. Different types of figure may be revealed, depending on how the wood is cut (see pages 14–15). Quartersawn oak, for example, can reveal the beautiful ray figure known as 'silver grain', whereas if the same wood is flatsawn, the resulting surface is unlikely to have such interesting figure.

It is important not to confuse figure with grain. 'Grain' refers to the alignment of the wood elements in relation to the timber's longitudinal axis; the contrast in density and colour between early- and latewood in timbers such as Douglas fir *(Pseudotsuga menziesii)* is a grain characteristic. Grain is only one of the features that contribute to figure.

Although each piece of wood is unique, there are recognized patterns of figure markings that have become accepted – many of them associated with particular woods, such as bird's-eye figure in maple. The names of these patterns often give a good clue to their appearance. I have listed some key terms here, but specialists in figured veneers will use more.

Bird's-eye figure in hard maple (*Acer saccharum*)

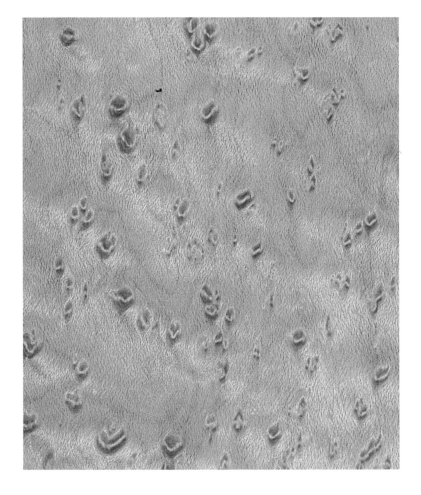

Burr (burl) on an elm trunk (*Ulmus* sp.)

Burr (burl) of brown mallee (*Eucalyptus* sp.)

Cutting through the centre of the crotch produces this classic **crotch** figure

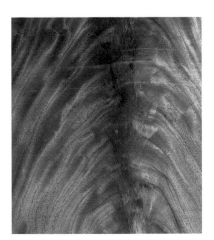

Cat's-paw figure on a chest of drawers in oak (*Quercus* sp.)

angel step	a staircase-like curly figure caused by cutting across the stump or butt sections of a tree; frequently found in walnut (*Juglans* spp.), but can also occur in ash (*Fraxinus* spp.) and maple (*Acer* spp.).
bee's wing	a small-scale, very tight mottle figure, found in East Indian satinwood (*Chloroxylon swietenia*), mahogany (*Swietenia* spp.), bubinga (*Guibourtia demeusei*) and some eucalypts. **Block mottle** is similar, but larger in scale.
bird's eye	a pattern of small, rounded, lustrous spots, found almost exclusively in hard maple (*Acer saccharum*).
blister	a figure resembling billowing clouds, or on occasion bubble-like forms; the surface looks blistered, even when perfectly smooth. An uneven contour in the growth rings can create this effect when a log is rotary- or half-round-cut for veneer (see page 15). It is similar to **pommelé**, but with sparser, larger figure.
burr (burl)	a wartlike, deformed growth, normally on the root or trunk, but sometimes on the branches. These usually form as the result of some injury to or infection under the bark, or an unformed bud that does not grow properly. As the tree grows the burrs can grow with it, causing the surrounding growth wood to be twisted or wavy, which results in very beautiful figure. Burr figure is often found in European elm (*Ulmus* spp.), ash (*Fraxinus* spp.), poplar (*Populus* spp.), California redwood (*Sequoia sempervirens*) and walnut (*Juglans* spp.), amongst others.
butt	a wavy, rippled pattern caused by grain distortion where the root joins the stump. American walnut (*Juglans nigra*) can produce very interesting butt figure, which is exploited in stumpwood veneer.
button	a pattern of buttons or flakes against a straight-grained background, revealed when wood with large medullary rays is quartersawn to expose the hard, shiny rays. Found particularly in American sycamore (*Platanus occidentalis*), white oak (*Quercus alba*) and lacewood (*Platanus* spp.). See also **flake**.
cathedral	a series of stacked or inverted V-shapes; this can occur in plain-sliced veneer.
cat's paw	a variety of pippy or burr wood which looks as though a cat has walked over it and left footprints; found particularly in oak (*Quercus* spp.) and cherry (*Prunus* spp.).
crossfire	any marking that goes across the grain in a rolling curl, such as in **fiddleback** and **mottle**. It can look very spectacular.
crotch	a typically Y-shaped pattern formed where a branch joins the trunk of a tree. **Burning bush**, **feather**, **flame**, **plume** and **rooster-tail** are all varieties of crotch figure. Mahogany and walnut veneers (*Swietenia*, *Juglans* spp.) are the best sources.
curly	contortions in grain direction give the appearance of undulating waves as they reflect light differently. Curly figure is particularly common in maple and birch (*Acer*, *Betula* spp.). A staircase-like curl is often referred to as **angel steps** (see above), and a rolling curl as a form of **crossfire**.

Sideboard with panels of **pippy** oak (*Quercus* sp.)

Bowl in **quilted** soft maple (*Acer saccharinum*)

fiddleback	a form of curly figure exposed by quartersawing, giving very straight grain with almost perpendicular curls from edge to edge. The name derives from the use of this figure for the backs of violins, which are traditionally made of European sycamore (*Acer pseudoplatanus*). It is not common but can be found in maple (*Acer* spp.), African mahogany (*Khaya* spp.), makoré (*Tieghemella heckelii*), blackbean (*Castanospermum australe*) and koa (*Acacia koa*).
flake, fleck or **ray fleck**	a lustrous effect found in lacewood (European plane, *Platanus hybrida*), oak (*Quercus* spp.) and sycamore (*Acer pseudoplatanus*), when the wood is cut parallel or nearly parallel to the medullary rays, thus exposing some parts of the rays.
flame	see **crotch**.
flower grain	a diagonal ripple pattern, occurring in small, irregular patches, sometimes found in European spruce (*Picea abies*).
mottle	another type of cross-grain figure, where spiral interlocked grain combines with wavy grain to give a blotchy, wrinkled effect. The pattern can be random, or in something of a chessboard form (**block mottle**), and a finer, smaller form is known as **bee's wing** (see above). Mottle figure can occur in mahoganies (*Swietenia* spp.), sapele (*Entandrophragma cylindricum*), bubinga (*Guibourtia demeusii*) and koa (*Acacia koa*), amongst others.
peanut shell	some woods that are susceptible to quilted or blister figure can be rotary-cut to produce a peanut figure, which has some similarity to a **quilted** or **pommelé** figure. The wood surface appears bumpy and pitted, even when flat. Peanut-shell figure is found particularly in Japanese ash (*Fraxinus mandschurica*), but can occur in other woods.
pippy	a random scattering of numerous little spots; typical in yew (*Taxus baccata*) and sessile oak (*Quercus petraea*).
pommelé	a pattern of small circles or ovals that sometimes overlap each other; it has been likened to a puddle surface during light rain. Resembling a finer form of **blister** figure, it is common in some African woods such as bubinga (*Guibourtia demeusii*), African mahogany (*Khaya ivorensis*) and sapele (*Entandrophragma cylindricum*).
quilted	a pillow-like, three-dimensional effect caused when an uneven or wavy interlocking pattern, forming a bumpy surface on the log, is rotary- or half-round-cut. It is a larger, more emphatic form of **pommelé** or **blister** figure.
ribbon stripe	an effect resembling a slightly twisted ribbon, found in quartersawn mahogany (*Swietenia* spp.) and sapele (*Entandrophragma cylindricum*).
ripple	any figure with a ripple-like appearance, such as **fiddleback** (see above).
roe or **roey figure**	short, broken stripe or ribbon figure in certain quartersawn hardwoods, arising from interlocked grain.
roll	a pattern of large rolls or twists that can run diagonally; if bookmatched (see page 22), the resulting pattern is known as **herringbone**.
silver grain	another name for lustrous ray fleck on quartersawn timber, especially oak (*Quercus* spp.).
swirl	a gentler type of **crotch** figure, where the grain swirls, meanders and sometimes appears to fold in on itself; common in cherry (*Prunus* spp.), mahogany (*Swietenia* spp.), maple (*Acer* spp.) and walnut (*Juglans* spp.).

DEFECTS IN WOOD

Being a natural material, exposed to differing and unpredictable conditions as it grows, wood often develops features which are undesirable to the woodworker. The most important of these are listed below. Remember, however, that what is a defect to one worker may be a 'feature' to another. Fungal stains such as spalting, for example, may be considered attractive, provided they do not weaken the wood too much for its intended purpose. Adventurous and experienced woodturners and furniture makers may enjoy using wood with splits, bark inclusions and other features which are normally avoided.

bark inclusion or **pocket**	a piece of bark wholly or partially enclosed within the wood, which is weakened as a result. **bark**
blackheart	abnormal black or brown discoloration of the heartwood, which is not necessarily decayed. Ash (*Fraxinus* spp.) can be prone to this.
blue stain, sap stain or **sapwood stain**	a bluish or light grey discoloration of sapwood, brought about by the growth of dark-coloured fungi in the interior and on the surface of the wood.
bow	the form of warping in which a board is bent or bowed lengthwise.
brittleheart	heartwood that snaps easily across the grain as a result of compression failure in fibres during growth.
canker	a disease-damaged area of a tree, usually caused by bacteria or fungus .
case-hardening	a defect of seasoning, where the surface of the wood dries faster than the core. This causes permanent stresses and 'set' (deformation) that are released when the wood is cut, resulting in severe distortion.
check	a longitudinal crack that does not go through the whole log or plank; usually caused by too-rapid seasoning.
chipped grain	torn grain due to poor machining or finishing.
collapse	a caved-in cell structure, caused during drying, giving a shrivelled or irregular appearance.
common furniture beetle	*Anobium punctatum*, commonly known as 'woodworm', one of the most widespread insect pests. The damage is done by the grub, which can live in the wood for up to two years before emerging as an adult.
compression wood	see **reaction wood**.
crack	a large radial check, caused by tangential shrinkage being greater than radial shrinkage.
crook	similar to bow, but curving in the plane of the thin edge, rather than the wide side of a board. Also, a tree typified by a sharp bend in the stem.

This adult **common furniture beetle** (shown approximately 6 times life size) died while emerging from an insecticide-treated log of English elm (*Ulmus procera*)

cupping	bending as a result of shrinkage across the width of a board.
cup shake	a split caused by lack of cohesion between the annual rings.
death-watch beetle	*Xestobium rufovillosum*, a beetle that is about $^1/_4$in (6mm) long and very destructive to structural beams. The adults make a ticking noise, hence the name.
end check	the separation of wood cells along the grain at the end of a piece of wood, caused by uneven drying.
gum, **sap** and **pitch**	resinous liquids found on the surface or in pockets in the interior of certain woods.
gum canal	an intercellular cavity, found in woods that may contain gum, latex or resins.
heart pith	the soft, spongy heart of a tree, which may appear on the surface of sawn timber.
heart shake	a split that starts at the heart of a log.
honeycombing	a network of checks in the interior of timber, not seen on the outside.
knot	a section through a branch or twig which became embedded in the tree as the trunk continued to grow around it. Several types may be distinguished:
branched knot	two or more knots coming from a common centre.
dead, **encased** or **loose knot**	formed when the trunk grew round a dead branch. The knot is surrounded by a ring of bark and is often decayed. It may fall out, leaving a **knot hole**.
live, **intergrown** or **tight knot**	the base of a living branch, surrounded by growth rings and firmly fixed in the surrounding wood.
pin knot	a knot whose diameter does not exceed $^1/_2$in (13mm).
spike or **splay knot**	a knot which has been sawn lengthwise when the wood was converted. It may be tight at the base, but loose near the surface of the log.
lyctid borer	see **powder-post beetle**.
machine burn	burn marks on the surface of converted wood as a result of poor sawing or machining.
pitch pocket	a typically lens-shaped space, containing liquid or solid resin, that extends parallel to the annual growth rings in certain coniferous woods.
powder-post beetle	a beetle (*Lyctus* spp.) which attacks the sapwood of hardwoods with large pores, including ash (*Fraxinus* spp.) and oak (*Quercus* spp.).
reaction wood	abnormal wood formed under the stress of compression or tension during growth, such as on the underside of a branch or leaning trunk (**compression wood**), or the upper side of a branch near the trunk (**tension wood**). The cells are typically shorter and thicker-walled, with spiral markings. The wood tends to be of a poorer quality and not desirable for commercial purposes.
ring check, **ring failure** or **ring shake**	a separation of the wood fibres parallel to and between annual rings in the growing tree.

Cross section of a log showing different kinds of **shake**

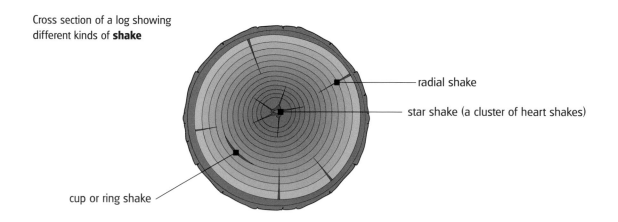

radial shake

star shake (a cluster of heart shakes)

cup or ring shake

Turned bowl in **spalted** beech (*Fagus sylvatica*)

Wormholes in beech (*Fagus sylvatica*)

rot	a generic term for several types of fungal decay, such as:
brown rot	the cellulose and associated carbohydrates are attacked, but not the lignin. This usually gives a light brown stain and a friable texture. At an advanced stage the wood will split along rectangular planes as it shrinks; this is referred to as **cubical rot**.
butt rot	a common disease in which fungal infection degrades the roots and stem of a living tree. Frequently caused by the fungus *Heterobasidion annosum*.
dry rot	a general term applying to any crumbly rot, but particularly one in which the wood is easily crushed into a powder; typically caused by *Serpula lacrymans* fungus.
soft rot	this occurs in the outer layers of wood in very wet conditions, such as in boats. The secondary cell walls are attacked by microfungi that destroy the cellulose content. Typically caused by the fungus *Chaetomium globosum*.
wet rot	usually occurs in persistently damp conditions, and can be caused by a wide variety of fungi.
white rot	a variety of fungus that attacks lignin and cellulose, creating a spongy, stringy mass, which is usually whitish, but may have shades of light brown, yellow or tan.
sap or **sapwood stain**	see **blue stain**.
shake	a split in wood, normally parallel to the growth rings.
skip	an area of a board that the planer has failed to surface.
spalting	partial fungal decay that often causes discoloration or fine irregular lines. It can be attractive for decorative turnery and the like, but the wood has lost its strength qualities.
twist	a type of warping in which the ends twist in opposing directions.
wane or **waney edge**	the presence of the outer surface of the trunk on the edge or corner of a board; bark may be present, or part of the edge may be missing.
warping	any deviation from a true or flat surface. This can include bowing, crooking, cupping, twisting or a combination of these.
wormhole	any hole made by boring insects or their larvae.

GLOSSARY OF WOOD TERMINOLOGY

Note that terms which have already been defined in the sections on **Figure** and **Defects** are not repeated here.

Like every discipline, the world of wood has its own terminology, which is really quite extensive and can vary in different parts of the English-speaking world, and even from workshop to workshop. Common names for woods, in particular, can differ greatly from place to place. Australian white birch (*Schizomeria ovata*) is also known as crab apple, humbug and squeaker in Australia, and bea bea, malafelo and hambia in the Solomon Islands. An American's 'lumber' is an English person's 'timber' or 'wood'. Here is a brief list of key 'woody' terminology.

air-dried or **air-seasoned**	naturally seasoned in the open air, and generally protected from the sun and rain.
angiosperms (Angiospermae)	botanical name for all plants whose seeds are carried inside an ovary, including what are commonly referred to as **hardwoods**: those trees which are broad-leaved, flowering and fruit-bearing. Most are deciduous.
annual or **growth rings**	concentric rings of wood added yearly to the growing tree in temperate zones.
arboreal	related to or connected with trees.
arboriculture	the management of trees, or groups of trees, for their amenity value.
adult or **mature wood**	wood produced when the tree is already established; it will typically have a relatively constant cell size, stable physical behaviour and structural patterns that are well developed.
back cut	the final cut when felling a tree, which is made on the opposite side to the direction of fall.
backsawn	sawn so that the growth rings are inclined at less than 45° to the wide face. A backsawn log is converted in such a way as to provide the maximum number of cuts tangential to the growth rings; see illustration on page 14.
bast	the soft, fibrous tissue between the bark and the inner cell structure.
beating up	replacing trees that have died soon after planting.
billets	small-diameter round timber cut to length.
blaze	to mark a tree with paint or by slicing off bark with an axe, either to earmark it for felling or to delineate boundary lines.
board foot	144 cubic inches of wood; for example, a board 12 x 12 x 1in. Used chiefly in North America; elsewhere, cubic feet or cubic metres are preferred.
bole	the part of the trunk or stem of a tree from above the root butt to the first branch or limb, normally of timber size over 8in (200mm) in diameter.
bookmatching	the mirror-image effect obtained, especially in veneering, when adjacent sheets from a **flitch** are opened in the manner of a book, the back of one sheet being matched to the face of the next.
box the heart	to leave a square piece at the heart when converting a log.
breast height	the point at which the girth or diameter of a standing tree is measured on the highest side; dbh = diameter at breast height. Breast height is normally regarded as 4ft 6in (1.37m).
bucking	cutting trees into shorter lengths such as logs and cordwood.
bummer	a truck for hauling logs.
butt	the base of a tree.
butt cut	the first cut above the stump of a tree.
butt log	the first log cut above the stump of a tree.
cambium	the layer of cells in a tree that divides to produce new tissue.
cheese block	a wedge to stop a log from rolling.
chromated copper arsenate (CCA)	the most frequently used preservative chemical for pressure-treating timber.
clean	free from knots.

Bookmatched pieces of Brazilian rosewood (*Dalbergia nigra*) for a guitar back

Butt of European sycamore (*Acer pseudoplatanus*) with incipient spalting

clear	free from visible defects.
cleft	split with an axe or similar tool rather than sawn (see also **riven**).
clinometer	an instrument used for measuring slopes and the height of trees.
close-grained	having narrow growth rings.
conversion	sawing logs into smaller sections in preparation for use.
conversion loss	the difference between the volume of a standing tree and the volume of the boards cut from it. This is normally given as a percentage of the standing volume. Typical range: 8–20%.
coppicing	the practice of cutting down a woody stem to ground level to encourage growth of several stems from one root system. It is used with trees such as ash (*Fraxinus* spp.), Spanish chestnut (*Castanea sativa*), hazel (*Corylus avellana*) and willow (*Salix* spp.), whose stems are used for commercial purposes such as basket and hurdle making.
cordwood	low-quality, small-diameter wood suitable for pulp, firewood or chips.
corestock	the core layer or layers of wooden strips, plies, woodchips or particles used in manufacturing man-made boards such as blockboard, plywood and particleboard.
crosscut	to cut wood across the grain.
crown	the uppermost branches and foliage of a tree.
crown-sawn	a less common term for **flatsawn**.
debarker	a sawmill machine that removes tree bark by chipping or grinding prior to sawing.
diameter at breast height (dbh)	see **breast height**.
dicotyledons (Dicotyledonae)	an order of plants within the Angiospermae that have two cotyledons or seed leaves. All hardwood trees are dicotyledons.
diffuse-porous	(of a hardwood) having pores that are typically of uniform size throughout the growth ring.
earlywood	the first part of the annual ring, which is laid down in the spring, and typically has lower density and larger cells.
end grain	the grain shown on a **crosscut** surface, revealing the cut ends of the wood fibres.
end-rearing	storing boards for seasoning vertically instead of horizontally; this can help reduce fungal staining, and is recommended particularly for European sycamore (*Acer pseudoplatanus*).
equilibrium moisture content (EMC)	Wood is hygroscopic and can therefore absorb or lose moisture at any time. When no water is being lost or given back, the moisture content is said to be in equilibrium. EMC is not a constant, but varies with temperature.
extractives	substances, such as resins, deposited in the **heartwood** that give it its distinctive colour and odour. Extractives may affect the wood's compressive strength, hardness, permeability, and resistance to decay and insect attack.
exudates	secretions such as gum, oil, latex or resin on the surface of timber. The secretion of exudates can sometimes be exacerbated by kilning in some species.
flatsawn	cut tangentially to the growth rings; also referred to as **crown-sawn**.

(Right)
Interlocked grain in sapele (*Entandrophragma cylindricum*). Each change of colour or lustre represents a change in grain orientation

(Far right)
Detail of a console table in oak (*Quercus* sp.), stainless steel and glass. The oak has been scrubbed, stained with iron salts and **limed** to accentuate the grain

flitch	a log or piece of wood prepared for conversion, especially into veneers. Also, a pack of about 500 pieces of veneer.
forwarder	a specialist tractor that extracts timber lifted clear of the ground.
fuming	a process for darkening woods that contain tannic acid by exposure to ammonia fumes in an airtight container before final finishing. The longer the exposure, the darker the wood will become. Due to its high level of tannic acid, oak (*Quercus* spp.) is especially suitable.
genus	a group of closely related plants, sufficiently distinct not to interbreed. A genus normally consists of several species. The plural of *genus* is *genera*.
girdling	the practice of cutting away the bark around the circumference of a tree before felling, so as to partially kill the tree and reduce moisture content.
girth tape	a tape used to measure the diameter of a tree. The tape is placed round the girth but is calibrated in such a way that it gives a measurement of the diameter.
grain	the arrangement of the fibres that make up the wood, or the pattern produced by these fibres on the surface of the wood. Many types of grain pattern are distinguished, such as fine, coarse, plain, interlocked, etc. The word *grain* tends to refer to the regular pattern of the wood, whereas *figure* (see pages 16–18) refers to interesting irregularities.
granny	an old tree – often European larch (*Larix decidua*) or Scots pine (*Pinus sylvestris*) – surrounded by young trees growing vigorously.
green tonne	a unit of measurement of freshly felled timber before any drying.
green wood	freshly cut wood that is not seasoned or dried and is still 'wet'.
gymnosperms (Gymnospermae)	the conifers and related plants, whose seeds are not contained within an ovary; they have needle-like leaves, and produce the softwoods.
hardwood	wood from a broad-leaved (dicotyledonous) tree – usually harder than softwood, but not always.
harvester	a forestry machine that cuts a tree from its roots, de-branches it and then cuts it to preset lengths.
heartwood or **true wood**	the non-functioning xylem tissue toward the centre of the trunk, which provides the hardest and most durable part of the timber.
hewn timber	timber finished to size with an axe or adze.
hypsometer	an instrument used from ground level to measure the height of trees. A **clinometer** is a type of hypsometer.
interlocked grain	grain that exhibits periodic changes in the direction and pitch of the fibres, often producing a ribbon-like figure.
juvenile wood	wood produced in the first years of growth, up to about five years. Juvenile wood is normally of lower strength, has thinner cell walls and higher lignin content than mature wood.
kerf	the cut made by a saw blade; also, the width of this cut.

Horse chestnut (*Aesculus hippocastanum*), one year after **pollarding**

A **palmate** leaf

Lammas growth	a second spurt of growth in late summer in some tree species, such as oak (*Quercus* spp.).
latewood	the part of the annual ring formed later in the growing season, which has smaller cells and is denser, usually resulting in darker rings.
liming	the filling of an open-grained wood – typically oak or ash (*Quercus*, *Fraxinus* spp.) – with lime slurry, which leaves a milky-white colour in the filled pores for decorative effect. Nowadays 'liming wax' is usually substituted.
longitudinal shrinkage	shrinkage along the grain, resulting in the shortening of the wood during drying; this is usually minimal.
mallee	a shrubby form of eucalyptus (*Eucalyptus* spp.) that grows in the desert regions of Australia.
medullary rays	vertical ribbons or sheets of tissue formed radially across the annual rings, which are very distinctive in some woods, such as oak (*Quercus* spp.), and barely visible in others.
moisture content (MC)	The moisture content of wood decreases dramatically during seasoning. The completely dry (oven-dry) weight of a given species is a constant, and the moisture content of the wood at any given time can be expressed as a percentage of this constant. The formula: MC = weight of water present in sample ÷ oven-dry weight of sample x 100.
movement	a general term to describe shrinkage and distortion due to stresses or water loss in the wood.
old growth	forest or wood with trees regenerated by natural succession, containing a substantial number of old trees and some dead wood. Old growth is often preferred to less mature timber, but there are negative ecological results of harvesting too much old-growth wood.
oven-dry weight	the weight of a piece of wood which has been dried in a kiln until there is no further weight loss.
palmate leaves	leaves whose lobes are arranged like the fingers of a hand.
pedunculate	(of fruit) borne on a stalk.
phloem	the inner bark, used for food transport in the growing tree.
pith	the soft core in the centre of a tree trunk, branch or twig.
plainsawn	same as **flatsawn**.
pluck-out or **pull-out**	a blemish in wood that has been caused by a tool pulling a clump of fibres away from the body of the wood; this can occur with part-decayed or decayed wood.
pollarding	the lopping of tree branches at head height or above, either to encourage shoots to form higher up a tree out of reach of browsing animals, or simply to reduce the size of the tree.
prime	the best quality of timber.
pulpwood	wood suitable for manufacturing paper.
quartersawn	cut radially from the bark to the heart, often producing ribbon figure.
refractory wood	wood that is difficult to dry, machine, process using conventional methods, and impregnate with preservatives.

Distinct growth rings in a **ring-porous** hardwood: Japanese ash (*Fraxinus mandschurica*)

regrowth	trees that have grown within a forest after the older or original trees have been felled or removed.
ring-porous	having more conspicuous pores in the earlywood than in the latewood.
rip	to cut along the grain.
rip cut	a cut made parallel to the grain.
riven	similar to **cleft**, but refers specifically to the splitting of wood into small sections such as traditional plasterers' laths.
roundwood	small branches and logs.
sanitation cutting	removing diseased or damaged stems to prevent the spread of insects or disease.
sapwood	the relatively soft and perishable wood from the outer part of the trunk; a non-technical term for **xylem**.
sawlogs	timber of typically $5^1/2$in (140mm) diameter or more at the small end, which can be sawn economically into planks and boards.
sensitizer	any wood (or other substance) which, after initial exposure, will invariably cause an allergic reaction in the user when encountered again. This may take the form of dermatitis, other skin disorders, or respiratory and associated problems. Yew (*Taxus baccata*), for example, can be a sensitizer for some woodworkers.
silviculture	the cultivation of forest trees to produce wood products.
skidder	a tractor used to drag logs out of the forest.
snedding	removing branches from a felled tree.
softwood	wood from a coniferous (gymnosperm) tree – usually softer than hardwood, but not always.
species	a subdivision of a genus; a group of individual plants of the same kind that share many of the same characteristics. The genus *Quercus* encompasses all types of oak, whereas *Quercus robur* is the name of one particular species of European oak.
sticks or **stickers**	pieces of wood of uniform size placed between stacked boards to aid drying and give support. They should be of a neutral wood that will not stain the boards.
sweep	a long, gentle, natural bend in a log or tree.
tangential shrinkage	shrinkage at right angles to the grain, that could cause cupping on flatsawn wood.
wolf or **wolf tree**	a larger than average, older tree with a spreading crown and limited timber value, though often of great value to wildlife.
woolly grain	a woolly or fuzzy surface with frayed, rather than cleanly cut, fibres after machining. It can occur with **tension wood**, or can be a feature of certain species.
xylem	the living tissue in the outer layers of the tree trunk, serving to transport sap and store food; known as **sapwood** when converted to timber.

TOXIC WOODS

Although wood looks and feels such a beautiful and safe material, it really can put your health at risk, and in extreme situations actually kill you – not because of accidents when felling trees, or unsafe operation of woodworking machinery, but because of the toxic effects of the wood itself.

Excessive exposure to certain kinds of wood dust can cause ailments including bronchial asthma, rhinitis (a constantly runny nose), alveolitis allergica (hypersensitivity pneumonia), ODTS (organic dust toxic syndrome), bronchitis, allergic dermatitis and conjunctivitis. Nasal cancers are rare, but they can occur, especially to those working a long time in the furniture industry. Cancer of the upper respiratory tract can be caused by many kinds of wood dust, especially beech and oak (*Fagus, Quercus* spp.).

Some woods, such as yew (*Taxus* spp.), can act as sensitizers. When first used, there is no reaction, but after repeated exposure the user may become sensitized so that each contact with the wood produces an almost immediate allergic reaction. Normally this is irreversible, the only logical outcome being to avoid using that particular wood. Other sensitizers include beech, mahogany, sequoia or redwood, willow and teak (*Fagus, Swietenia, Sequoia, Salix, Tectona* spp.). If you are allergic to aspirin, be cautious of willow and birch (*Salix, Betula* spp.), as they can have a similar effect.

Micro-organisms in bark and fungus can induce bronchial asthma, rhinitis and allergic dermatitis. In North America, maple bark strippers' disease is due, apparently, to the mould *Cryptostroma corticale* that grows between the sapwood and the bark of maple and birch trees (*Acer, Betula* spp.). This can cause severe respiratory allergies. Spalted maple is known to cause respiratory problems, and I have come across one case where a turner developed pneumonia from it, and eventually had to give up work as a result.

Some people are more susceptible than others, and if you are a smoker the risk of illness from inhalation of wood dust is greatly increased.

Subtropical and tropical woods noted for allergic effects include western red cedar (*Thuja plicata*), sequoia or redwood (*Sequoia sempervirens*), obeche (*Triplochiton scleroxylon*), cocobolo (*Dalbergia retusa*) and mansonia (*Mansonia altissima*). Woods from temperate climes tend to produce a less extreme effect; those which should be treated with caution include larch, walnut, oak, beech, yew and pine (*Larix, Juglans, Quercus, Fagus, Taxus, Pinus* spp.).

Precautions

All woodworkers should take precautions to minimize the risk of allergic reactions, particularly from wood dust and extractives such as tannin and resins. Some useful guidelines are:

- Work in a well-ventilated area.
- Wash and shower frequently.
- Wash work clothes frequently.
- Avoid particularly toxic woods.
- Wear gloves if necessary.
- Use a powered respirator helmet, or at least a face mask.
- Install effective dust extraction in addition to the mask or respirator.
- Avoid working unseasoned wood.
- Do not use known sensitizing woods for such things as handles.
- Be especially cautious with dust from bonded wood products such as plywood and MDF.

Woods and their hidden health risks

The chart which follows, compiled from a variety of reliable sources, shows a wide selection, but by no means all, of the toxic and allergic effects of wood. It should be used as a guideline only. Woods vary from subspecies to subspecies, and the type of soil a tree grows in can affect its toxicity. There are other woods not shown in the chart which can also be toxic, and dust from *any* source in quantity is dangerous if breathed in.

WOOD	ADVERSE REACTION	TOXIC PARTS
Balsam fir *Abies balsamea*	Sensitizer; skin and eye irritation	Leaves, bark
Mulga *Acacia aneura*	Irritation to nose, throat, eyes; headaches, vomiting	Dust
Brigalow *Acacia harpophylla*	Dermatitis; irritation to nose, eyes, throat, groin	Bark dust, wood dust
Australian blackwood *Acacia melanoxylon*	Dermatitis, asthma, nose and throat irritation; sensitizer	Dust, wood
European maple *Acer campestre*	Sensitizer; decrease in lung function	Dust
Bigleaf maple *Acer macrophyllum*	Dermatitis, rhinitis, allergic bronchial asthma	Dust
Boxelder *Acer negundo*	Dermatitis, rhinitis, allergic bronchial asthma	Dust
Soft maple *Acer rubrum*, *A. saccharinum*	May affect lung function	Dust
Hard maple *Acer saccharum*, *A. nigrum*	May affect lung function	Dust
Yellow buckeye *Aesculus flava*	Nuts and twigs contain aescin, a cytotoxin	Nuts, twigs
Afzelia/doussié *Afzelia* spp.	Dermatitis, respiratory problems, nose and throat irritation	Dust
Albizia *Albizia (Paraserianthes) falcataria*	Irritation to nose, eyes, alimentary tract; dermatitis; nausea	Dust
Kokko *Albizia lebbeck*	Irritant to eyes, nose and throat	Dust
Red siris *Albizia toona*	Dermatitis, nosebleeds, conjunctivitis, giddiness	Dust
Alder *Alnus* spp.	Dermatitis, rhinitis, bronchial problems	Dust
Cashew *Anacardium occidentale*	Sensitizer; blisters from sap; dermatitis	Dust, wood, sap
Peroba rosa *Aspidosperma peroba*	Skin irritation, headache, nausea, sweating, respiratory problems, fainting, drowsiness, stomach cramps, weakness, blisters	Dust, wood
Gonçalo alves *Astronium fraxinifolium*	Sensitizer; dermatitis, irritation to skin and eyes	Wood, dust
Gaboon/okoumé *Aucoumea klaineana*	Irritant to skin and eyes; asthma, coughing	Dust, wood
Tatajuba *Bagassa guianensis*	Contact dermatitis, allergic reactions	Dust, wood
Rhodesian teak *Baikiaea plurijuga*	Respiratory irritation	No information
Pau marfim *Balfourodendron riedelianum*	Dermatitis, rhinitis, asthma	Dust
Pink ivory *Berchemia zeyheri*	Bark and fruit are poisonous; sap can cause dermatitis	Fruit, bark, sap
Yellow birch *Betula alleghaniensis*	Dermatitis, respiratory problems	Dust
Paper birch *Betula papyrifera*	Dermatitis, respiratory problems	Dust
Silver birch *Betula pendula*	Sensitizer; dermatitis, respiratory problems	Dust, wood
Rose butternut *Blepharocarya involucrigera*	Dermatitis, conjunctivitis	Dust
Sucupira *Bowdichia* spp.	Allergic contact dermatitis	Dust, wood
Muhuhu *Brachylaena hutchinsii*	Dermatitis	Dust, wood
Satiné *Brosimum* spp.	Nausea, excessive salivation, thirst	Dust
Snakewood *Brosimum guianense*	Thirst, salivation, respiratory tract irritation, nausea	Dust, wood
Cocuswood *Brya ebenus*	Dermatitis	Dust, wood
Boxwood *Buxus sempervirens*	Sensitizer; dermatitis; irritant to eyes, nose and throat	Dust, wood
White cypress pine *Callitris glauca*	Dermatitis, swollen eyelids, asthma, nasal irritation, nasal cancer	Dust, wood
Jacareuba *Calophyllum brasiliense*	Dermatitis, loss of appetite, possible kidney damage, fainting, insomnia	Dust, wood
Australian silky oak *Cardwellia sublimis*	Dermatitis	Dust, green wood

Sweet chestnut *Castanea sativa*	Dermatitis	Bark, lichens
Blackbean *Castanospermum australe*	Dermatitis; irritation to nose, eyes, throat, armpits, genitals	Dust
South American cedar *Cedrela fissilis*	Dermatitis, asthma; nose and throat irritation, skin blistering, inflammation of eyelids, possible nasal cancer	Dust, wood
Cedar of Lebanon *Cedrus libani*	Respiratory disorders, rhinitis, chest tightness	Dust
Coachwood *Ceratopetalum apetalum*	Dermatitis	Dust
Port Orford cedar *Chamaecyparis lawsoniana*	Dermatitis, irritation to eyes and lungs, violent earache, giddiness, stomach cramps. Inhalation of odour from freshly milled wood can cause kidney problems	Dust, extractives
Greenheart *Chlorocardium rodiaei*	Splinters go septic; cardiac and intestinal disorders, severe throat irritation; sensitizer	wood, dust
Ceylon satinwood *Chloroxylon swietenia*	Dermatitis, headache, swelling of scrotum, nasal irritation	Dust, wood
Camphor laurel *Cinnamomum camphora*	Dermatitis, shortness of breath	Dust
Freijo/cordia *Cordia goeldiana*	Possibly a skin sensitizer	Dust, wood
Spotted gum *Corymbia citriodora*	Dermatitis	Dust, wood
Red bloodwood *Corymbia gummifera*	Irritation to eyes and skin, dermatitis, violent headache, giddiness, stomach cramps, asthma, bronchitis	Dust
New Zealand white pine *Dacrycarpus dacryoides*	Dermatitis, irritation to nose and throat	Dust
Rimu *Dacrydium cupressinum*	Eye and nose irritant	Dust
Rosewood *Dalbergia* spp.	Irritation, dermatitis, respiratory problems; sensitizer	Dust, wood
Kingwood *Dalbergia cearensis*	Eye and skin irritant	Dust
African blackwood *Dalbergia melanoxylon*	Acute dermatitis, conjunctivitis, sneezing, asthma	Dust
Cocobolo *Dalbergia retusa*	Sensitizer; irritant to skin, nose and throat; conjunctivitis, nausea, bronchial asthma, wheezing, chest tightness, headache	Dust, wood
Ebony (Macassar and African) *Diospyros* spp.	Irritant; dermatitis, conjunctivitis, sneezing; possibly a skin sensitizer	Dust, wood
Persimmon *Diospyros virginiana*	Possible dermatitis	Heartwood, dust
Ayan/movingui *Distemonanthus benthamianus*	Dermatitis	Dust
Jelutong *Dyera costulata*	Possible contact allergy	Wood, dust
Miva mahogany *Dysoxylum muelleri*	Dermatitis, lung congestion, nose bleeds, inflammation of nose and eyes, loss of appetite, headache	Dust
Gedu nohor *Entandrophragma angolense*	Dermatitis	Wood, dust
Sapele *Entandrophragma cylindricum*	Skin irritation, sneezing	Dust
Utile *Entandrophragma utile*	Skin irritant	Dust, wood
Guanacaste *Enterolobium cyclocarpum*	Possible mucous membrane irritation, allergies	Dust
Southern blue gum *Eucalyptus* spp.	Dermatitis	Dust, wood
Tasmanian oak *Eucalyptus delegatensis, E. obliqua, E. regnans*	Dermatitis, asthma, sneezing; irritant to eyes, nose and throat	Dust
Blue gum *Eucalyptus globulus*	Dermatitis	Dust, wood
Yellow gum *Eucalyptus leucoxylon*	Irritant to nose and throat	Dust
Jarrah *Eucalyptus marginata*	Irritant to eyes, nose and throat	Dust
Grey box *Eucalyptus microcarpa*	Irritant to skin, throat and nose; eczema	Dust, wood

Coolibah *Eucalyptus microtheca*	Dermatitis	Bark, wood dust
Sydney blue gum *Eucalyptus saligna*	Contact dermatitis, nose and throat irritation	Dust, wood
American beech *Fagus grandifolia*	Dermatitis, eye irritation, decrease in lung function, rare incidence of nasal cancer	Dust
European beech *Fagus sylvatica*	Dermatitis, eye irritation, decrease in lung function, rare incidence of nasal cancer	Leaves, bark, dust
Crows' ash *Flindersia australis*	Dermatitis	Dust
Queensland maple *Flindersia brayleyana*	Dermatitis	Dust, wood
Ash *Fraxinus americana, F. excelsior*	Rhinitis, asthma, decrease in lung function	Dust
Japanese ash *Fraxinus mandschurica*	Can affect lung function	Dust
Rengas *Gluta* spp.	Irritant; dermatitis, blistering, chronic intestinal ulcers	Bark, sap, dust
African boxwood *Gonioma kamassi*	Irritation to nose and throat, asthma, fainting, headache, shortness of breath	Dust, extractives
Ramin *Gonystylus macrophyllum*	Dermatitis; sharp fibres cause skin irritation; breathing difficulties, coughing, shivering, sweating, tiredness	Bark, splinters
Agba/tola *Gossweilerodendron balsamiferum*	Dermatitis	Dust
Lignum vitae *Guaiacum officinale*	Dermatitis	Dust
Guarea *Guarea cedrata*	Skin and mucous membrane irritation, visual disturbance, nausea, headache, dermatitis, asthma	Dust, extractives
Bubinga *Guibourtia demeusei*	Dermatitis, possible skin lesions	Dust, extractives
Cooliman tree *Gyrocarpus americanus*	Can apparently cause blindness	No information
Bibu *Holigarna arnottiana*	Skin blisters from sap, eye irritation	Sap
Courbaril *Hymenaea courbaril*	Skin irritant	Dust
Merbau *Intsia bijuga*	Dermatitis, rhinitis; irritant dust	Dust
Caroba *Jacaranda caroba*	Dermatitis	Dust
Butternut *Juglans cinerea*	Irritant to skin and eyes	Dust
American walnut *Juglans nigra*	Irritant to eyes and skin	Dust, wood
European walnut *Juglans regia*	Dermatitis, irritation of nose, eyes and throat, possible nasal cancer	Dust
Virginian pencil cedar *Juniperus virginiana*	Respiratory problems, possible dermatitis	Dust
African mahogany *Khaya ivorensis*	Dermatitis, rhinitis, respiratory problems, nasal cancer	Dust
Laburnum *Laburnum anagyroides*	Seeds highly toxic	Seeds
European larch *Larix decidua*	Dermatitis, possibly from bark lichens; nettle rash, respiratory irritation	Bark, dust
Western larch *Larix occidentalis*	Dermatitis, rhinitis, allergic bronchial asthma	Dust
American sweet gum *Liquidambar styraciflua*	Dermatitis	Dust
American whitewood *Liriodendron tulipifera*	Dermatitis, allergic reactions	Dust
Bollywood *Litsea glutinosa*	Skin irritation	Dust
Ekki *Lophira alata*	Dermatitis and itching	Dust, wood
African walnut *Lovoa trichilioides*	Irritation to mucous membranes and alimentary tract; nasal cancer	Dust
Jacarandá pardo *Machaerium villosum*	Contact dermatitis, allergic symptoms	Wood, dust
Osage-orange *Maclura pomifera*	Dermatitis	Sap
Red lancewood *Manilkara huberi*	Dermatitis	Dust

Mansonia *Mansonia altissima*	Splinters go septic; nosebleeds, sneezing, skin irritation, asthma, respiratory problems, headache, nausea, vomiting, cardiac disorders. Bark highly toxic	Dust, wood, bark
Rata *Metrosideros robusta*	Irritation to nose and eyes	Dust
Zebrano *Microberlinia brazzavillensis*	Sensitizer; irritant to eyes and skin; asthma, breathing difficulties	Dust, wood
Iroko *Milicia excelsa*	Dermatitis, furunculosis, asthma, nettle rash, oedema of eyelids, respiratory problems, sneezing, giddiness	Dust
Wengé *Millettia laurentii*	Splinters go septic; irritation of eyes, skin and respiratory system; dermatitis, giddiness, drowsiness, visual problems, stomach cramps; sensitizer	Dust, wood
Abura/bahia *Mitragyna ciliata* (*Hallea ledermannii*)	Vomiting, nausea, giddiness, eye irritation; short splinters hard to remove	Dust, splinters
Opepe *Nauclea diderrichii*	Dermatitis, mucous membrane irritation, giddiness, visual disturbance, nosebleeds, blood spitting	Dust, wood
Oleander *Nerium oleander*	Cardiac problems, malaise, nausea	Dust, wood, leaves, bark
Tasmanian myrtle *Nothofagus cunninghamii*	Irritation to mucous membranes	Dust
Stinkwood *Ocotea bullata*	Nasal irritant	Dust
Imbuia *Ocotea* (syn. *Phoebe*) *porosa*	Irritant to nose, eyes, skin	Dust
European olive *Olea europaea*	Irritant to eyes, skin and respiratory system	Dust
East African olive *Olea hochstetteri*	Irritant to eyes, skin, nose and lungs	Dust
Desert ironwood *Olneya tesota*	Rhinitis, sneezing	Fine dust
White peroba *Paratecoma peroba*	Dermatitis, nasal irritation, asthma; splinters go septic	Dust
Purpleheart *Peltogyne pubescens*	Nasal irritation, nausea	Dust, wood
Afrormosia *Pericopsis elata*	Skin and eye irritation; splinters go septic; effects on the nervous system; possible rhinitis and asthma	Dust, splinters
Spruce *Picea abies*	Respiratory problems, irritation to nose and throat	Dust, wood
Sitka spruce *Picea sitchensis*	Respiratory irritation, asthma, rhinitis, dermatitis	Dust
Pine (various) *Pinus* spp.	Irritant; decrease in lung function, allergic bronchial asthma, rhinitis, dermatitis	Dust, wood
Dahoma *Piptadeniastrum africanum*	Irritant; dermatitis, sneezing, coughing, nose bleeds	Dust, wood
Taun *Pometia pinnata*	Dermatitis, rhinitis	Dust
Poplar (various) *Populus* spp.	Dermatitis, sneezing, eye irritation, asthma, bronchitis	Dust, wood
Mesquite *Prosopis juliflora*	Dermatitis, respiratory irritation	Dust
American cherry *Prunus serotina*	Wheezing, giddiness	Dust
Douglas fir *Pseudotsuga menziesii*	Dermatitis, nasal cancer, rhinitis, respiratory problems; splinters go septic	Dust, wood
Padauk *Pterocarpus* spp.	Dermatitis, itching, nasal irritation, eyelid swelling, vomiting, asthma; sensitizer	Dust, wood
Muninga *Pterocarpus angolensis*	Dermatitis, bronchial asthma, nasal irritation	Dust
Amboyna *Pterocarpus indicus*	Dermatitis, asthma, nausea	Dust
American white, red oak *Quercus alba, Q. rubra*	Asthma, sneezing, irritation to nose and eyes, nasal cancer	Dust
Japanese oak *Quercus mongolica*	Dermatitis, sneezing, nasal cancer	Dust
European oak *Quercus robur, Q. petraea*	Dermatitis, sneezing, nasal cancer	Dust
Sumac *Rhus* spp.	Blisters from bark; dermatitis	Dust, bark
Robinia *Robinia pseudoacacia*	Irritant to eyes and skin; nausea, malaise	Dust, leaves, bark

Willow *Salix alba*	Sensitizer; allergic reaction similar to aspirin	Dust, wood, leaves, bark
Sassafras *Sassafras officinale*	Sensitizer; irritant to skin and respiratory system; possible nasal cancer	Dust, wood, leaves, bark
Needlewood *Schima wallichii*	Skin irritation	Bark
Quebracho *Schinopsis* spp.	Dermatitis, respiratory and nasal irritation, nausea, malaise; possible carcinogen	Dust, leaves, bark
Sequoia (redwood) *Sequoia sempervirens*	Asthma, wheezing, dermatitis, nasal cancer, hypersensitivity pneumonia; respiratory irritant	Dust
Lauan/meranti *Shorea* spp.	Irritation, dermatitis	Dust
White lauan *Shorea contorta*	Dermatitis, irritation of nose, eyes, throat	Dust
Tamboti *Spirostachys africana*	Irritant to skin and eyes; blisters; possible blindness	Bark, sap, dust
American mahogany *Swietenia macrophylla*	Dermatitis, respiratory problems, giddiness, furunculosis, vomiting	Dust
Turpentine *Syncarpia glomulifera*	Irritant to mucous membranes	Dust
Ipê *Tabebuia serratifolia*	Yellow dust can cause skin and eye irritation. Possible shortness of breath, headache, visual disturbance	Dust
Bald cypress *Taxodium distichum*	Sensitizer; respiratory problems	Dust
Yew *Taxus baccata*	Headaches, nausea, fainting, intestinal irritation, visual disturbances, lung congestion, reduction in blood pressure; sensitizer. Highly toxic to humans and cattle	Dust, wood, leaves
Pacific yew *Taxus brevifolia*	Highly toxic; irritant; dermatitis	All parts
Teak *Tectona grandis*	Dermatitis, conjunctivitis, irritation to nose and throat, swelling of the scrotum, nausea, oversensitivity to light	Dust
Indian laurel *Terminalia alata*	Irritant	Dust
Idigbo *Terminalia ivorensis*	Skin and respiratory problems; possible irritant	Dust
Afara/limba *Terminalia superba*	Splinters go septic; nettle rash, nose and gum bleeding, decrease in lung function	Dust, wood
Western red cedar *Thuja plicata*	Asthma, rhinitis, dermatitis, mucous membrane irritation, nosebleeds, stomach pains, nausea, giddiness, disturbance to central nervous system	Dust, wood, leaves, bark
Makoré *Tieghemella heckelii*	Dermatitis, nose and throat irritation, nosebleeds, nausea, headaches, giddiness. Can affect blood and central nervous system	Dust, wood
Australian red cedar *Toona ciliata*	Irritant to nose and throat; dermatitis, violent headache, giddiness, stomach cramps, asthma, bronchitis	Dust
Obeche *Triplochiton scleroxylon*	Dermatitis, nettle rash, asthma, lung congestion, sneezing, wheezing	Dust, wood
Western hemlock *Tsuga heterophylla*	Dermatitis, rhinitis, eczema, bronchial problems, possible nasal cancer	Dust
Avodiré *Turraeanthus africanus*	Dermatitis, nosebleeds, respiratory irritation, possible internal bleeding	Dust
American elm *Ulmus americana*	Dermatitis; irritant to nose and eyes	Dust
Wych elm *Ulmus glabra*	Dermatitis; irritant; nasal cancer	Dust
Dutch elm *Ulmus hollandica*	Dermatitis, irritation of nose and throat, nasal cancer	Dust
English elm *Ulmus procera*	Dermatitis; irritation of nose, eyes, throat; nasal cancer	Dust
Rock elm *Ulmus thomasii*	Dermatitis, skin irritation	Dust
Myrtle *Umbellularia californica*	Sensitizer; respiratory problems	Leaves, bark, dust
West Indian satinwood *Zanthoxylum flavum*	Dermatitis, giddiness, nausea, lethargy, visual disturbances	Dust

WOOD DIRECTORY

Woods listed
alphabetically by
botanical names

INTRODUCTORY NOTE

Each species is listed first under the name by which it is most commonly known in the English-speaking world, followed by the botanical name (see Introduction, pages 9–10). Alternative names, including local ones where known, are then given under the heading 'Also called'. The entries are arranged in alphabetical order according to their *botanical* names, for a variety of reasons:

- Botanical names are (in principle) definitive and uncontroversial, whereas vernacular names are often vague and vary from place to place.

- Botanical nomenclature ensures that closely related species, such as the maples and European sycamore (*Acer* spp.), are grouped together, whereas unrelated species with misleadingly similar common names, such as European oak and Tasmanian oak (*Quercus* and *Eucalyptus* spp.), are not.

- Botanical names are always listed in the order genus–species, whereas 'Australian silky oak', for example, might be listed under A, S or O, making it time-consuming to find.

To locate a species whose botanical name you do not know, simply look up one of its common names in the Index.

For those woods that are notorious for their toxicity, clear information is given. In some cases data concerning possible health risks is unavailable, but this does not necessarily mean that there are no risks. Some woods, like apple (*Malus sylvestris*), are non-toxic and can safely be used for kitchenware or containers for foodstuffs. However, the inhalation of dust created by machining *any* wood is a health hazard. For further information on wood toxicity and recommended precautions, see pages 27–32.

No information has been given about the availability of particular species, since this changes constantly. In any given country only a modest range of species will be classed as 'commercial', but independent suppliers catering for turners, carvers, musical instrument makers and other specialist users may carry a much greater range – and many such workers take especial pleasure in searching out hard-to-find species.

A number of the woods listed are now classified as endangered species, and the author and publishers would like to make it clear that they do not condone the felling of these timbers, or the sale or use of such timbers recently felled. They are included here because they may be met with in antique furniture, and reclaimed material may sometimes be available for restoration projects. Up-to-date information on endangered species can be obtained from CITES, the Convention on International Trade in Endangered Species of Wild Flora and Fauna (www.cites.org).

Key to symbols used

 Softwood

 Hardwood

The main photograph of each species has been reproduced as close to life size as possible. Where more than one species is listed in the heading to an entry, the main photograph shows the first species mentioned, unless otherwise stated. Every effort has been made to render the colours accurately, but please bear in mind that all reprographic processes have their limitations.

The watercolour illustrations show the shape of a typical tree, the leaves, the (male) flowers and the fruit, for every species for which reliable information could be obtained. In a few cases, colour information was not available.

To benefit fully from the information given in the Wood Directory, it is helpful to be familiar with some of the key specialist vocabulary used in the descriptions:

■ The **typical dry weight** is usually measured at a moisture content of 12%.

■ **Specific gravity**, also referred to as density or relative density, is the ratio of the mass of a substance to that of water. The higher the number, the heavier and more dense the material is. Material with an SG of over 1.00, such as lignum vitae (*Guaiacum officinale*), will not float in water.

■ **Movement in use** (or in service) is indicated as follows:
Small: less than 3%
Medium: 3–4.5%
Large: more than 4.5%.

■ **Stiffness** refers to the wood's ability to resist a change in shape from external pressures, as in a loaded beam.

■ **Bending strength** indicates the degree of curvature to which wood can be bent before breaking, without special treatment such as steaming.

■ **Crushing strength** is the ability of the wood to withstand compression, either parallel or perpendicular to the grain.

■ **Resistance to shock loads** is the ability to withstand sudden impact loads.

■ **Durability** is the wood's ability to resist decay, without preservative treatment.

Finally, always remember that wood is a natural material, and its growth is affected by many factors, such as the amount and direction of sunlight received by the growing tree, and the mineral composition of the soil. This may result in considerable differences between one specimen and another, in colour, weight, grain formation and many other properties. We have made every effort to show representative samples, and to give information which is true of 'average' specimens, but in the final analysis, every piece of wood is unique.

KOA

Acacia koa (Leguminosae)

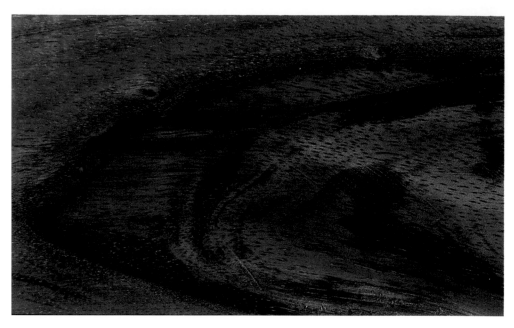

Also called: black koa, curly koa, Hawaiian mahogany, koaia, koa-ka

Description

The pale brown sapwood is clearly demarcated from the heartwood. The heartwood is most commonly reddish-brown, but can vary in colour from tree to tree, from pale blond through golden-brown to deep chocolate. Koa yellows quickly in sunlight. The curly and wavy grain is moderately to severely interlocked, which can produce beautiful fiddleback and rainbow figure. The growth rings show as black lines on longitudinal surfaces. Koa has a moderately coarse texture and is highly lustrous.

Typical dry weight: 41lb/ft³ (670kg/m³)
Specific gravity: .67

Properties

Koa has medium stiffness and bending strength, good resistance to shock loads and high crushing strength. It works fairly easily with both hand and machine tools, except that figured material is difficult to work by machine. Wood with curly grain may require a reduced cutting angle for planing, and end grain needs very sharp tools. Koa has a medium blunting effect on tools. It screws, nails, stains, varnishes and turns well, but can be difficult to glue. The surface can be brought to a high polish.

Seasoning

It dries easily with little or no degrade. There can be some surface checking on thicker stock. It is stable in use and retains its shape.

Durability

Koa is durable and resistant to insect and fungal attack. It is highly resistant to preservative treatment.

Typical uses

Koa is prized for making musical instruments, including Hawaiian ukuleles, violin bows and organ pipes. It is also used for cabinets and fine furniture, interior joinery and panelling, boats and canoes, gunstocks, and novelties. It yields decorative veneer with a fiddleback figure.

Grows
Hawaiian Islands
Typical height: 80–100ft
(24–30m)
Trunk diameter: 3–4ft
(0.9–1.2m)

⚠ **Possible health risks**
Not known

AUSTRALIAN BLACKWOOD
Acacia melanoxylon (Leguminosae)

Also called: Tasmanian blackwood, black wattle

Description
The sapwood ranges from straw to greyish-white in colour, and is clearly differentiated from the heartwood. The latter is golden to dark brown, with chocolate-brown zones marking the growth rings. The grain is most commonly straight, but may sometimes be wavy or interlocked, producing a beautiful fiddleback figure on quartersawn surfaces. The wood has a lustrous surface with an even, fine to medium texture.
Typical dry weight: 41lb/ft³ (665kg/m³)
Specific gravity: .66

Properties
Australian blackwood has high crushing strength and resistance to impact, with good bending properties and medium stiffness. It has a moderate blunting effect on cutters, and a reduced angle should be used for machine planing. The wood nails and screws well, but has variable gluing properties. Australian blackwood works satisfactorily with hand tools, stains well, and the surface can be brought to an excellent finish.

Seasoning
It dries easily without degrade, but wide boards can cup unless the stack is weighted down. There is little movement in service.

Durability
The heartwood is durable, but vulnerable to attack by common furniture beetle and termites. It is strongly resistant to preservative treatment. The powder-post beetle can attack the sapwood.

Typical uses
Being a very decorative wood, it is used for cabinetmaking, ornamental turning, musical instruments, shop fittings (store fixtures), bank interiors, gunstocks, billiard tables and boatbuilding. It yields decorative veneers which are used for doors and panelling.

▲ Burr (burl)

Grows
South-eastern Australia, Tasmania, New Zealand, South Africa, India, Sri Lanka, Chile, Argentina
Typical height: 80ft (24m)
Trunk diameter: 5ft (1.5m)

⚠ **Possible health risks**
Dermatitis, asthma, nose and throat irritation; sensitizer

The genus *Acer*
Maples and European sycamore

The *Acer* genus contains up to 150 species that are native to the northern hemisphere, some of which can be found as far south as Mexico. Maples are customarily divided into two groups, hard and soft, depending on the width of their medullary rays. Hard maples are tougher than soft maples, and about 35% harder on average. In North America the maples generally classified as hard are rock or sugar maple (*A. saccharum*) and black maple (*A. nigrum*). The soft species include silver or soft maple (*A. saccharinum*), red maple (*A. rubrum*), bigleaf maple (*A. macrophyllum*) and boxelder (*A. negundo*). European sycamore (*A. pseudoplatanus*) would come under the soft category.

The typically five-lobed maple leaf is well known as the national symbol of Canada, though not all maple leaves are of this form. The seeds of the *Acer* genus have a distinctive winged form, which allows them to be carried on the wind easily. The wood tends to be pale and bland, but there are many interesting varieties of figure to be found in the different *Acer* species. It is easy to work and, being generally odourless, it is often used for kitchen utensils and food containers.

Maple syrup is obtained by tapping certain species – most commonly the sugar maple (*A. saccharum*) and black maple (*A. nigrum*), but also, to a lesser extent, red maple (*A. rubrum*) and silver maple (*A. saccharinum*).

◀ Chest of drawers in weathered ripple sycamore (*A. pseudoplatanus*) and bog oak (*Quercus* sp.)

▶ Workstation in bird's-eye maple (*A. saccharum*), plain maple and rosewood (*Dalbergia* sp.)

▼ Norway maple (*A. platanoides*)

EUROPEAN MAPLE

Acer campestre and related species (Aceraceae)

Also called: field maple, Ahorn, Feldahorn (German), **érable** (French), **arce** (Spanish)
The wood is very similar to **Norway maple (A. platanoides)** and **Bosnian maple
(A. platanus)**, which are also called 'European maple'

Description

The heartwood is creamy-white when freshly cut, but ages to a light tan. The grain is usually straight, but can be wavy or curly, and has a smooth, fine texture. The wood has a high natural lustre, especially on quartered surfaces. The sapwood is not normally distinct from the heartwood.
Typical dry weight: 43lb/ft³ (690kg/m³)
Specific gravity: .69

Properties

The wood has low resistance to shock loads and low stiffness, with medium crushing and bending strengths. European maple steam-bends well. It works well and easily with both hand and machine tools, but has a moderate blunting effect on cutting edges. When machine-planing wavy or curly stock, a reduced cutting angle is advised, and pre-boring is recommended for nailing. The wood stains and glues well, turns particularly well, and can be brought to an excellent polished finish.

Seasoning

It dries slowly with little degrade, but there can be problems with staining. Rapid but careful kiln-drying is advised if the natural whitish colour is to be preserved. There is only small movement in service.

Durability

The heartwood is non-durable and can be subject to attack by decay fungi and other wood-destroying organisms. The sapwood is susceptible to attack from the common furniture beetle. The sapwood is permeable for preservative treatment, but the heartwood is resistant.

Typical uses

It is used for turnery, furniture and interior joinery, brush backs and woodenware. Selected wood is sliced to make very decorative veneers, and it can also be treated with chemicals to produce grey **harewood**, which is used for veneers and marquetry.

▲ Bowl in maple burr (burl)

Grows
Europe, including UK;
Turkey; USA
Typical height: 65ft (20m)
Trunk diameter: 1–2ft
(0.3–0.6m)

⚠ **Possible health risks**
Dust can cause a decrease in lung function; sensitizer

BIGLEAF MAPLE

Acer macrophyllum (Aceraceae)

Also called: maple, broadleaf maple, bugleaf maple, Californian maple, Oregon maple, Pacific coast maple, western maple, white maple

Description

The wood is pale pinkish-brown to almost white, normally with no clear distinction between heartwood and sapwood. It has a close, fine grain with uniform colour, and is not dissimilar to birch and cherry (*Betula*, *Prunus* spp.) with regard to the contrast in growth rings.
Typical dry weight: 34lb/ft3 (545kg/m3)
Specific gravity: .55

Properties

Bigleaf maple comes into the medium-density category. It displays medium stiffness, bending strength and shock resistance. The wood machines, nails and screws well, and is excellent for turning. It also sands well, and accepts stains and other finishes readily and uniformly to achieve a good finish. It takes glue moderately well.

Seasoning

The wood dries quite slowly with little degrade and shows medium movement in service.

Durability

It is non-durable, and has a moderate resistance to preservative treatment. The permeable sapwood can be liable to insect attack.

Typical uses

Furniture, turnery, carvings, musical instruments, doors, shutters, mouldings, kitchen cabinets, woodware utensils, pallets and paper products.

Grows

USA and Canada, from California to British Columbia
Typical height: 60ft (18m), sometimes higher
Trunk diameter: 1–3ft (0.3–0.9m)

⚠ Possible health risks

Allergic bronchial asthma, dermatitis and rhinitis

BOXELDER

Acer negundo (Aceraceae)

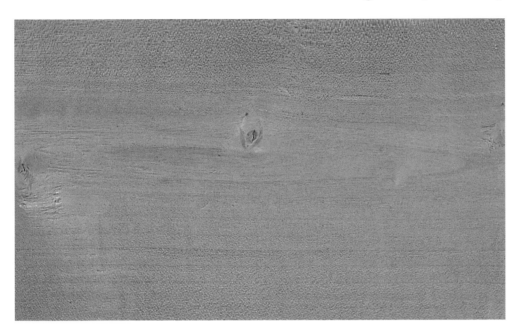

Also called: ashleaf maple, Manitoba maple, maple, négondo (French), **Eschenahorn** (German)

Description

Boxelder is the lightest of the American maples. The yellowish-brown heartwood merges gently into greenish-yellow sapwood. Coral-red streaks allegedly caused by a pigment of the fungus *Fusarium reticulatum* (syn. *F. negundi*) are sometimes present. It is weak, light and porous, and close-grained. It sometimes has wavy or curly figure.

Typical dry weight: 28lb/ft³ (450kg/m³)
Specific gravity: .45

Properties

The wood is relatively low in strength properties, and is of average density. Its steam-bending qualities are rated as good. Boxelder is workable with both machine and hand tools, and has a medium blunting effect on cutters. Its gluing properties are variable, and care is needed when nailing. The wood planes and stains well, and can be polished to an excellent finish.

Seasoning

It dries slowly with little degrade, and is stable in service.

Durability

The heartwood has little resistance to decay, and is vulnerable to insect attack. The boxelder bug can attack the growing tree. The heartwood has moderate resistance to preservative treatment, and the sapwood is permeable.

Typical uses

Some artistic use is made of the red-streaked boxelder for decorative turning and sculpture. It is also used for inexpensive furniture, woodware, crates and boxes, cooperage, pulp and charcoal.

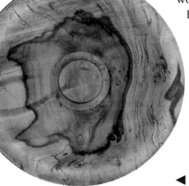

◀ Bowl in figured boxelder

Grows Canada and USA
Typical height: 30–60ft (9–18m)
Trunk diameter: 2ft 6in (0.8m)

⚠ **Possible health risks**
Allergic bronchial asthma, dermatitis, rhinitis

JAPANESE MAPLE
Acer palmatum and *A. mono* (Aceraceae)

No other names

Description
The heartwood is creamy-tan or pale brown to pinkish-brown, and is not distinct from the sapwood. The grain can be wavy or curly, but is usually straight. Japanese maple has a fine, even texture, and the growth rings can show fine brown lines on longitudinal surfaces.
Typical dry weight: 41lb/ft³ (670kg/m³)
Specific gravity: .67

Properties
It is heavy and dense, rated as medium in all strength categories, and very good for steam bending. The wood is highly resistant to abrasion and quite tough to work, with a moderate blunting effect on cutters. A reduced angle is advised for planing. It requires pre-boring for nailing, and glues and sands well. Staining and polishing qualities are rated as excellent.

Seasoning
The wood dries slowly with minimum degrade, but can have a high tendency to warp while drying. There is medium movement in service.

Durability
It has little natural resistance to decay, and is vulnerable to attack from the common furniture beetle. The sapwood is permeable but the heartwood is difficult to treat with preservatives.

Typical uses
Furniture and cabinetmaking. Because of its resistance to abrasion, the wood is also used for flooring of many types, including industrial, domestic, roller-skating rinks, squash courts, dance halls and bowling alleys. It is also used for piano actions, kitchen cabinets, shuttles, rollers in textile mills, and plywood. Interesting logs are also sliced for decorative veneers.

Grows
Japan
Typical height: 30ft (9m)
Trunk diameter: 1ft (0.3m)

⚠ **Possible health risks**
Not known

EUROPEAN SYCAMORE

Acer pseudoplatanus (Aceraceae)

Also called: sycamore plane, great maple, plane (Scotland), **érable sycomore, faux platane** (French), **Bergahorn** (German), **gewone esdoorn** (Dutch). Not to be confused with the plane *Platanus occidentalis*, which is called 'sycamore' in the USA

Description
The creamy-white or yellowish-white heartwood darkens to light golden-brown on exposure. The sapwood is not distinct. Though typically straight-grained, the wood can produce excellent lacy or fiddleback figuring. It has a fine, even texture and is highly lustrous.
Typical dry weight: 38lb/ft³ (610kg/m³)
Specific gravity: .61

Properties
It has medium bending and crushing strength, very low stiffness, low resistance to shock loads, and steam-bends very well. It works easily with machine and hand tools, with a moderate blunting effect. Very sharp tools are advised for a clean finish. It planes, bores, turns, moulds, glues, mortises, screws, sands and paints well, carves easily, and nails, stains and polishes very well. Fiddleback sycamore is best finished by scraping.

Seasoning
The wood kiln-dries well, but is prone to staining unless end-reared. Rapid kilning will preserve the white colour; slower kiln-drying will give a pink-brown 'weathered' colour. The heartwood can suffer ring failure, honeycombing and water pockets during drying. There is medium movement in service.

Durability
Sycamore decays easily if untreated, but is permeable for preservative treatment. The sapwood is vulnerable to common furniture beetle and other insects.

Typical uses
Furniture and turnery. Fiddleback sycamore is used for violins and related instruments. Other uses include domestic flooring, dairy utensils, food containers, cooperage, textile rollers, brush handles, bobbins, and decorative and dyed veneers. When chemically treated to produce shades of grey, it is called **harewood**.

Grows
Central and southern Europe, UK and western Asia; also planted in USA
Typical height: 100ft (30m)
Trunk diameter: 5ft (1.8m)

⚠ **Possible health risks**
Not known

◀ Spoon box in fiddleback sycamore

SOFT MAPLE

Acer rubrum and *A. saccharinum* (Aceraceae)

Ambrosia figure

Quilted figure

Also called: Carolina red maple, Drummond red maple, maple, red maple, scarlet maple, swamp maple, water maple, silver maple

Grows
Canada and eastern USA
Typical height: 60–100ft
(18–30m)
Trunk diameter: 2ft 6in (0.8m)

⚠ **Possible health risks**
Dust may affect lung
function

Natural-topped hollow
form in burr maple ▶

Description
The heartwood is light to dark reddish-brown, and can have a faint purplish hue or a greyish or greenish tinge from time to time. The grain is normally straight and close, but can be wavy or curly, and pith flecks are often present. The sapwood is white to greyish-white.
Typical dry weight: *A. rubrum* 39lb/ft³ (630kg/m³); *A. saccharinum* 34lb/ft³ (550kg/m³)
Specific gravity: *A. rubrum* .63; *A. saccharinum* .55

Properties
Soft maples are about 25% softer than the hard maples. The wood is good for steam bending, but has low stiffness and resistance to shock loads, with medium crushing and bending strengths. It works satisfactorily with hand and machine tools, and has a moderate dulling effect on cutting edges. Soft maple planes and bores well, nails and screws satisfactorily, but is difficult to glue. It can be stained and polished to an excellent finish.

Seasoning
Soft maple dries slowly and easily with little degrade. There can sometimes be problems with ring failure and honeycombing due to wet wood. If the airflow during drying is not adequate, blue staining can occur.

Durability
The heartwood is not durable and can be attacked by decay-causing fungi and insects. The sapwood is permeable for preservative treatment, but the heartwood is fairly difficult to treat.

Typical uses
Furniture, including office furniture and kitchen cabinets; musical instruments, domestic flooring, interior joinery, corestock and truck bodies. It is also rotary-cut for plywood and sliced for figured decorative veneers.

HARD MAPLE

Acer saccharum and *A. nigrum* (Aceraceae)

Bird's-eye figure

Ripple figure

Also called: rock maple, sugar maple, white maple (*A. saccharum*); black maple, black sugar maple, hard rock maple (*A. nigrum*). Both are sold as 'hard maple' or 'rock maple'

Description

The heartwood is a uniform pale reddish-brown or light tan, the sapwood white with a reddish tinge. It has a typically straight grain, which can sometimes be wavy or curly, and a fine, even texture. The classic **bird's-eye** form has brownish dots on a whitish background. Other kinds of decorative figuring which are commonly found include fiddleback, leaf, blistered and burr maple.
Typical dry weight: 45lb/ft³ (720kg/m³)
Specific gravity: .72

Properties

It has medium stiffness, is rated high in all other strength categories, and has very good steam-bending qualities. The hard maples are about 35% harder than the soft maples, and are resistant to abrasion. The wood has a moderate blunting effect and can be quite difficult to work. Sawing and planing can present difficulty, but the wood turns, bores, moulds and paints well. It is rated as satisfactory for gluing and polishing, and requires pre-boring for nailing and screwing.

Seasoning

Hard maple dries slowly, but is quite easy to season. Shrinkage is high and there is a moderate tendency to warp. Movement in service is rated as medium.

Durability

Although more durable than some of the other maples, hard maple has little natural resistance to insects and fungi, and can be attacked by common furniture beetle. The sapwood is permeable for preservative treatment, but the heartwood is resistant.

Typical uses

Furniture, musical instruments and interior joinery. Because of its resistance to abrasion, hard maple is suitable for heavy-duty flooring, and is used for roller-skating rinks, dance floors, squash courts and bowling alleys. It is also used for butchers' blocks, rollers in the textile industry, sports goods, casks and woodenware. Selected figured stock is peeled for bird's-eye figurc, or sliced to make fiddleback, mottled, curly or blistered veneers.

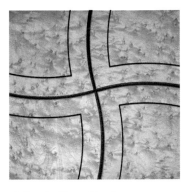

▲ Interlocking tables in bird's-eye maple

Grows
Canada and USA
Typical height: *A. saccharum* 70–120ft (20–37m); *A. nigrum* 80ft (24m)
Trunk diameter: 2–3ft (0.6–0.9m)

⚠ **Possible health risks**
Dust can affect lung function

YELLOW BUCKEYE

Aesculus flava (Hippocastanaceae)

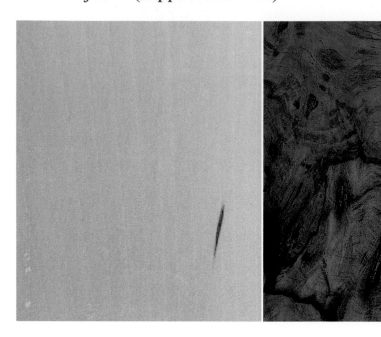

Syn.: *A. octandra*
Also called: buckeye, big buckeye, large buckeye, sweet buckeye. The closely related
Ohio buckeye (*A. glabra*) is also a commercial species

Description
The sapwood is white and merges gradually into a creamy, yellowish or yellow heartwood. The centres of logs can often discolour to a greyish brown. Buckeye generally has a uniform texture and fine grain which may be either straight or wavy.
Typical dry weight: 25lb/ft3 (360kg/m3)
Specific gravity: .36

Properties
Yellow buckeye is light and soft, with low shock resistance. The wood works easily with hand tools, but has poor machining qualities for boring, mortising, shaping and copy-turning.

Seasoning
Generally the wood seasons with few checking or cracking problems.

Durability
Yellow buckeye has only slight resistance to heartwood decay.

Typical uses
Furniture, artificial limbs, splints, coffins, wood pulp, woodware, decorative turning. It has similar uses to aspen (*Populus tremula*), basswood (*Tilia americana*) and American whitewood (*Liriodendron tulipifera*).

Grows
USA: Pennsylvania to Nebraska, Alabama to Texas
Typical height: 30–70ft (9–21m)
Trunk diameter: 2ft (0.6m)

⚠ **Possible health risks**
The nuts and twigs are poisonous; they contain aescin, a cytotoxin

◄ Natural-edged bowl in buckeye burr (burl)

HORSE CHESTNUT

Aesculus hippocastanum (Hippocastanaceae)

Also called: European horse chestnut, conker tree, marronnier d'Inde (French), **Rosskastanie** (German), **witte paardekastanje** (Dutch), **castaña de Indias** (Spanish)

Description
The heartwood is usually creamy-white or yellowish. If the tree is felled in the early winter the wood can be very white, whereas those felled later can vary from yellow to light brown. There is no clear delineation between sapwood and heartwood. Horse chestnut can be cross-, spiral- or wavy-grained, with tiered rays frequently producing ripple or mottle figure on longitudinal surfaces. It has a fine, close, uniform texture.
Typical dry weight: 31lb/ft³ (510kg/m³)
Specific gravity: .51

Properties
Horse chestnut has very low stiffness and low bending strength. Steam-bending properties are, however, good. The crushing strength is rated as medium. It works easily with both machine and hand tools, and has only a slight dulling effect on cutting edges. It glues, screws and nails without difficulty, and planes easily, but a reduced cutting angle is advised for machine planing. Horse chestnut stains and polishes satisfactorily.

Seasoning
The wood dries quickly and easily with little degrade, but can be liable to distortion and end-splits. Movement in service is small.

Durability
It has little or no resistance to decay fungi, the sapwood being vulnerable to the common furniture beetle. The heartwood, which is perishable, is permeable for preservative treatment.

Typical uses
Furniture, cabinetmaking, turnery, interior trim and construction, kitchen utensils, food containers, baskets, fruit storage trays and racks. It is also sliced for decorative veneers, and may be dyed as **harewood** (cf. sycamore, *Acer pseudoplatanus*) for marquetry veneers.

Grows
Europe, including UK; related species found in USA (**buckeye**, *A. glabra* and other spp.), China and Japan
Typical height: 70ft (21m)
Trunk diameter: 2ft (0.6m)

⚠ **Possible health risks**
Not known

◀ Vase in horse chestnut burr

AFZELIA

Afzelia spp. (Leguminosae)

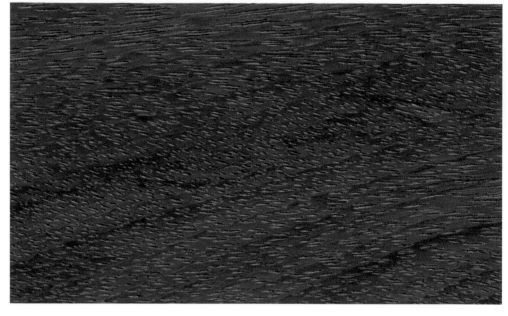

Also called: doussié (Cameroon), **apa, aligna** (Nigeria), **lingué** (Ivory Coast), **chamfuta** (Mozambique), **mkora** (Tanzania), **bolengo, m'banga, papao, uvala**

A. quanzensis

Grows
Tropical West Africa and East Africa
Typical height: 80–100ft (25–30m)
Trunk diameter: 4ft (1.2m)

⚠ Possible health risks
Dermatitis, respiratory problems, sneezing, nose and throat irritation

Description
The reddish-brown heartwood is clearly differentiated from the pale straw-coloured sapwood. The heartwood matures to a mahogany-like colour on exposure to the air. The grain is irregular and interlocked, giving the wood a coarse though even texture. Yellow or white deposits can cause staining.
Typical dry weight: 51lb/ft³ (820kg/m³)
Specific gravity: .82

Properties
Afzelia has only a moderate bending classification, because it is liable to distort and exude resin during steaming. It has high crushing and bending strength, low resistance to shock loads and medium stiffness. It is a hard wood to work, since it has a high resistance to cutting, causing moderate blunting of tools. It polishes well when the grain is filled, but is difficult to stain. Pre-boring is advised for nailing and screwing. Afzelia is difficult to plane and requires a very low cutting angle when planing by machine.

Seasoning
It can be kiln-dried satisfactorily, provided it is dried slowly from green. There may be slight distortion, the extension of existing shakes and some fine checking. There is only small movement in service.

Durability
The sapwood can be vulnerable to powder-post beetle attack, but the heartwood is extremely durable and stable, with great resistance to preservative treatment and impregnation.

Typical uses
Afzelia is prized for furniture, interior and exterior joinery, shop (store) counters, boatbuilding, bridges, floors in public buildings, parquet flooring, outdoor furniture, ships' rails, heavy construction work, and as vats for acids and chemicals. It is also used for shingles and plywood, and is sliced decorative veneers.

KAURI PINE

Agathis spp. (Araucariaceae)

Also called: New Zealand kauri (*A. australis*), Queensland kauri (*A. robusta*, *A. palmerstonii*, *A. microstachya*), East Indian kauri (*A. dammara*), Fijian kauri (*A. vitiensis*); also known as agathis, almaciga, bindang, dakua makadre, damar minyak, menghilan, tolong

A. robusta

Description

Kauri heartwood can range from pale biscuit, through pink to dark red-brown. It is normally straight-grained, has a fine, uniform, silky texture, and can show an attractive streaked or mottled figure with a lustrous surface.

Typical dry weight: New Zealand kauri 36lb/ft³ (580kg/m³), Queensland kauri 30lb/ft³ (480kg/m³)

Specific gravity: New Zealand .58, Queensland .48

Properties

It has high stiffness with medium bending and crushing strength and medium resistance to shock loads. Kauri is not suitable for steam bending. It is easy to work with both hand and machine tools, with only a slight dulling effect on cutting edges. It is easy to carve, and planes, moulds, nails, turns and stains well. The wood screws, glues and varnishes satisfactorily, and takes a high polish.

Seasoning

Kauri dries well at a moderate rate, but it does have a tendency to warp. It is stable in service.

Durability

The wood is moderately durable and resistant to preservative treatment. Kauri is vulnerable to attack from the common furniture beetle.

Typical uses

Depending on the grade and the exact type, kauri may be used for cabinetwork, joinery and panelling, boatbuilding, patternmaking, blind (shade) rollers, domestic flooring, shuttles, boxes and crates. Other uses include machinery, construction, vats and tanks, battery separators and plywood. It is also a source of decorative veneers.

Grows
Australia, New Zealand, Papua New Guinea, Philippines, Fiji, Indochina, Indonesia and Malaysia
Typical height: 150ft (45m)
Trunk diameter: 5–6ft (1.5–2m)

⚠ **Possible health risks**
Not known

KOKKO
Albizia lebbeck (Leguminosae)

Also called: acacia amarilla, East Indian walnut, barba de caballero, West Indies ebony, woman's tongue, lebbek, siris. There are over 100 species of *Albizia*

Description

The sapwood, which is clearly demarcated from the heartwood, is beige-white. When newly cut, the heartwood is golden-brown, but turns to a rich dark brown or dark walnut colour, often with lighter streaks. It has a strongly interlocked grain and a coarse texture, with heavy flecking and a lustrous surface. Radial surfaces can show a ribbon figure. The wood is often confused with the mahoganies because of its colour and texture, but it is neither a true mahogany nor a true walnut.
Typical dry weight: 39lb/ft³ (635kg/m³)
Specific gravity: .63

Properties

Kokko has medium crushing and bending strengths, medium resistance to shock loads, low stiffness and a good steam-bending rating. Its irregular or interlocked grain and woolly texture make it difficult to work, and a reduced cutting angle is required for planing. It sands to a good lustrous finish. Kokko has a moderate blunting effect on cutting edges, which

should be kept sharp. Turning, boring, mortising and moulding can be fairly difficult with normal tools. The wood nails and screws well, and gluing, varnishing and polishing are satisfactory.

Seasoning

Kokko is moderately difficult to season, with marked longitudinal shrinkage and risk of end splitting and surface checking. Initial conversion when green is advised. There is medium movement in use.

Durability

The heartwood is moderately durable, but can be attacked by termites and marine borers. The sapwood is permeable for preservative treatment, but the heartwood is very resistant.

Typical uses

Furniture and cabinetmaking, including office furniture, rustic furniture and kitchen cabinets; carving, interior joinery, flooring including parquet, boatbuilding. It is also sliced for decorative veneer.

Grows
South-East Asia, China, India, Fiji, New Caledonia, Andaman Islands, Florida and many other tropical areas
Typical height: 90ft (27m) max.
Trunk diameter: 3ft (0.9m)

⚠ **Possible health risks**
Machining dust can be an irritant to the eyes, nose and throat

SHEOAK

Allocasuarina fraseriana (Casuarinaceae)

Lace figure

Syn.: *Casuarina fraseriana*
Also called: she-oak, Western Australian sheoak, condil. Other related *Casuarina* species from eastern Australia are also referred to as sheoak

Description
The heartwood ranges from orangey-red-brown through burgundy to dark red, but the sapwood is lighter. It has a moderately fine, straight grain with an even texture. Sheoak has large rays – a feature which is common to all *Casuarina* and *Allocasuarina* timbers – and this is probably why European settlers referred to it as oak. It is alleged that the name 'she' oak derives from the fact that it is not as tough as true oak (*Quercus* spp.).
Typical dry weight: 46lb/ft³ (730kg/m³)
Specific Gravity: .73

Properties
The wood is hard and of medium weight and strength. It machines and cuts reasonably well and a smooth surface can be achieved. There is only a slight blunting effect on cutting tools. It holds screws quite well, but can split when nailed, so pre-drilling or extra care is advised. Sheoak glues and steam-bends well, and can be brought to a reasonably high polish.

Seasoning
It can be difficult to dry, as it has a tendency to warp and check with high shrinkage. However, when dry it displays only a small amount of movement and is stable in service.

Durability
Sheoak sapwood can be susceptible to attack from lyctus borers, but the heartwood is durable.

Typical uses
Due to its relatively small dimensions it is used mainly for panels, inlays and decorative turning, but also for furniture and flooring. In the past it was used by settlers for roof shingles and beer barrels.

Grows
South-western Australia
Typical height: 50ft (15m)
Trunk diameter: 1ft 6in–3ft (0.5–1m)

⚠ **Possible health risks**
Not known

COMMON ALDER
Alnus glutinosa (Betulaceae)

Also called: black alder, grey alder, Japanese alder, aune (French), **eis** (Dutch), **Erle, Schwarzerle** (German), **hannoki** (Japanese)

Description
There is little difference between the sapwood and the heartwood. The wood is generally dull in appearance, being a lustreless bright orange-brown when freshly cut. It matures on exposure to a light reddish-brown with darker streaks or lines formed by broad rays. It has straight grain and a fine, close texture. It can be burry, and sound burrs (burls) can be highly figured.
Typical dry weight: 33lb/ft³ (530kg/m³)
Specific gravity: .53

Properties
It has a moderate bending rating with a low bending strength, and moderate steam-bending properties. Common alder has low resistance to shock loads, medium crushing strength and low stiffness. Straight-grained wood works well with hand tools, and it has only a slight dulling effect on cutters. It can be glued well, and takes nails and screws satisfactorily. Alder can be stained and polished to a good finish.

Seasoning
Alder dries fairly rapidly and well, with little degrade.

Durability
The wood is vulnerable to attack from the common furniture beetle. It is permeable for preservative treatment, but perishable.

Typical uses
Domestic woodware, woodcarving, turnery, broom handles, brush backs, utility plywood. Picturesquely gnarled pieces are prized in Japan for sculpture, turnery and carving.

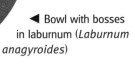

◄ Bowl with bosses in laburnum (*Laburnum anagyroides*)

RED ALDER

Alnus rubra (Betulaceae)

Also called: western alder, Oregon alder, Pacific coast alder

Description
Red alder is a fairly straight-grained wood of uniform texture, the heartwood being pale yellow to reddish-brown. Heartwood and sapwood are not clearly distinct. It has a pleasant but not outstanding figure.
Typical dry weight: 33lb/ft³ (530kg/m³)
Specific gravity: .53

Properties
Red alder is a weak, soft wood of medium density, with low bending strength and shock resistance, very low stiffness and medium crushing strength. Its steam-bending qualities are very good, however. Apart from a slight tendency for the grain to pick up on planing, it works well. The wood nails and glues without difficulty, and takes finishes well. There is only a slight blunting effect on tools. Red alder works well with hand tools and peels easily for veneers.

Seasoning
Red alder dries fairly rapidly and easily with almost no degrade. It moves very little in service.

Durability
The wood is vulnerable to the common furniture beetle, and both the heartwood and sapwood are permeable for preservation treatment. It is perishable.

Typical uses
Furniture, cabinetwork, rustic furniture, turnery and carving, woodware, interior construction, electric guitar bodies, umbrella handles and utility plywood. Red alder can also produce interesting veneers with burr (burl) clusters, streaks and knots.

> **Grows**
> Pacific coast of USA and Canada
> **Typical height:** 70–120ft (21–36m)
> **Trunk diameter:** 1–4ft (0.3–1.2m)

⚠ **Possible health risks**
Dermatitis, rhinitis, bronchial problems

CEREJEIRA

Amburana cearensis (Leguminosae)

Also called: amburana (USA), **cumaré** (Brazil), **ishpingo, palo trebol** (Argentina), **cerejeira rajada, Brazilian oak, roble del pais**

Description
The heartwood is a uniform yellow to mid-brown with an orange-pink tint, but darkens when exposed to the air. The sapwood is not distinct from the heartwood. Cerejeira has a moderately interlocked and irregular grain, with a medium to coarse texture. The wood feels and looks waxy and has a medium to high natural lustre.
Typical dry weight: 37lb/ft³ (600kg/m³)
Specific gravity: .60

Properties
Cerejeira is classified as moderate for steam bending, and has good strength properties in relation to its weight. Pre-boring is necessary for nailing and screwing, and the wood takes glue well. It works well with both hand and machine tools, but cutting edges need to be kept very sharp, and there is a moderate blunting effect on tools. A reduced angle is advised for machine planing. Cerejeira accepts stains and polishes well.

Seasoning
The wood needs to be dried slowly to avoid tangential shrinkage. It has good dimensional stability in service.

Durability
Cerejeira is naturally resistant to insect attack and decay, and highly resistant to preservative treatment.

Typical uses
Furniture, interior joinery, boatbuilding, flooring, vehicle bodies, construction; also sliced for decorative veneers.

Grows
Eastern Brazil, Central and South America
Typical height: 100ft (30m)
Trunk diameter: 2–3ft (0.6–0.9m)

⚠ **Possible health risks**
Not known

LATI *

Amphimas pterocarpioides (Leguminosae)

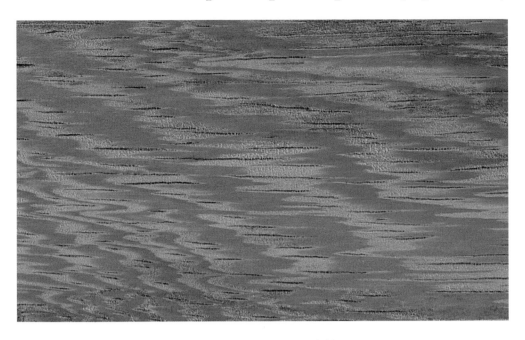

Also called: asanfran, bokanga, edjin, adzi, muizi, salaki, yaya

Description
The heartwood is orange when freshly cut, and darkens to orange-brown on exposure to the air. It has very distinct growth rings, and ripple marks are frequently present. Lati is straight-grained and has a moderately coarse texture. The sapwood is yellowish-white or pale brown, and is clearly differentiated from the heartwood.
Typical dry weight: 46lb/ft³ (740kg/m³)
Specific gravity: .74

Properties
Lati has good strength qualities in all categories. It is a compact, heavy and elastic wood that has considerable resistance to abrasion. Because of its toughness, it is difficult to work. It has a moderate to severe blunting effect on cutting edges, and is difficult to saw. Although not easy to plane, it is capable of being planed to a smooth surface. The wood turns, glues and sands well. It also accepts stains, paints and polishes readily, but requires pre-boring for nailing and screwing.

Seasoning
It dries rather slowly, with a tendency to warp, check and distort. Very slow kiln-drying is recommended. The wood is stable in service, with small movement.

Durability
Lati is moderately durable, but it is vulnerable to attack from the powder-post and common furniture beetles. The heartwood is difficult to treat with preservative, and the sapwood is only moderately responsive.

Typical uses
Furniture, interior and exterior joinery, office furniture, domestic and factory flooring, parquet flooring, furniture parts, railway sleepers (railroad ties), shingles, decorative veneer and panelling.

Grows
Tropical West and Central Africa
Typical height: 150ft (45m)
Trunk diameter: 3–6ft (0.9–1.8m)

⚠ **Possible health risks**
Not known

ANGELIN
Andira inermis (Leguminosae)

Also called: partridgewood, red cabbage bark, rode kabbas, red kabbas, maquilla, macaya, pheasantwood, angelim, andira, moca, acapurana

Description
The sapwood is a yellowish-white or pale brown to greyish-yellow, and usually clearly defined from the heartwood. The heartwood is typically yellowish-brown to a dark reddish-brown with distinctive lighter stripes, which resemble the markings on a partridge's wing. Its grain is straight to slightly interlocked or moderately irregular, with a very coarse texture and a low lustre.
Typical dry weight: 40lb/ft³ (640kg/m³)
Specific gravity: .64

Properties
Angelin is a tough, strong wood, with a very high bending strength. It works fairly well, but its alternating bands of hard and soft tissue make planing to a smooth finish difficult. The wood has a moderate blunting effect on cutting edges. It saws and mortises easily, turns, bores, stains, nails and screws well, and glues satisfactorily. Angelin carves very well, and can be polished and varnished to a good finish if the grain is filled.

Seasoning
It dries at a moderate rate with little degrade, but it can be slightly prone to check and distort while drying. There is little movement in use.

Durability
The heartwood is resistant to decay-causing organisms, and has a moderate resistance to dry-wood termites. Its sapwood is vulnerable to attack from the powder-post beetle. The heartwood is difficult to treat with preservatives, and the sapwood is relatively difficult to treat.

Typical uses
Furniture and cabinetmaking, turnery, and decorative objects such as umbrella handles and walking sticks. In contrast, it is also used for heavy construction, parquet flooring, exterior trim and cladding (siding), house framing and sills. Angelin also yields decorative veneers.

MERSAWA

Anisoptera laevis and related species (Dipterocarpaceae)

A. polyandra

Also called: krabak, kaunghmu, palosapsis, phdiek, ven ven

Description

When freshly cut, the heartwood is yellow-brown with a pink tinge; it darkens to a straw-brown on exposure. The sapwood is lighter, and not clearly demarcated from the heartwood. Mersawa has an interlocked grain with a moderately coarse and even texture. When quartersawn, a silver-grain figure created by the prominent rays is often visible.

Typical dry weight: 40lb/ft³ (640kg/m³)
Specific gravity: .64

Properties

The wood has medium crushing strength, low resistance to shock loads, low bending strength, very low stiffness and a poor steam-bending classification. The high silica content in the wood, combined with the interlocked grain, causes severe blunting of cutting edges. A reduced angle and very sharp cutters are required for effective machine planing, and the interlocked grain can affect mortising and moulding qualities. The wood turns, glues, nails and screws well, and stains and polishes satisfactorily.

Seasoning

The wood dries very slowly. There can be problems with drying the core of thicker stock, and there can be slight distortion during seasoning. There is medium movement in service.

Durability

Mersawa is moderately durable, with some natural resistance to attack by decay fungi. The sapwood is vulnerable to attack from the powder-post beetle. The heartwood has moderate resistance to preservative treatment.

Typical uses

Furniture, interior joinery, flooring including parquet, beams, corestock, heavy construction, boat planking, structural and utility plywood. Interesting logs are sliced for decorative veneers.

Grows
Malaysia and South-East Asia
Typical height: 100–150ft (30–45m)
Trunk diameter: 3–5ft (1–1.5m)

⚠ **Possible health risks**
Not known

PARANÁ PINE
Araucaria angustifolia (Araucariaceae)

Also called: Brazilian pine, pin, pinheiro do Brasil, pino Paraná

Grows
Brazil, Argentina, Paraguay
Typical height: 80–100ft
(24–33m)
Trunk diameter: 5ft (1.5m)

⚠ **Possible health risks**
Not known

Description
The heartwood ranges from beige to pale brown with a darker inner core, and is often streaked with dark pink, red or rusty red, which can be very attractive. The grain is typically straight, and the wood has a uniform close texture with a slight lustre, and growth rings that are usually barely visible. Attractive small, tight knots may sometimes be present, but these do not affect the strength of the wood. Despite its name, it is not a true pine.
Typical dry weight: 33lb/ft³ (540kg/m³), but with wide variation
Specific gravity: .54

Carving after Michelangelo ▶

Properties
Paraná pine has medium crushing and bending strength, very low resistance to shock loads, low stiffness, and a poor steam-bending rating. It works well with both hand and machine tools, with a slight to moderate blunting effect on cutting edges. It planes, moulds and sands to a smooth finish, and glues, stains, polishes, nails, screws, varnishes and paints well.

Seasoning
It is a difficult wood to dry; the darker-coloured wood tends to distort, split and dry slowly. The wood is rated as moderate for movement in service, but it can distort with changes in moisture content.

Durability
It is not durable, and is susceptible to attack from powder-post beetles and some other insects. The sapwood is permeable for preservative treatment, and the heartwood is moderately permeable.

Typical uses
Interior joinery, cabinetmaking, domestic and office furniture, framing, kitchen cabinets, turnery, domestic flooring including parquet, food containers, matches and matchboxes, panelling, blockboard, truck bodies, railway sleepers (railroad ties), telephone poles and wood pulp. It is also sliced for decorative veneer, and peeled for making plywood.

HOOP PINE

Araucaria cunninghamii (Araucariaceae)

Also called: Australian araucaria, arakaria, Dorrigo pine, colonial pine, Norfolk Island pine

Description

The heartwood ranges from white to pale yellow-brown. The sapwood, which can be as much as 6in (150mm) thick, is white, and not clearly distinct from the heartwood. The wood has straight grain and a fine to very fine uniform texture, which lends it a somewhat grainless appearance. Despite its common name, it is not a true pine.

Typical dry weight: 35lb/ft³ (560kg/m³)
Specific gravity: .56

Properties

Hoop pine is a soft, light wood that has medium to low stiffness and bending strength, a medium resistance to shock loads, and medium crushing strength. It is not suitable for steam bending. It works easily with both hand and machine tools, and has little blunting effect on cutting edges. Cutting edges must be kept very sharp to avoid pick-up and tearing around knots. The wood nails, screws and glues well, and the surface can be brought to a good finish.

Seasoning

The wood dries rapidly and well without degrade, but care is needed to avoid blue stain. It exhibits only a small degree of movement in service.

Durability

The heartwood is not durable and can be attacked by the hoop pine borer in tropical areas, and by the common furniture beetle. The sapwood is generally permeable for preservative treatment, and the heartwood moderately resistant.

Typical uses

Furniture, interior joinery, mouldings, panelling, boxes, flooring; also used to make plywood and particleboard.

Grows
Australia and Papua New Guinea; plantation-grown in Indonesia and South Africa
Typical height: 100–150ft (30m–45m) or more
Trunk diameter: 2–4ft (0.6–1.2m) or broader

⚠ **Possible health risks**
Not known

MADRONA
Arbutus menziesii (Ericaceae)

Also called: arbuti tree, madroño, jarrito, arbutus, Pacific madrone, coast madrone, strawberry tree, manzanita

▲ Miniature chest of drawers in yew (*Taxus baccata*) and madrona burr (burl)

Grows
Canada and USA
Typical height: 20–80ft
(6–24m)
Trunk diameter: 2–3ft
(0.6–0.9m)

⚠ Possible health risks
Not known

Description
The heartwood is light pink to pale reddish-brown, and sometimes has deep red spots. The growth rings can form an irregular pattern that makes the wood very attractive. The fine grain is usually straight to irregular and has a fine, smooth, even texture. The sapwood is whitish to cream and can have a pinkish cast.
Typical dry weight: 48lb/ft³ (770kg/m³)
Specific gravity: .77

Properties
Madrona is hard, tough and heavy. It has a high crushing and bending strength, with medium resistance to shock loads and medium stiffness. The wood is rated as moderate for steam bending. Despite being hard, madrona works satisfactorily with both hand and machine tools, giving a clean surface on planed and machined material. It has a moderate blunting effect on cutting edges. The wood turns, bores, nails, sands, screws and stains well, and polishes to a high finish; but gluing can be difficult.

Seasoning
Madrona is very difficult to dry. When green it has a very high moisture content, and this can lead to warping, checking, excessive shrinkage and collapse. If tension wood is present then uneven shrinkage can result. The wood should be air-dried very slowly before kilning. It is very stable in service.

Durability
It has very low natural resistance to decay, but is moderately resistant to common furniture beetle and powder-post beetle. The sapwood is permeable to preservative treatment, but the heartwood is resistant.

Typical uses
Quality furniture, decorative turnery, flooring, interior construction, corestock, and charcoal for making gunpowder. It is also sliced to make decorative veneers for cabinets and panelling. The sliced burr (burl) is highly prized for marquetry and furniture inlay.

PEROBA ROSA

Aspidosperma polyneuron (Apocynaceae)

Syn.: *A. peroba*
Also called: amarello, amargosa, ibri romi, palo rosa, red peroba, peroba rosa. There are many different names for different-coloured perobas

Description

The heartwood is pinkish-brown, but can vary widely, from pink to red with purple, orange or yellow streaks. The wood darkens on exposure. The yellowish sapwood is not very distinct from the heartwood. Grain ranges from straight to irregular, with a fine to very fine texture, and the wood has a low to medium lustre.
Typical dry weight: 47lb/ft³ (750kg/m³)
Specific gravity: .75

Properties

Peroba rosa is a hard, heavy timber with a high crushing strength, low stiffness, medium resistance to shock loads and medium bending strength. It is not suitable for steam bending. It works well with hand tools, but has a moderate blunting effect on cutting edges. A reduced cutting angle is recommended when planing stock with irregular grain, but straight-grained wood is easy to work. Peroba rosa carves, nails, stains and glues well, and is satisfactory for boring, mortising, varnishing and painting. It can be polished to an excellent finish.

Seasoning

The wood dries rapidly with considerable shrinkage, so care needs to be taken to reduce degrade, which usually takes the form of splitting and distortion. The wood shows medium movement in service.

Durability

The heartwood is very durable and highly resistant to preservative treatment. It is generally resistant to decay-causing organisms, but susceptible to attack from dry-wood termites. The sapwood is permeable for preservative treatment.

Typical uses

Cabinetmaking, interior and exterior joinery, floor joists, panelling, parquet flooring, building construction and shipbuilding; also sliced for decorative veneer.

Grows
Argentina and Brazil
Typical height: 90ft (27m)
Trunk diameter: 2ft 6in (0.75m); but can be taller and broader

⚠ **Possible health risks**
The dust and wood can cause skin irritation, headache, sweating, respiratory problems, nausea, stomach cramps, fainting, drowsiness, weakness and blisters

◀ Turned box in amarello (*Aspidosperma* sp.)

GONÇALO ALVES

Astronium fraxinifolium and *A. graveolens* (Anacardiaceae)

Also called: zorrowood, zebrawood, tigerwood, mura, bois de zèbre, bossona, urunday-para

Description

The clearly defined sapwood is up to 4in (100mm) wide and is grey or brownish-white. The heartwood is light golden-brown to reddish-brown, with irregular black and brown streaks. The grain is irregular and normally interlocked or wavy, with alternating bands of harder and softer wood. The texture is usually fine, and the wood has a medium to dull lustre. It is a very attractive wood.
Typical dry weight: 59lb/ft³ (950kg/m³)
Specific gravity: .95

Properties

Gonçalo alves is a hard, dense and heavy wood, which is very tough. It is not suitable for steam bending. Cutting normally requires tungsten carbide-tipped (TCT) blades, and planing can be difficult because of the hard and soft banding. Gluing can be tricky, but less so if a solvent is used to remove extractives. The wood needs pre-boring for nailing and screwing. It turns well and can easily be brought to a good polished finish.

Seasoning

It is advisable to dry the wood slowly to avoid degrade, otherwise there can be excessive warping and checking.

Durability

The wood is highly durable, and is resistant both to beetle attack and to preservative treatment.

Typical uses

Cabinetmaking, quality turnery, boatbuilding, flooring, jewellery boxes and other ornamental articles, decorative panelling, butts for billiard or pool cues, bobbins, knife handles and veneers.

Three-centre spire box ▶

Grows
Brazil, Paraguay and Uruguay
Typical height: 120ft (37m)
Trunk diameter: 2–3ft (0.6–1m)

⚠ **Possible health risks**
Dermatitis, irritation to skin and eyes; sensitizer

GABOON
Aucoumea klaineana (Burseraceae)

Also called: angouma, combogala, mofoumou, n'goumi, okoumé

Description
Gaboon has a white or pale grey sapwood. This is not clearly differentiated from the heartwood, which is salmon-pink to light brown or reddish-brown. The wood can attain a mahogany colour after exposure to light. The grain is usually straight or slightly interlocked, but it can sometimes be curly or wavy, which shows as a mottled or striped figure when the wood is quartersawn. It has a medium to moderately fine texture and a good satin-like lustre.
Typical dry weight: 27lb/ft³ (430kg/m³)
Specific gravity: .43

Properties
This is a weak, low-density wood with very low stiffness, low bending strength, poor steam-bending qualities and medium crushing strength; it also dents and scratches easily. It does, however, have a high silica content, and for this reason it can have a moderate to severe blunting effect on cutting edges. It works fairly easily with machine or hand tools, but surfaces can be woolly if care is not taken. It glues and nails well, stains satisfactorily, and can be brought to a lustrous finish.

Seasoning
Gaboon dries quickly and well. Degrade is very low, but there can be slight distortion and checking.

Durability
The heartwood has low resistance to decay, and can be attacked by marine borers. The sapwood is vulnerable to attack from the powder-post beetle. It does not take preservative treatment well.

Typical uses
Much of the wood used is made into plywood, blockboard and particleboard. Gaboon is also used for furniture, cabinetmaking, interior joinery, cigar boxes, construction, and as a substitute for mahogany.

Grows
Congo, Equatorial Guinea, Gabon
Typical height: 100–130ft (30–40m)
Trunk diameter: 3–8ft (0.9–2.4m)

⚠ **Possible health risks**
Asthma, coughing, skin and eye irritation

TATAJUBA

Bagassa guianensis (Moraceae)

Also called: bagasse, gele bagasse, amapa rana, cow-wood, garrote

Description

The narrow sapwood is yellowish-white to pale yellow and clearly demarcated from the heartwood. The heartwood is yellow when newly cut, but matures to a lustrous golden-brown or russet, and can be streaked. Its grain can be irregular, straight or interlocked, with a medium to coarse texture, distinct rays, and a lustrous surface. The interlocked grain can produce a broad stripe.

Typical dry weight: 50lb/ft³ (800kg/m³)
Specific gravity: .80

Properties

Tatajuba is a heavy, dense and hard wood, with high bending and crushing strengths and good steam-bending properties. It works easily with both machine and hand tools, and has only a slight blunting effect on cutting edges. Pre-boring is recommended for nailing and screwing, and these fixings hold well. Interlocking grain may cause tear-out when planing, but generally a clean finish can be obtained. The wood turns, moulds, mortises, carves and bores well. It takes glue, stains, paints and varnishes well, and is capable of being brought to a highly lustrous finish.

Seasoning

The wood is slow-drying with little degrade, but there is a risk of slight checking and distortion. Tatajuba is very stable in use.

Durability

It is durable, and resistant to white and brown rot fungi. The heartwood is difficult to treat with preservative.

Typical uses

Boatbuilding, decking, heavy construction and decorative veneers; also furniture and cabinetwork, including office furniture and kitchen cabinets.

Grows

Amazonian Brazil, French Guiana, Guyana and Surinam
Typical height: 90ft (27m)
Trunk diameter: 1ft 8in–2ft (0.5–0.6m)

⚠ **Possible health risks**

Contact dermatitis, allergic reactions

RHODESIAN TEAK

Baikiaea plurijuga (Leguminosae)

Also called: mukushi, mukusi, umgusi, Zambesi redwood

Description

The narrow sapwood, which is clearly demarcated from the heartwood, is pinkish-brown. The heartwood is reddish-brown, sometimes marked with irregular dark brown or black lines or flecks. It has a straight or slightly interlocked grain, with a fine, even texture and a low lustre. The tannin content of the wood can react with ferrous metals to cause staining. It is not a true teak.

Typical dry weight: 56lb/ft³ (900kg/m³)
Specific gravity: .90

Properties

Rhodesian teak is hard and heavy, and has a high abrasion resistance. It has high crushing and bending strengths, low shock resistance and stiffness, and a moderate steam-bending classification. The high silica content has a severe blunting effect on cutting edges, so tungsten carbide (TCT) cutters are advised, but these can gum up with resin if the wood is sawn green. A reduced cutting angle is recommended for planing, but a lustrous, smooth finish can be obtained. The wood can char when being bored. Pre-boring is required for nailing and screwing. The wood glues and stains well and can be brought to an excellent finish. It also turns excellently.

Seasoning

It dries slowly but easily, with only slight degrade, which can be in the form of distortion and surface checking if drying is too rapid. Movement in use is small.

Durability

The heartwood is very durable, with a high resistance to decay and a moderate resistance to termites. The sapwood is vulnerable to attack from the powder-post beetle, and is moderately resistant to preservative treatment; the heartwood is highly resistant to it.

Typical uses

Furniture and cabinetwork, carving, turnery, shop fittings (store fixtures), decorative and heavy-duty flooring, parquet flooring, railway sleepers (railroad ties) and decorative veneer.

Grows
Botswana, Zambia and Zimbabwe
Typical height: 50–60ft (15–18m)
Trunk diameter: 2ft 6in (0.8m)

⚠ **Possible health risks**
Respiratory irritation

PAU MARFIM

Balfourodendron riedelianum (Rutaceae)

Also called: guatambú, pau liso, marfim, moroti, kyrandy, ivorywood

Grows

Argentina, Brazil and Paraguay
Typical height: 40–80ft (12–24m)
Trunk diameter: 1–4ft (0.3–1.2m)

⚠ **Possible health risks**
Dermatitis, rhinitis and asthma

Description

There is no real contrast between the sapwood and the heartwood. The colour ranges from near-white through pale yellowish-brown or cream to lemon. It can have a greyish tinge and darker streaks. The grain may be either straight or irregular, and is sometimes interlocked, with a fine to very fine uniform texture and a medium lustre.
Typical dry weight: 50lb/ft³ (800kg/m³)
Specific gravity: .80

Properties

It is a very hard, dense wood, which is very hard-wearing, and is rated high in all the strength categories. Pau marfim is too strong for steam bending. It works well with both machine and hand tools, but does have a fairly severe blunting effect on cutting edges. When planing or moulding wood with irregular grain, tearing may occur, but it gives a smooth finish on straight-grained stock. It carves, nails, screws, stains and paints well, glues satisfactorily, and can be brought to a highly polished finish.

Seasoning

The wood dries easily and readily with little degrade. There is only small movement in service.

Durability

The wood is vulnerable to insect attack and decay, and has little natural resistance. The sapwood is permeable for preservative treatment, but the heartwood is resistant.

Typical uses

Cabinetmaking, interior joinery, kitchen cabinets, interior trim, boatbuilding and oars, domestic and office furniture, domestic flooring, textile rollers, bobbins, shoe lasts, handles and marquetry. It is also sliced to make decorative veneers and plywood.

PINK IVORY WOOD

Berchemia zeyheri (Rhamnaceae)

Syn.: *Rhamnus zeyheri*
Also called: red ivory wood, pink ivory, pau preto, umgoloti, mucarane, sungangona

Description

The heartwood is yellowish-brown, with a rich golden-red cast. It has a straight to interlocked grain with a moderately fine and even texture and a fine pore structure. The wood has a pinkish-red striped figure that is created by alternating bands of dark and light wood in the growth rings.
Typical dry weight: 56lb/ft³ (900kg/m³)
Specific gravity: .90

Properties

Pink ivory is a tough, very hard and heavy wood that is extremely strong in the majority of categories, but has a low steam-bending rating. It is fairly difficult to work with hand tools, having a medium to severe blunting effect on cutting edges. A reduced cutting angle is advised when planing quartersawn wood. Pre-boring is required for nailing and screwing, and cutting edges must be very sharp. The wood glues, sands and stains well, and has excellent turning and carving qualities. It can be brought to a highly polished finish.

Seasoning

It is difficult to air-dry, and kiln-drying requires careful control, otherwise degrade can be excessive.
High differential shrinkage can cause serious distortion. It exhibits large movement in use.

Durability

The wood is not durable, with low resistance to wood-destroying insects and decay-causing fungi. The sapwood is permeable for preservative treatment, but the heartwood is very resistant.

Typical uses

Furniture, interior joinery, panelling, light flooring, carving, inlay, chess pieces and vehicle parts. Choice logs are sliced for decorative veneer.

◀ Pill box

Grows
Mozambique; also south and south-eastern Africa
Typical height: 20–40ft (6–12m)
Trunk diameter: 7–12in (18–30cm)

⚠ **Possible health risks**
Not known

The genus *Betula*
Birches

▲ Lidded bx in heavily spalted birch

▲ Birches have distinctive peeling bark, often strikingly coloured; some decorative varieties are pure white

The *Betula* genus contains up to 60 species of trees and shrubs that are native to the northern hemisphere. Birch trees can be found as far north as the Arctic, with European white birch (*B. pubescens*, also known as downy or hairy birch) surviving at 70 degrees north – it is one of the few species of tree to grow in Iceland. The subspecies Arctic white birch (*B. pubescens* ssp. *tortuosa*) is the only tree native to Greenland. Birch trees feature largely in the folklore and culture of northern European countries, especially in Scandinavia and Russia; the Beriozka tourist shops of the Soviet era were named after the birch tree. In North America the bark of the paper birch (*B. papyrifera*) was used for the construction of canoes by the Native Americans, and also for writing on – hence the name.

Birch trees are typified by constantly shedding their outer bark (rind) in strips around the stem; the silver birch (*B. pendula*), familiar in Europe, is a particularly good example of this. Birch bark is often grey or white, but there can be many exceptions to this. Birches typically have fine twigs and foliage, with their flowers forming in catkins.

Tilt-hinge box in rippled silver birch (*B. pendula*)▶

YELLOW BIRCH

Betula alleghaniensis (Betulaceae)

Also called: hard birch, betula wood, Canadian yellow birch, Quebec birch, swamp birch

Description

The sapwood is whitish, pale yellow or light reddish-brown, whereas the heartwood is reddish-brown. Colours can vary, however. Yellow birch has a fine, even texture and is close-grained. The grain is mostly straight, but wavy and curly grain can occur, resulting in a pleasing figure.
Typical dry weight: 44lb/ft³ (710kg/m³)
Specific gravity: .71

Properties

When yellow birch is air-dried, bending strength is very high. The wood also has a high resistance to shock loads, and high crushing strength. Both nailing and screwing properties are somewhat poor, and pre-boring is required. Gluing needs care, and must be carried out in controlled conditions. Planing can be difficult when the grain is irregular, but is satisfactory on straight grain. The wood has a moderate dulling effect on cutters, but otherwise works fairly easily with both machine and hand tools. Yellow birch takes stain and polish very well.

Seasoning

It dries quite slowly with little degrade, but shrinkage tends to be pretty high. It can develop end and surface checks, and wet heartwood can lead to honeycombing and collapse. There is a lot of movement in use, giving poor dimensional stability.

Durability

The heartwood is fairly resistant to preservative treatment and the wood has little natural resistance to decay.

Typical uses

Furniture, quality joinery, turnery, rustic furniture, upholstery frames, decorative and marquetry veneers, violin bows and flooring. Also crates, cooperage, shuttles and best-quality plywood.

Grows
Eastern Canada and eastern USA
Typical height: 70–100ft (21–30m)
Trunk diameter: 2ft 6in (0.8m)

⚠ **Possible health risks**
Dermatitis, respiratory problems

PAPER BIRCH

Betula papyrifera (Betulaceae)

Also called: white birch (Canada), **American birch** (UK), **canoe birch, western paper birch, Canadian white birch**

Description
The heartwood is creamy-white, often with a brownish central core. It is straight-grained with a fine, even texture, and it can have an attractive natural figure.
Typical dry weight: 39lb/ft³ (620kg/m³)
Specific gravity: .62

Properties
This is a heavy wood that has quite a good bending classification, with medium strength for crushing and resistance to shock loads. Its steam-bending category is moderately low and its stiffness is low. It has a moderate blunting effect on cutters and works well with machine and hand tools. It can chip and tear on planing, so a reduced cutting angle is advised. Pre-boring is advised for nailing and screwing. It glues well if care is taken. It polishes well, and takes dyes and clear stains better than heavily pigmented finishes.

Seasoning
It air-dries slowly with little degrade, but extractives can cause brownish stains. It shows very little movement in service.

Durability
Paper birch has little natural resistance to decay. The sapwood is permeable for preservative application, but the heartwood is fairly resistant to treatment.

Typical uses
Fine furniture, office furniture, rustic furniture and panelling. It is used widely for turnery such as spools, dowels, domestic ware and toys. It is also used for boxes and crates, ice-cream spoons, medical spatulas (tongue depressors), fruit baskets and decorative veneers. Paper birch is rotary-cut for making plywood, and pulped to make writing paper. Native Americans traditionally made their canoes from the bark.

Grows
Canada and eastern USA
Typical height: 50–70ft (15–21m)
Trunk diameter: 1–2ft (0.3–0.6m)

⚠ **Possible health risks**
Dermatitis, respiratory problems

EUROPEAN BIRCH

Betula pendula and *B. pubescens* (Betulaceae)

Ripple figure

Spalted

Syn. for *B. pendula*: *B. verrucosa*
Also called: silver birch (*B. pendula*), downy or **hairy birch (*B. pubescens*), European**
white birch, bouleau (French), **Birke, Sandbirke** (German); also English, Swedish, Finnish
birch, according to origin. Additionally according to figure: **flame, ice, curly, masur birch**

Description

The wood is creamy-white to pale brown and somewhat featureless, with no colour distinction between sapwood and heartwood. It is generally straight-grained and of a fine, even texture, with a lustrous appearance. Grain irregularities can cause flame and curly figure. Masur birch is caused by larvae attacking the cambium, giving a beautiful flecked, swirling figure.
Typical dry weight: 41lb/ft³ (660kg/m³)
Specific gravity: .66

Properties

A heavy, dense wood, it steam-bends well, but there may be problems with knots or irregular grain. It has medium stiffness and resistance to shock loads, with high bending and crushing strength. It tends to be woolly, but generally works well with hand or machine tools. It has a moderate blunting effect on cutters; a reduced planing angle of 15° will prevent tearing on cross-grained wood. Birch requires pre-boring for nails and screws. It can be polished and stained to a good finish, and glues well. It is very good for turnery.

Seasoning

It must be dried rapidly to prevent fungal attack, and has a slight tendency to warp. There is only small movement in service.

Durability

Birch is perishable and vulnerable to attack from the common furniture beetle, but immune to the powder-post beetle. The permeable sapwood is moderately resistant to preservative treatment.

Typical uses

Furniture making and interior joinery. Also quality turnery, brooms, brushes, cabinet interiors and flooring. Much used for plywood. Figured veneers, produced by slicing or peeling, are valued for marquetry and panelling.

Grows
Europe, including UK and Scandinavia. Found as far north as Lapland, which is further north than any other broad-leaved tree
Typical height: 60–70ft (18–21m)
Trunk diameter: 2–3ft (0.6–1m)

⚠ **Possible health risks**
Dermatitis and respiratory problems; sensitizer

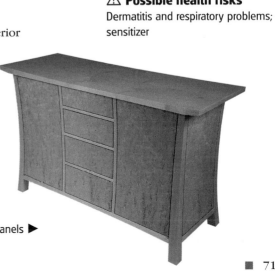

Sideboard with masur birch panels ▶

SUCUPIRA

Bowdichia virgilioides and related species (Leguminosae)

Also called: alcornoque, sapupira, sucupira parda, sucupira preta, paricarana, black sucupira, cœur dehors (French)

Description
The heartwood is a dull chocolate to reddish-brown, with light yellow markings that show as a striped figure on quartered surfaces. It has an irregular and interlocked grain, which is sometimes wavy, and a coarse texture with a harsh feel. The sapwood is whitish and clearly demarcated from the heartwood.
Typical dry weight: 62lb/ft³ (1000kg/m³)
Specific gravity: 1.00

Properties
The wood has high strength in all categories, but is not suitable for steam bending. Its high density and interlocked grain make it difficult to work. A reduced cutting angle is advised for planing, and a lot of sanding is required to get a smooth finish. It holds nails and screws well, glues and turns well and can be brought to a good polished finish if pre-filled.

Seasoning
A difficult wood to dry, it is prone to checking and cupping when kiln-dried. It exhibits medium movement in use.

Durability
Sucupira is highly durable, and not vulnerable to insect attack or decay.

Typical uses
Furniture, turnery, boatbuilding, domestic flooring, durable heavy construction and railway sleepers (railroad ties). It is also sliced for decorative veneers used in panelling, doors and inlay.

Grows
Brazil, Venezuela and the Guianas
Typical height: 150ft (45m)
Trunk diameter: 4ft (0.2m)

⚠ **Possible health risks**
Allergic contact dermatitis

MUHUHU

Brachylaena hutchinsii (Compositae)

Also called: mkarambaki, muhugive, muhugwe

Description

The heartwood is bright yellow-brown when freshly cut, but darkens to a dark yellowish-brown, which frequently has darker streaks and a greenish hue. The grain is closely interlocked and sometimes wavy or curly, with a fine, even texture. The sapwood, which is distinct from the heartwood, is greyish-white. Muhuhu has an aromatic scent similar to that of sandalwood (*Santalum album*).
Typical dry weight: 58lb/ft³ (930kg/ft³)
Specific gravity: .93

Properties

Muhuhu is a very heavy wood and has a very high resistance to wear, abrasion and indentation. It has a very low resistance to shock loads, a medium bending strength, low stiffness, but high crushing strength. The wood is rated as moderate for steam bending. Due to its high density and irregular grain, muhuhu has a moderate blunting effect on cutting edges, and there can be gum build-up when sawing. A reduced cutting angle is advised for planing. The wood turns, stains, polishes, varnishes and paints well, but gluing can be difficult, and pre-boring is required for nailing.

Seasoning

As the wood is very dense, slow drying is recommended to reduce degrade. End splitting and surface checking are typical drying defects. There is small movement in service.

Durability

The heartwood is resistant to decay, and has moderate resistance to marine borer and termite attack. It is extremely resistant to preservative treatment.

Typical uses

Carvings, turnery, parquet and heavy-duty flooring, heavy construction, bridge decking and railway sleepers (railroad ties). Muhuhu is used in crematoria in India as a substitute for sandalwood.

Grows
East Africa
Typical height: 80–90ft (24–27m)
Trunk diameter: 2ft (0.6m)

⚠ **Possible health risks**
Dermatitis

SNAKEWOOD

Brosimum guianense (Moraceae)

Syn.: *Piratinera guianensis*
Also called: letterwood, letterhout, amourette, gateado, palo de oro, burokoro, cacique carey, leopardwood, speckled wood, lechero

Description

Snakewood owes its name to its appearance: it has markings resembling snakeskin, though sometimes it can be more leopard-like and spotty. The heartwood is dark red to reddish-brown, and has irregular black markings or vertical black stripes, which can appear alone or in juxtaposition with speckles. The very thick sapwood is yellowish-white and has an irregular border with the heartwood. Snakewood has a moderately fine to fine, uniform straight grain with a medium to high lustre.
Typical dry weight: 81lb/ft³ (1300kg/m³)
Specific gravity: 1.30

Properties

The wood is extremely hard and heavy and extremely strong in all categories, but is not suitable for steam bending because of gum exudation. On account of its hardness it is very difficult to work, and has a severe blunting effect on cutting edges. Gluing can be tricky because of the resin content. Snakewood finishes smoothly straight from the tool, turns very well and can be polished to a splendid high finish.

Seasoning

Drying can be difficult, with some warping and degrade. The wood exhibits medium movement in use.

Durability

The heartwood is highly durable and immune to insect attack, and is highly resistant to preservative treatment.

Typical uses

Inlay, violin bows, walking sticks, decorative turnery, fishing-rod butts, drumsticks, jewellery, cutlery handles and archery bows. Snakewood is also sliced into decorative veneers for cabinetwork and marquetry.

Grows
Central and tropical South America
Typical height: 80ft (25m)
Trunk diameter: 1–3ft (0.3–0.9m)

⚠ **Possible health risks**
Thirst, salivation, respiratory tract irritation and nausea

EUROPEAN BOXWOOD

Buxus sempervirens (Buxaceae)

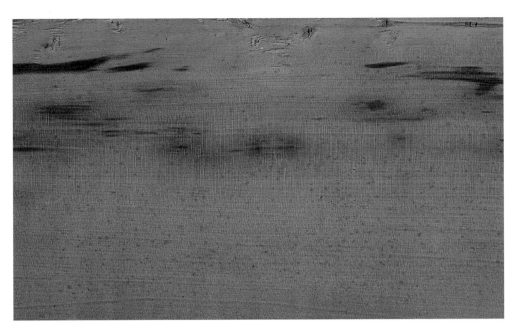

Also called: box, buis (French), **Buchs, Buchsbaum** (German), **gewone palm** (Dutch); also by origin: **Turkish, Iranian,** etc.

Description
The colour is a uniform yellow, individual specimens varying from butter to lemon; heart and sapwood are not distinct. Small, tight knots are fairly common. The grain is usually straight, but can be irregular. Boxwood has a fine, uniform texture.
Typical dry weight: 57lb/ft³ (910kg/m³)
Specific gravity: .91

Properties
Box is a hard, dense and heavy wood. It has good crushing strength and resistance to shock loads, high stiffness and good steam-bending qualities. It has a moderate blunting effect on cutters and is rather difficult to plane, although it turns well. Pre-boring is required for nailing and screwing, and it glues satisfactorily.
It stains and polishes well. Boxwood takes detail very well when carved or turned.

Seasoning
It needs very slow seasoning under cover to prevent end splitting, which can be severe if it is dried in the round without end coating. It is very stable in service.

Durability
The heartwood can be vulnerable to the common furniture beetle, but it is a durable wood. For the type of articles made from it, preservative treatment is not normally required.

Typical uses
Carving, ornamental turnery, chess pieces, inlay work, woodwind instruments, rules, shuttles, handles and veneer.

▲ Rules and scales, 19th and 20th centuries

Grows
UK, southern Europe, Turkey and western Asia
Typical height: 20–30ft (6–9m)
Trunk diameter: 8in (0.2m)

⚠ **Possible health risks**
Sensitizer; dermatitis; dust irritates eyes, nose and throat

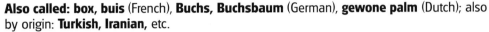

◀ Lidded box

BRAZILWOOD

Caesalpinia echinata (Leguminosae)

Syn.: *Guilandina echinata*
Also called: Bahia wood, Para wood, Pernambuco wood, pau Brasil, Brazil ironwood, brasilete

Grows
Eastern Brazil
Typical height: 25–40ft (8–12m)
Trunk diameter: 20–27in
(0.5–0.7m)

⚠ **Possible health risks**
Can cause irritation to the eyes and skin, headaches and nausea, visual disturbances

Description
This is the wood after which the country of Brazil was named. It was originally prized for its dyeing properties. The heartwood is a bright orange-red, which matures to a deep red-brown. The sapwood is nearly white. The figure varies from stripy to marble-like, and may have pin knots to add to the interest. The grain can be straight to interlocked, with a fine, even texture and a natural lustre.
Typical dry weight: 75–80lb/ft³
(1200–1280kg/m³)
Specific gravity: 1.2

Properties
Brazilwood is very hard and heavy, with exceptional shock resistance, stiffness, bending and compression strength. It is not suitable for steam bending. Due to its hardness it can be difficult to work, and has a severe blunting effect on cutting tools. Pre-drilling is required for nailing and screwing. It glues well and can be polished to an excellent lustrous finish.

Seasoning
The wood needs very slow drying to avoid degradation and checking.

Durability
A highly durable wood, which is resistant to decay and insect attack.

Typical uses
A highly prized wood for making violin bows, it is also used for gunstocks, quality turnery, parquet flooring, exterior joinery and inlay work, and may be sawn into decorative veneers for furniture.

Turned box ▶

YELLOW CEDAR

Callitropsis nootkatensis (Cupressaceae)

Syn.: *Xanthocyparis nootkatensis, Chamaecyparis nootkatensis, Cupressus nootkatensis*
Also called: Alaska cedar, Alaska yellow cedar, Pacific coast yellow cedar, yellow cypress, Sitka cypress, Nootka false cypress

Description

The heartwood is a bright, clear yellow or pale yellow when first cut, and darkens on exposure. The sapwood is very narrow, and near-white to yellowish-white; it is not very distinct from the heartwood. The texture is fine to medium, and the grain is usually straight and even. It is not a true cedar.
Typical dry weight: 31lb/ft³ (500kg/m³)
Specific gravity: .50

Properties

It has low resistance to shock loads and low stiffness, with medium crushing and bending strengths. Its steam-bending classification is poor. It has excellent nailing and screwing characteristics, and very good gluing properties. The blunting effect on cutting edges is very slight, and it works well with both hand and machine tools. A reduced cutting angle is advised so as to avoid pick-up when planing wavy-grained stock. The wood can be brought to an excellent finish, and stains, varnishes and paints well. It is acid-resistant.

Seasoning

Yellow cedar dries well, but slow drying is advised to avoid end splitting. Thick stock can experience some surface checking. There is little movement in service.

Durability

Yellow cedar has a naturally high resistance to decay fungi, and responds poorly to the application of preservatives.

Typical uses

Quality joinery, boatbuilding, canoes, exterior joinery, office furniture, sporting goods, rustic furniture, shingles, posts and marine piling. Yellow cedar is also used for battery separators, and interestingly figured logs are sliced for decorative veneers.

Grows
From Alaska to Oregon, including the Canadian Pacific coast
Typical height: 50–100ft (15–30m), but can reach 170ft (50m) in Canada
Trunk diameter: 1–4ft (0.3–1.2m)

⚠ **Possible health risks**
Not known

JACAREUBA

Calophyllum brasiliense (Guttiferae)

Also called: Santa Maria (Central America), **aceite, alfaro, barillo, cachicambo, guanandi, pau de Maria, leche de Maria**

Description

The sapwood is pale and merges into the heartwood without a clear differentiation. The heartwood ranges in colour from pink, yellowish-pink or pale red to brick red or a rich reddish-brown. It usually has an interlocked to highly interlocked grain, with a medium homogeneous texture and a low to medium lustre. The grain can also be straight, frequently with dark red stripes showing on flatsawn surfaces, and a ribbon figure on quartered surfaces.
Typical dry weight: 37lb/ft³ (590kg/m³)
Specific gravity: .59

Properties

The wood is heavy and dense; it has medium shock resistance and bending properties, high crushing strength and low stiffness. Steam bending is rated as moderate. It saws easily, but brown gum and interlocked grain can be problems. Planing qualities may be below average; a low cutting angle reduces tear-out. The blunting effect is usually moderate, but can be severe if gum is present. The wood glues, stains and polishes well, and carves easily when straight-grained. Pre-boring is advised for screwing and nailing.

Seasoning

It is difficult to air-dry. The rate of drying is variable but generally slow, and there can be severe warping; slight surface checking, a high level of knot splitting and case hardening can also occur.

Durability

The heartwood is moderately resistant to decay-causing organisms, but susceptible to dry-wood insects and marine borers; it is extremely difficult to treat with preservatives. The sapwood is permeable.

Typical uses

Furniture, interior and exterior joinery, flooring including parquet, boat and ship building, construction work, shop fittings (store fixtures), decks, cooperage, shingles and plywood. Selected logs are sliced into decorative veneers for panelling and cabinets.

DEGAME

Calycophyllum candidissimum (Rubiaceae)

Also called: lemonwood (USA), **degame lacewood** (UK), **alazano, betun, dagame, guayabo, palo camarón, madroño** (but not to be confused with *Arbutus menziesii*)

Description

Degame has a very broad zone of sapwood, which varies in colour from white to light brown. The heartwood is variegated and ranges from light brown through oatmeal to olive-brown; sometimes it can be greyish. The grain is very irregular, and varies from straight to interlocked. The wood has an exceptionally fine, uniform texture and a low to medium lustre.
Typical dry weight: 51lb/ft³ (820kg/m³)
Specific gravity: .82

Properties

Degame is a very hard, tough and heavy wood, with exceptionally high bending strength and good steam-bending qualities. It works well, whether machine or hand tools are used, and has only a slight blunting effect on cutting edges. The wood glues, screws and nails well, with little risk of splitting, is satisfactory for planing, and has very good staining properties. It can be polished to an excellent finish.

Seasoning

It both air- and kiln-dries well, but there can be some surface and end checking in planks. Warping can occur, and there is a risk of twisting with samples that have irregular grain.

Durability

The heartwood is non-resistant to decay, but is highly resistant to marine borers. The typical uses of this wood do not require preservative treatment.

Typical uses

Cabinetmaking, quality joinery and turnery; also domestic and factory flooring, fishing rods, archery bows, handles, shuttles, organ building and sporting goods.

> **Grows**
> Central America, Colombia and Venezuela
> **Typical height:** 40–60ft (12–18m)
> **Trunk diameter:** 2ft 6in (0.75m)

⚠ **Possible health risks**
Not known

AUSTRALIAN SILKY OAK

Cardwellia sublimis (Proteaceae)

Also called: northern silky oak, bull oak, Queensland silky oak

Description
On quartered surfaces, silky oak has large rays that produce a very clearly marked silver-grain ray figure. The wood is pink to reddish-brown, maturing to a darker red-brown with age. It has a moderately coarse but even texture. It sometimes has narrow gum lines, or ducts. Except where the fibres pass around the rays, it is straight-grained. As its name implies, the wood has a natural golden sheen, and the figure can range from a small lacelike pattern to a large splashlike form. It is not a true oak.
Typical dry weight: 33lb/ft³ (530kg/m³)
Specific gravity: .53

Properties
In relation to its density it is below average strength, especially for bending and compression. It does, however, have a good steam-bending classification. It is easy to work with hand and machine tools, but some problems can occur due to the crumbling of the large ray-cell walls, particularly when planing or shaping. It has a medium blunting effect on tools. A reasonable finish can be obtained, and it can be stained, screwed, nailed and glued satisfactorily.

Seasoning
This is a difficult wood to season, and cupping may occur on wide boards. It needs to be dried slowly, and may suffer checking or splits.

Durability
The sapwood is vulnerable to attack from the powder-post beetle. However, it is moderately durable and has moderate resistance to preservative treatment.

Typical uses
Quality grades are used for domestic and rustic furniture, shop fittings (store fixtures), kitchen cabinets, block flooring and cask staves. It is used in Australia instead of softwood for shuttering and building. Regarded as a medium-quality wood, it is also used as a substitute for oak in joinery.

EUROPEAN HORNBEAM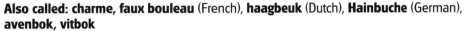
Carpinus betulus (Betulaceae)

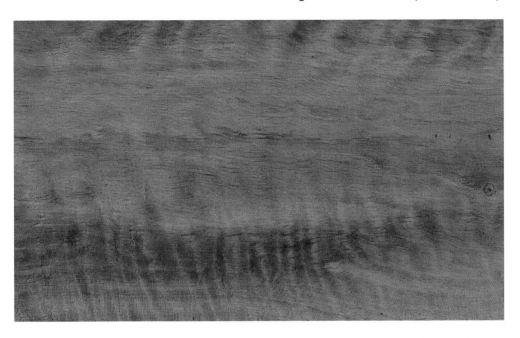

Also called: charme, faux bouleau (French), **haagbeuk** (Dutch), **Hainbuche** (German), **avenbok, vitbok**

Description
There is no real distinction between sapwood and heartwood. The wood is a dull white in colour, with green streaks. It normally has a crossed or irregular grain and a fine, even texture. Quartersawn surfaces may show a flecked appearance, produced by the broad medullary rays.
Typical dry weight: 47lb/ft³ (750kg/m³)
Specific gravity: .75

Properties
Hornbeam is a hard, heavy wood. It has high crushing and bending strength, medium stiffness and resistance to shock loads, and very high steam-bending properties. The wood exhibits excellent shear strength and resistance to splitting. It has good wearing qualities and is somewhat difficult to work, with a moderate blunting effect on cutting edges. Pre-boring may be necessary where nailing is required. The wood planes and cuts satisfactorily, and has good gluing, turning and staining qualities. It can be polished to a high finish.

Seasoning
It dries readily and well, with little degrade. However, it is dimensionally unstable in service.

Durability
Hornbeam has little natural resistance to decay. It can be vulnerable to attack from the forest longhorn beetle when in log form, and the sapwood can be susceptible to the common furniture beetle. The wood absorbs preservatives easily.

Typical uses
Turnery, including drumsticks and billiard or pool cues. Also musical instrument parts including organ pipes; mallets, pegs, pulleys, tools and tool handles. Due to its hard-wearing qualities, hornbeam is good for light industrial flooring. It is also used for veneer.

Grows
Europe, Turkey, Iran
Typical height: 50–80ft
(15–24m)
Trunk diameter: 3–4ft
(0.9–1.2m)

⚠ **Possible health risks**
Not known

HICKORY

Carya spp. (Juglandaceae)

C. ovata

C. tomentosa

Syn.: *Hicoria*
Also called: pignut hickory (*C. glabra*), mockernut hickory (*C. tomentosa*), shellbark hickory (*C. laciniosa*), shagbark hickory, scalybark hickory (*C. ovata*)

Description

There are four commercial species of hickory, and the wood is almost the same from all of them. The sapwood is pale and clearly demarcated from the heartwood, and is sold as 'white hickory'. The heartwood is brown to reddish-brown, and marketed as 'red hickory'. Usually straight-grained, it can be wavy or irregular, with a coarse texture, and it has a medium lustre.
Typical dry weight: 51lb/ft³ (820kg/m³)
Specific gravity: .82

Properties

Hickory is very dense and has high crushing, stiffness, bending and toughness qualities. It has exceptionally good shock resistance, and good steam-bending properties. The wood is quite difficult to work, especially with hand tools, and has a moderate to severe blunting effect on cutting edges. Pre-boring is required for nailing, and it is difficult to glue. Hickory sands, turns, stains and polishes well.

Seasoning

It dries fairly rapidly, and this must be managed with care. High shrinkage, twisting and warping can be a problem. Hickory shows high stability in service.

Durability

The wood is non-durable, with little resistance to decay. It can be vulnerable to attack from the forest longhorn and buprestid beetles, and the sapwood is at risk from powder-post beetle. It is moderately responsive to impregnation with preservatives.

Typical uses

Hickory is much used for the handles of striking tools, such as axes and hammers. It is also used for furniture, ladders, vehicle parts, cutting surfaces, violin bows, piano keys, sporting goods, flooring, handles and baseball bats.

Grows
Canada and USA
Typical height: 50–100ft
(15–30m)
Trunk diameter: 2ft 6in (0.8m)

⚠ **Possible health risks**
Not known

PECAN

Carya illinoiensis (Juglandaceae)

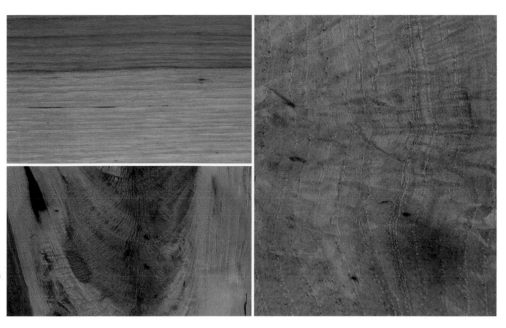

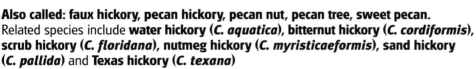

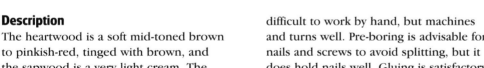

Crotch figure

Also called: faux hickory, pecan hickory, pecan nut, pecan tree, sweet pecan.
Related species include **water hickory (*C. aquatica*)**, **bitternut hickory (*C. cordiformis*)**,
scrub hickory (*C. floridana*), **nutmeg hickory (*C. myristicaeformis*)**, **sand hickory
(*C. pallida*)** and **Texas hickory (*C. texana*)**

Description

The heartwood is a soft mid-toned brown to pinkish-red, tinged with brown, and the sapwood is a very light cream. The tight grain is generally straight but can be wavy or mottled, with a medium to coarse texture. The various species of hickory and pecan are very closely related and there is some confusion between them; many pecans are referred to as hickories. The two groups are distinguished by their microanatomy: pecan hickories have parenchyma bands in their earlywood and 'true' hickories do not. True hickory is typically heavier than pecan and is considered to be of slightly higher quality.
Typical dry weight: 46lb/ft³ (750kg/m³)
Specific Gravity: .75

Properties

The wood has high crushing and bending strength, high stiffness and very high shock resistance. It is excellent for steam-bending. It is good for uses where elasticity and strength are important. Being hard, it has a moderate to severe blunting effect on cutting edges. It is difficult to work by hand, but machines and turns well. Pre-boring is advisable for nails and screws to avoid splitting, but it does hold nails well. Gluing is satisfactory. It sands, polishes and stains well.

Seasoning

Pecan kiln-dries well, and air-dries rapidly. Shrinkage is high, but it generally seasons quickly with little degrade. However, there can be a problem with warping and twisting when air-dried. It exhibits small movement in service.

Durability

It is non-durable with slight resistance to heartwood decay, and is extremely resistant to preservative treatment.

Typical uses

Furniture, chairmaking, tool handles, turnery, sports goods such as baseball bats and archery equipment, ladder rungs, flooring, decorative veneer and plywood. It is also used for smoking meats, and for charcoal, and the pecan tree is a source of edible nuts.

Grows
Midwest to eastern USA, Mexico
Typical height: 100–140ft (30–43m)
Trunk diameter: up to 4ft (1.2m)

⚠ **Possible health risks**
Not known

AMERICAN CHESTNUT

Castanea dentata (Fagaceae)

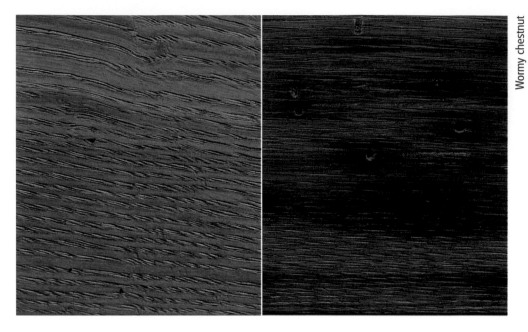

Also called: chestnut, wormy chestnut

Description

The heartwood is greyish-brown to brown, and can age to a darker brown. The wide growth rings can create an interesting figure on certain cuts. It often has wormholes as a result of chestnut blight. The sapwood is whitish to light brown, and narrow. The wood normally has straight grain, but it can be spiral-grained. American chestnut is classified as fairly coarse to coarse in texture. There is some similarity to oak, but without the distinctive broad rays.
Typical dry weight: 30lb/ft³ (480kg/m³)
Specific gravity: .48

Properties

American chestnut has very low resistance to shock loads, and also very low stiffness. It has low bending strength, medium crushing strength and a moderate steam-bending classification. It is fairly difficult to plane and saw, but otherwise works well with either machine or hand tools. Pre-boring is required for nailing and screwing, and it glues well. The blunting effect on cutters is fairly slight. Contact with ferrous metals is liable to cause blue stain. The wood can be stained and polished to a very good finish.

Seasoning

Drying is slow and difficult, with a tendency to dry unevenly, resulting in honeycombing and collapse. Iron staining can be a problem.

Durability

It has a high natural resistance to decay. The durable heartwood is very resistant to treatment with preservatives, but the sapwood is vulnerable to attack from the common furniture beetle and the powder-post beetle.

Typical uses

Furniture, interior construction, barrels, coffins, posts, railway sleepers (railroad ties) and handles. The wormy form is favoured for decorative veneers and picture frames.

Grows
Eastern USA and southern Ontario, Canada
Typical height: 20ft (6m)
Trunk diameter: Prior to the decimation of the chestnut by chestnut blight in 1904, trees could grow to 60–100ft (18–30m) with trunks of 2–4ft (0.6–1.2m) across

---

⚠ **Possible health risks**
Not known

SWEET CHESTNUT

Castanea sativa (Fagaceae)

Also called: European chestnut, Spanish chestnut, châtaignier (French), **Edelkastanie, Esskastanie** (German), **tamme kastanje** (Dutch)

Description

The heartwood of sweet chestnut is a biscuit-like yellowish-brown, similar to that of oak in its overall appearance, but with finer medullary rays. The sapwood is thin and pale, and clearly differentiated from the heartwood. The grain is typically straight, though spiral grain is not uncommon, and the texture is coarse. Shakes can frequently be found in older trees.

Typical dry weight: 34lb/ft³ (540kg/m³)
Specific gravity: .54

Properties

Sweet chestnut has medium crushing strength, very low stiffness and resistance to shock loads, and good steam-bending properties. Contact with iron is liable to result in blue-black iron stains, and the wood can in turn cause corrosion in metals because of its acid content. It works well with both hand and machine tools, and has only a slight dulling effect on cutting edges. Sweet chestnut takes screws, nails, glues and stains well, and the wood can be either polished or varnished to an excellent finish.

Seasoning

Chestnut dries slowly and can degrade severely, with collapse, honeycombing and moisture pockets. Movement in service is small.

Durability

The sapwood is vulnerable to attack from the common furniture beetle and powder-post beetle. The heartwood is durable and very resistant to preservative treatment. In old structures in some areas the death-watch beetle can attack both sapwood and heartwood.

Typical uses

Sometimes used as a substitute for oak in furniture, built-in kitchens, coffins, casks, stakes, turnery, umbrella handles and kitchen utensils. Decorative veneers are sliced from selected logs.

◀ Platter in figured sweet chestnut

Grows
Europe, chiefly south-west and Mediterranean area
Typical height: 100–115ft (30–50m)
Trunk diameter: 5ft (1.5m)

⚠ **Possible health risks**
Dermatitis, possibly caused by bark lichens

BLACKBEAN
Castanospermum australe (Leguminosae)

Also called: beantree, Moreton Bay bean, Moreton Bay chestnut

Description
The sapwood is white to yellowish and the heartwood medium to chocolate brown, sometimes with darker streaks. It can darken to black with age. The grain is generally straight, but may be a little interlocked. The texture is medium to coarse, and the wood has an oily feel. Quartersawn wood is attractively striped.
Typical dry weight: 44lb/ft³ (700kg/m³)
Specific gravity: .70

Properties
Blackbean is hard and heavy. It has medium strength in most respects, but will not withstand shock loads due to its brittleness, and has a very poor steam-bending classification. It has a moderate blunting effect on cutting tools, due to a high mineral content. Planing and moulding can be difficult: some lighter patches may crumble unless the cutters are very sharp. Due to the wood's oily nature, gluing results can be variable. It nails and screws satisfactorily, and stains and polishes to an excellent finish. It has very high electrical resistance.

Seasoning
It is difficult to dry. If care is not taken, honeycombing and collapse can occur. Kilning needs to be preceded by very slow air-drying. Movement in service is medium.

Durability
The heartwood is naturally durable, but the sapwood is vulnerable to attack from powder-post beetle. The sapwood is moderately resistant to preservative treatment, and the heartwood is said to be untreatable.

Typical uses
Blackbean is a prized cabinetmaking wood in Australia. It is also used for joinery, office furniture, turning, carving, electrical appliances, and as inlay, veneers, and for making blockboard.

Grows
Eastern Australia; also plantation-grown in the USA, and as an ornamental tree and for its edible nuts in India, Malaysia and Sri Lanka
Typical height: 120ft (37m)
Trunk diameter: 3–4ft (1.0–1.2m)

⚠ Possible health risks
Dermatitis and irritation to the nose, eyes, throat, armpits and genitals

SOUTH AMERICAN CEDAR

Cedrela fissilis (Meliaceae)

Also called: Brazilian cedar, Peruvian cedar, cigar-box cedar, cedro batata, cedro rosa, cedro vermelho (red)

Description

Not a true cedar (these are softwoods), this wood belongs to the same family as mahogany (*Swietenia macrophylla*). It probably gets its name from the cedar fragrance of its oil, which may show on the surface as a sticky resin. The colour varies, but normally ranges from pale pinkish-brown to dark reddish-brown. The grain can be shallowly interlocked or straight, with a fairly coarse texture.
Typical dry weight: 30 lb/ft³ (480kg/m³), but with wide variation
Specific gravity: .48

Properties

It has a moderately good steam-bending classification, and is of medium strength and density in its other properties. Provided edges are kept sharp to avoid woolliness, it works easily with both hand and machine tools. Gluing is satisfactory, and it holds nails and screws well. Staining and polishing can be a little tricky because of the presence of gum, but it can be taken to a good finish.

Seasoning

It dries rapidly. There may be slight checking and minor warping. Movement in service is minimal.

Durability

Resistant to termites but vulnerable to the powder-post beetle, it is a durable wood. The sapwood is permeable for preservative treatment, but the heartwood is very resistant to it.

Typical uses

Cabinetwork, quality joinery, boatbuilding, organ soundboards, cigar boxes, canoes, decorative veneers, and as panel corestock and plywood.

Grows

South and Central America, except Chile
Typical height: 65–95ft (20–30m)
Trunk diameter: 2–3ft (60–90cm)

⚠ Possible health risks

Nose and throat irritation, dermatitis, asthma, skin blistering, inflamed eyelids and possible nasal cancer

CEDAR OF LEBANON
Cedrus libani (Pinaceae)

Also called: true cedar, cèdre du Liban (French), **Zeder** (German), **Libanonceder** (Dutch)

Description

The heartwood is a warm brown, and there is a clear distinction between the latewood zones, which are darker and denser, and the earlywood zones, which are paler. The sapwood is whitish in colour, and thin. The grain is usually straight, and this soft, light timber has a medium to fine texture. Bark inclusions are fairly common, and the outer edges of the annual rings can be rippled or wavy. The wood has a distinctive scent resembling incense. There are many other woods marketed as 'cedar' which are in fact unrelated.

Typical dry weight: 35lb/ft³ (560kg/m³)
Specific gravity: .56

◀ Turned bowl

Properties

Cedar of Lebanon is brittle and soft, with a low classification in bending, stiffness, crushing and resistance to shock loads. It is not a good choice for steam-bending, because it exudes resin during this operation. It works well with both machine and hand tools, and has little dulling effect on cutters. Screws and nails hold well, and it stains, varnishes and polishes to a good finish. Large knots can be a problem.

Seasoning

There is a slight inclination to warp, but the wood dries easily. It has moderate stability in service.

Durability

It is a durable wood, but can be attacked by pinhole borers and the longhorn beetle. The heartwood resists preservative treatment, and the sapwood exhibits moderate resistance.

Typical uses

Joinery, outdoor furniture, building construction, gates and fences. Interesting logs are sliced into veneers for decorative panelling and plywood facing.

Grows

Middle East, UK and USA
Typical height: 80ft (24m)
Trunk diameter: 3ft (0.9m).
Very old trees can grow to 40ft (12m) in trunk diameter

⚠ Possible health risks

Respiratory problems, rhinitis, chest tightness

CEIBA

Ceiba pentandra (Bombacaceae)

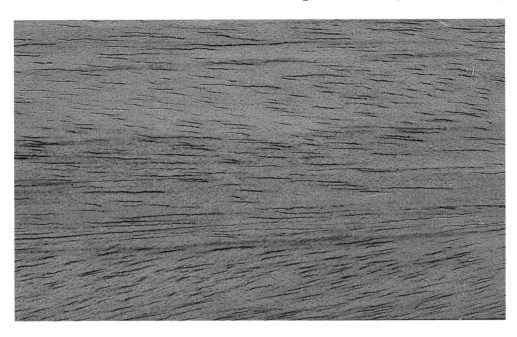

Also called: bonga, kapok tree, silk-cottontree, white silk-cottontree, pochota, fromager, sumauma, fuma

Description

The sapwood is not clearly differentiated from the heartwood, which is whitish, pale brown or pinkish-brown, and can often have greyish or yellowish streaks. The grain is interlocked and sometimes irregular, with a coarse texture and a low lustre. Ceiba is very soft; although twice the weight of balsa (*Ochroma pyramidale*), it is only slightly stronger.
Typical dry weight: 17lb/ft³ (260kg/m³)
Specific gravity: .26

Properties

It has low strength properties for its weight. It is easy to work with both hand and machine tools, but sharp cutting edges are essential, otherwise it will give a woolly finish. Ceiba does not hold nails or screws well, but it glues and sands well.

Seasoning

The wood dries well and easily, but seasoning should be carried out immediately after cutting to avoid fungal attack and staining.

Durability

Ceiba is not durable, and is vulnerable to attack from decay fungi and insects. The wood is permeable for preservative treatment.

Typical uses

Furniture parts, boxes, crates, corestock, packaging, plywood and wood pulp. The seed pods contain kapok fibre, used in insulation, stuffing and flotation.

Grows
West Africa, Malaysia, Indonesia, Mexico, Brazil
Typical height: 180ft (60m)
Trunk diameter: 6ft 6in (2m)

⚠ **Possible health risks**
Not known

HACKBERRY
Celtis occidentalis (Ulmaceae)

Also called: bastard elm, nettletree, hacktree, hoop ash. Sugarberry (*C. laevigata*) is also referred to as hackberry, and the two species are sold interchangeably

Description
The wide sapwood of hackberry ranges from pale yellow to greyish or greenish-yellow, and is frequently discoloured with blue sap stain. The heartwood is not very different from the sapwood, and is yellowish-grey to light brown, with yellow streaks. The wood is often said to resemble both ash and elm. The grain is sometimes straight, but can also be interlocked and irregular. The texture is fine and uniform.
Typical dry weight: 40lb/ft³ (640kg/m³)
Specific gravity: .64

Properties
Hackberry has moderate hardness. It is a heavy wood, and shows high shock resistance but low stiffness. The wood has only medium bending strength, but a good to very good steam-bending rating. It works well with both hand and machine tools, though it does have a moderate blunting effect on cutting edges. Pre-boring is advised for nailing and screwing. It takes glues, stains and polishes well.

Seasoning
The wood dries readily with minimal degrade. There is a chance of buckling with dry wood. It shows medium movement in service.

Durability
It has little or no resistance to attack by fungi and other wood-destroying organisms, and is vulnerable to attack from insects, especially the forest longhorn and buprestid beetles.

Typical uses
Furniture, kitchen cabinets, doors, mouldings, cooperage, crates and boxes, farm implements, sports and gymnasium equipment, plywood, decorative veneers.

Grows
Canada and USA
Typical height: 80ft (25m)
Trunk diameter: 1ft 6in–3ft (0.5–0.9m), but can be taller and broader

⚠ **Possible health risks**
Not known

COACHWOOD
Ceratopetalum apetalum (Cunonaceae)

Also called: scented satinwood. Not to be confused with *C. succirubrum*, which is known as PNG coachwood or satin sycamore

Description
Coachwood has a light brown to pinkish-brown sapwood and a slightly darker heartwood, which is not clearly differentiated from the sapwood. The grain is close and straight, with a fine, even texture. The wood has fine rays that form an attractive flecked figure on quartersawn surfaces.
Typical dry weight: 39lb/ft³ (630kg/m³)
Specific gravity: .63

Properties
Coachwood has medium resistance to shock loads, medium stiffness and bending strength, a high crushing strength, and a good steam-bending classification. It works reasonably easily with both machine and hand tools, and a smooth finish can be achieved. The wood has a tendency to chip out at tool exits when mortising or drilling, and pre-boring is necessary for nailing. Coachwood glues readily and takes stain well, and it can be brought to an excellent polished finish.

Seasoning
Since its natural rate of drying is fairly rapid, coachwood is liable to split and warp if not seasoned slowly and carefully. It exhibits medium movement in service.

Durability
The heartwood is non-durable, and the sapwood is susceptible to attack from the powder-post beetle. The wood is permeable for preservative treatment.

Typical uses
Because of its attractive flecked figure and fine texture it is used for cabinetmaking, turnery, panelling and quality furniture. It is also used for gunstocks, musical instruments, flooring and boatbuilding. It is sliced for decorative veneer, and used as plywood corestock.

Grows
Eastern Australia
Typical height: 60–80ft
(18–24m)
Trunk diameter: 1ft 6in–2ft 6in
(0.5–0.75m)

⚠ **Possible health risks**
Can cause dermatitis

PORT ORFORD CEDAR
Chamaecyparis lawsoniana (Cupressaceae)

Also called: Lawson cypress, Oregon cedar, Port Orford white cedar, white cedar

Description
It has a yellowish-white to pale yellowish heartwood, which can sometimes be pinkish-brown. As a rule, the sapwood is not clearly differentiated from the heartwood. The wood is usually non-resinous, but can sometimes exude an orange-yellow resin. Port Orford cedar has a straight and even grain with a fine, even texture. When freshly cut, it has a ginger-like odour. It is not a true cedar.
Typical dry weight: 30lb/ft³ (485kg/m³)
Specific gravity: .48

Properties
Port Orford cedar has medium crushing and bending strength, with low resistance to shock loads and also low stiffness. Its steam-bending classification is poor. This is an easy wood to work with both hand and machine tools, and it planes easily and well. The wood is also very suitable for turning and moulding. It holds screws and nails well, and its gluing properties are excellent. Port Orford cedar polishes well and can be stained without difficulty.

Seasoning
It dries readily with little degrade, and can be kilned from green.

Durability
The wood is particularly resistant to decay, and also to the corrosive properties of battery acid. There can be damage from the longhorn beetle. The sapwood is permeable to pressure treatment, but the heartwood is moderately resistant.

Typical uses
Cabinetwork and furniture, boatbuilding, oars and canoe paddles; construction, decks, formwork and mine timbers. Selected knotty specimens are used for decorative panelling.

Grows
Northern California and Oregon, USA; also introduced to New Zealand and UK
Typical height: 70–100ft (21–61m)
Trunk diameter: 2ft 6in–4ft (0.8–1.2m)

⚠ Possible health risks
Dermatitis, irritation to eyes and respiratory system, violent earache, giddiness, stomach cramps. Freshly milled wood gives off a pungent odour, and prolonged inhalation can lead to kidney problems.

SOUTHERN WHITE CEDAR

Chamaecyparis thyoides (Cupressaceae)

Also called: Atlantic white cedar, white cedar, false cypress, chilopsis

Description

Southern white cedar has a narrow whitish sapwood, while the heartwood is a light brown, often tinged with pink or red. The wood gives off a characteristic cedary scent (though it is not one of the true cedars) and has a slightly bitter, spicy taste. The grain is even and straight, and the wood is usually of a fine texture.
Typical dry weight: 23lb/ft³ (370kg/m³)
Specific gravity: .37

Properties

Southern white cedar is a soft wood, which is weak, with a very low stiffness rating and a medium classification for resistance to shock loads. Crushing and bending strength are also rated as medium, but its steam-bending classification is poor. The wood is easy to work, provided the cutting tools are kept sharp. It has only a minimal blunting effect on tool blades, and it holds screws and nails well. Southern white cedar has good staining and varnishing qualities, and it can also be brought to a fine finish by polishing.

Seasoning

The wood dries readily with little degrade, but care is needed with thicker stock to avoid defects such as internal honeycombing and collapse. It is dimensionally stable in service.

Durability

This is a very durable wood and has natural resistance to decay and to wood-boring insects. The heartwood is resistant to treatment by preservatives.

Typical uses

Southern white cedar weathers very well, and is therefore used on the outside of buildings, especially as shingles, and for fence posts, sleepers (railroad ties) and timber-framed houses. It is also used for canoes, casks, boxes and crates, and exterior trim. It was once popular with American settlers for building log cabins.

Grows
Eastern USA
Typical height: 50–90ft (15–27m)
Trunk diameter: 1ft 6in–2ft (0.5–0.6m)

⚠ **Possible health risks**
Not known

GREENHEART

Chlorocardium rodiaei (Lauraceae)

Syn.: *Ocotea rodiaei, Nectandra rodiaei*
Also called: Demerara greenheart, demerara, viruviru; also distinguished by colour:
yellow, brown, black, white greenheart

Description
The heartwood can vary greatly in its colour, from yellow-green, light olive, dark olive or yellowish-brown to dark brown or black. The grain is straight to roey, with a fine, uniform texture. The sapwood, which is not very distinct from the heartwood, is pale yellow or greenish.
Typical dry weight: 64lb/ft³ (1030kg/m³)
Specific gravity: 1.03

Properties
Greenheart is an extremely heavy and high-density wood. It has very high stiffness, bending and crushing strengths, and high shock resistance. It is said to be twice as hard as oak (*Quercus* spp.). The wood is difficult to work because of its hardness and interlocked grain. Pre-boring is required for nailing and screwing, and gluing is variable but usually fine. When machining, poisonous splinters can break out from end-grain wood. It has a moderate to high blunting effect on cutters, and a reduced cutting angle is required for planing. It polishes well to a lustrous finish. The acid content of the wood can have a slight corrosive effect on ferrous metals.

Seasoning
Greenheart dries slowly and there can be considerable degrade, especially in thick wood: shakes may extend, and end splitting and checking may occur.

Durability
It is highly durable and very resistant to pinhole and marine borers; it is suitable for saltwater applications. Greenheart is impermeable to preservative treatment.

Typical uses
Greenheart is a major timber for shipbuilding and other marine work. It is used for lock gates, piling, factory flooring, naval architecture, shuttles and chemical vats. Turnery uses include butts for billiard or pool cues, and fishing rods.

CEYLON SATINWOOD

Chloroxylon swietenia (Rutaceae)

Also called: East Indian satinwood, billu, burutu, behra, mutirai

Description

The heartwood is pale to lustrous golden-yellow and matures to a golden-brown with darker streaks. There is little distinction between the heartwood and the sapwood. The grain is narrowly interlocked and variegated, with a fine, close, uniform texture and a high satin lustre. The grain pattern produces attractive figure that includes bee's-wing, roey, ribbon and mottle effects.

Typical dry weight: 61lb/ft³ (980kg/m³)
Specific gravity: .98

Properties

Ceylon satinwood is a hard, heavy and dense wood that has a high crushing and bending strength, low resistance to shock loads and medium stiffness. The wood is somewhat difficult to work with both hand and machine tools, and has a moderate blunting effect on cutting edges. Planing quartersawn stock can easily result in torn grain. It is difficult to saw, sand, rout, bore, mould, mortise, glue and carve. Pre-boring is recommended for nailing and screwing. It is, however, an easy wood to turn. It takes stain well, and can be polished to a high finish after light filling.

Seasoning

Trees are commonly girdled for air drying, as this reduces degrade. The wood can be prone to surface cracking and some twisting and warping. It exhibits only small movement in use.

Durability

The heartwood is durable and highly resistant to attack from all fungus types, but not to termites; it is also vulnerable to marine borers and beetles. It is highly resistant to preservative treatment.

Typical uses

It is primarily used for high-quality furniture and cabinetmaking, and for inlay bandings, turnery, tool handles, bank fittings and bobbins. It is also sliced for decorative veneers.

Grows
India and Sri Lanka
Typical height: 45–50ft (14–15m)
Trunk diameter: 1ft (0.3m), but can be bigger

⚠ **Possible health risks**
Dermatitis, nasal irritation, headaches and swelling of the scrotum

ZIRICOTE
Cordia dodecandra (Boraginaceae)

Also called: ziracote, zircote, sericote, siricote, canalete, peterebi, laurel

Description
The brownish-yellow sapwood is clearly demarcated from the heartwood, which is red-brown with irregular wavy dark streaks. The dark markings can run at an angle to the main axis of the tree, giving an interesting and attractive pattern. It usually has straight or interlocked grain, a medium texture and a medium lustre.
Typical dry weight: 41–53lb/ft³ (650–850kg/m³), but can be heavier
Specific gravity: .65–.85

Properties
Ziricote is a hard, dense wood with good bending strength. It works well with hand and machine tools, and saws, planes, moulds, turns, carves, mortises, bores and glues well. It sands and nails very well, and can be brought to a very smooth finish and a high polish.

Seasoning
The wood is slow-drying and fairly difficult to season. It has a tendency to surface-check and develop end splits. It is stable in use.

Durability
Ziricote is moderately durable and resistant to decay fungi and wood-destroying organisms.

Typical uses
Because of its decorative qualities, ziricote is particularly prized for fine furniture and cabinetmaking, small decorative articles, turnery, panelling, and as a face veneer on plywood. It is also used for boatbuilding, kitchen cabinets, office furniture, rifle butts and flooring.

Grows
Belize, Guatemala and Mexico
Typical height: 60–90ft (20–28m), but often much shorter
Trunk diameter: 2ft 6in (0.75m) max.

⚠ **Possible health risks**
Not known

Turned bowl ▶

FREIJO

Cordia goeldiana (Boraginaceae)

Also called: cordia wood, jenny wood (USA), **Frei Jorge** (Brazil)

Description
The heartwood has some similarity to teak (*Tectona grandis*). It is golden-brown to dark brown, sometimes with dark streaks. When quartersawn, lighter and darker rays produce a contrasting figure. It has a straight grain with a uniform medium texture. Freijo can have a golden lustre in good lighting.
Typical dry weight: 37lb/ft³ (590kg/m³)
Specific gravity: .59

Properties
It is a heavy, high-density wood with medium strength classification in all categories except steam bending, which is poor. The wood saws easily, but sharp cutters are advised for planing. It works well with hand tools, and nails and screws satisfactorily, but pre-boring is advisable to avoid splitting. Gluing is usually good, and once filled it stains and polishes well. It weathers well, in a similar way to teak.

Seasoning
It both air- and kiln-dries well, with little degrade, and with little movement in use.

Durability
Freijo is a durable wood with high resistance to white and brown rot, but its sapwood is vulnerable to attack from the powder-post beetle.

Typical uses
This is an attractive wood that is used for cabinets, furniture, panelling, boatbuilding and decorative veneers. It is also used for flooring (including parquet), plywood, marine construction, naval architecture, cooperage and plywood.

Grows
Amazon basin, Brazil
Typical height: 40–60ft (12–18m)
Trunk diameter: 1ft 6in–2ft (0.45–0.60m)

⚠ **Possible health risks**
Possibly a skin sensitizer

DOGWOOD
Cornus florida (Cornaceae)

Also called: boxwood, bunchberry, flowering dogwood, Florida dogwood, cornel, arrow wood

Grows
Canada and USA
Typical height: 30ft (9m)
Trunk diameter: 8in (200mm)

⚠ **Possible health risks**
Not known

Description
The sapwood, which forms the bulk of the tree, is wide, and white to pinkish-brown in colour. The heartwood, if present, is yellowish or dark brown, and forms just a small central core. Dogwood has a very compact, interlocked grain with a fine, uniform texture.
Typical dry weight: 51lb/ft³ (820kg/m³)
Specific gravity: .82

Properties
This is a hard and heavy wood, with very high bending and compression strength. In spite of its hardness, it saws, turns and planes well because of its close grain. It glues easily and can be brought to a glossy finish, which it retains even when the surface is subjected to heavy wear.

Seasoning
Dogwood dries rather slowly, and care must be taken to minimize degrade, which takes the form of distortion or slight splitting. There is considerable movement in service.

Durability
The sapwood is non-durable and susceptible to decay.

Typical uses
The bulk of commercial use is for weaving shuttles. It is also used for mallet heads, spools, bobbins, golf-club heads, tool handles, machinery bearings, charcoal for gunpowder, and sporting goods.

◀ Woodcarving mallet

SPOTTED GUM

Corymbia citriodora and *C. maculata* (Myrtaceae)

Syn.: *Eucalyptus citriodora, Eucalyptus maculata*
Also called: lemon eucalyptus, lemon-scented gum (*C. citriodora*); spotted iron gum (*C. maculata*)

Description
The sapwood can be up to 2in (50mm) thick, and is normally white. The heartwood varies from light brown to dark red-brown, with a straight or wavy grain that sometimes produces a fiddleback figure. The grain is variable and moderately coarse-textured, and gum veins are common. The surface is greasy to the touch.
Typical dry weight: 61lb/ft³ (990kg/m³)
Specific gravity: .99

Properties
Spotted gum is very hard and strong, with a high density, and straight-grained stock steam-bends well. Despite its hardness it is relatively easy to work, with just a moderate blunting effect on cutting edges. Smooth results can be obtained when planing, but interlocked grain may cause chipping. It turns, moulds, bores, routs, screws, sands and stains well. Nailing can cause splitting. Gluing is satisfactory. The wood can be brought to a high polish.

Seasoning
It seasons satisfactorily, but there can be problems with checking and collapse. The wood is moderately stable in use.

Durability
The heartwood ranges from durable to moderately durable, but the sapwood is vulnerable to attack from the lyctus borer. The sapwood is permeable for preservative treatment, but the heartwood is highly resistant.

Typical uses
Fine furniture, joinery, turnery, internal and external flooring including parquet, boatbuilding, tool handles, mallet heads, cladding (siding), sporting goods, vehicle building, bent work, wine casks, ladder rungs and plywood.

Grows
Eastern Australia; also plantation-grown in Fiji, India and South Africa
Typical height: 132ft (40m)
Trunk diameter: 5ft (1.5m)

⚠ **Possible health risks**
Dermatitis

RIMU

Dacrydium cupressinum (Podocarpaceae)

Also called: red pine

Description

The heartwood is reddish-brown to yellow, with irregular dark streaks that are liable to fade on exposure to light. Rimu is a straight-grained wood with a fine, even, uniform texture, and is moderately lustrous. Seasoned heartwood tends to show a very attractive figure as a result of the rich pigments that are present in the wood. The sapwood is lighter in colour than the heartwood.
Typical dry weight: 33lb/ft³ (530kg/m³)
Specific gravity: .53

Properties

Rimu has a low resistance to shock loads and a low bending strength. It has medium crushing strength and a very low stiffness rating. Steam-bending qualities are poor. The wood works well with both hand and machine tools, and has only a slight blunting effect on cutting edges. It planes, bores, turns, sands and glues well, and holds screws firmly. Pre-boring is recommended for nailing. The wood stains and polishes well, especially when natural finishes are used.

Seasoning

The wood both air- and kiln-dries fairly well with just a slight tendency to surface-check. There is medium movement in use.

Durability

The heartwood is durable above ground, but the sapwood is non-durable. The sapwood is permeable for preservative treatment. The heartwood is resistant but, given the normal uses of the wood, this is not usually a problem.

Typical uses

Quality furniture, flooring, panelling, interior trim and structural work. It is rotary-cut for plywood, and choice logs are sliced for architectural veneers.

Grows
New Zealand
Typical height: 80–100ft (24–30m)
Trunk diameter: 6ft 6in (2m)
The tree can live up to 900 years.

⚠ Possible health risks

The dust can be an irritant to the eyes and nose

KINGWOOD

Dalbergia cearensis (Leguminosae)

Also called: violete (Brazil), **violetta, violet wood** (USA), **bois violet** (France)

Description

The heartwood displays a variety of colours, with a rich violet-brown as a background. It can shade almost to black, with streaks of dark violet, violet-brown and black, and sometimes of yellow also. The heartwood has a bright lustre, a very uniform texture and a smooth surface. The strongly differentiated sapwood is almost white, but the wood is invariably exported with the sapwood removed.
Typical dry weight: 75lb/ft³ (1200 kg/m³)
Specific gravity: 1.2

Properties

Kingwood is extremely dense and heavy. The wood is tough and strong in all categories, but it is principally reserved for decorative uses, since only small sizes are available. Because of its density and waxy properties, it can be brought to a high degree of finish. It holds nails and screws well, but does need pre-boring. Gluing requires some care. Kingwood works well with both hand and machine tools, but does have a moderate dulling effect on cutters.

Seasoning

It can split when being air-dried, if care is not taken. It will kiln-dry well without degrade, and is stable in use.

Durability

Kingwood is durable and extremely resistant to preservative treatment.

Typical uses

In antique restoration as *bois violet*, having been much used in Louis XIV, Louis XV and Georgian furniture. Also used as sliced veneer for marquetry, inlays and oyster veneering. Prized for decorative turnery, inlay bandings and small decorative items.

Grows
South America, mostly Brazil
Typical height: 50–100ft
(15–30m)
Trunk diameter: 4–8in
(100–200mm)

⚠ **Possible health risks**
Eye and skin irritant

◄ Box in kingwood and steamed pear (*Pyrus communis*)

BRAZILIAN TULIPWOOD
Dalbergia frutescens and related species (Leguminosae)

Also called: pau rosa, bois de rose, pinkwood, pau de fuso, jacarandá rosa. Some sources identify Brazilian tulipwood as **D. variabilis**. Not to be confused with American tulipwood or American whitewood (*Liriodendron tulipifera*), which is entirely unrelated

Description
The sapwood is a solid yellow colour.
The heartwood is particularly attractive and has a variegated striped figure with varying shades of pink, rose-red to violet on a straw-coloured background. There is some colour fading with age. The grain varies from straight to roey, and can be irregular and interlocked, with a rather fine texture and a high lustre. It is a very beautiful and highly prized wood.
Typical dry weight: 60lb/ft³ (960kg/m³)
Specific gravity: .96

Turned box ▶

Properties
Brazilian tulipwood is a heavy, hard, dense wood that is difficult to work, and can be splintery. The wood has a severe blunting effect on cutting edges, and a reduced planing angle is advised for quartered stock and irregular grain. Pre-boring is recommended for nailing and screwing, but it glues well. Brazilian tulipwood can be brought to a very highly polished finish.

Seasoning
It dries without difficulty, with a minimal risk of twisting and checking, and is stable in use.

Durability
The wood is not durable, but has some resistance to insect and fungal attack. It is very resistant to preservative treatment.

Typical uses
A classic cabinetmaker's wood, it is used for inlay, bandings, marquetry, antique restoration, fine cabinetwork, turnery and jewellery boxes. It is also sliced for decorative veneers.

Grows
Mainly north-eastern Brazil; also Colombia, Guyana and Venezuela
Typical dimensions: It is a small tree with an irregular trunk; the wood is sold in billets 2–4ft (0.6–1.2m) long by 2–8in (50–200mm) diameter

⚠ **Possible health risks**
Dermatitis, asthma; sensitizer

INDIAN ROSEWOOD

Dalbergia latifolia (Leguminosae)

Also called: Bombay blackwood, East Indian rosewood, Indian palisander, Java palisander, malabar, shisham, biti, eravadi, kalaruk

Description

The heartwood varies from rose to deep brown, and features darker purple-black lines, giving a very attractive figure. It has a narrowly interlocked or crossed grain, with a moderately coarse and uniform texture and a dull to medium lustre. When quartersawn, it can exhibit a beautiful ribbon figure. The sapwood is clearly defined from the heartwood and is yellowish-white, often with a purplish hue. When grown in commercial plantations, the wood is marketed as **sonokeling**.
Typical dry weight: 53lb/ft³ (850kg/m³)
Specific gravity: .85

Properties

Indian rosewood is heavy, with high crushing and bending strengths, medium resistance to shock loads, and low stiffness. Due to its hardness – 2½ times that of oak – it is difficult to work by hand or machine. Calcareous deposits in the wood can make it very difficult to saw and work, and can blunt cutting edges rapidly and severely. Slow speeds are advised for

mortising, and boring can be tricky. The wood turns, sands, screws and glues well, but is difficult to nail. It can be brought to an excellent polished or waxed finish after pre-filling.

Seasoning

It dries quite rapidly with minimal degrade, but if it is allowed to dry too rapidly surface checking and end splitting can occur. There is small movement in use.

Durability

The heartwood is very durable, resistant to preservative treatment, and highly resistant to attack from decay fungi and termites. The sapwood is vulnerable to attack from the powder-post beetle.

Typical uses

Quality furniture and cabinetmaking, musical instruments including organ pipes and violin bows, turnery, boatbuilding, bank and shop fittings, office furniture, kitchen cabinets, shuttles. It is also sliced for decorative veneers.

▲ Pembroke table in Brazilian mahogany (*Swietenia macrophylla*) with crossbanding of Indian rosewood

Grows
India
Typical height: 100ft (30m)
Trunk diameter: 2ft 6in (0.75m), but sometimes broader

⚠ **Possible health risks**
Dermatitis, asthma and respiratory problems; sensitizer

AFRICAN BLACKWOOD
Dalbergia melanoxylon (Leguminosae)

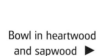

Also called: Mozambique ebony, mpingo (Tanzania)**, African grenadillo, pau preto**

Bowl in heartwood
and sapwood ▶

Description
Although sometimes referred to as an ebony, it is in fact related to the rosewoods. (The true ebonies are *Diospyros* spp.) The narrow sapwood is yellow-white in colour, contrasting with the heartwood which is dark purple-brown with black streaks. The grain is usually straight, but can be variable. The wood is slightly oily to the touch, extremely fine and even-textured. It is very heavy and hard.
Typical dry weight: 75lb/ft³ (1200kg/m³)
Specific gravity: 1.2

Properties
The wood is very strong and tough in all categories, but is not normally used for steam bending due to its weight and density. African blackwood has a severe blunting effect on tools; Tungsten-carbide-tipped (TCT) tools are required for conversion. It is difficult to work but turns well. Pre-boring is necessary for nailing and screwing, and screw threads can be tapped into it almost as well as in metal. It glues fairly well, takes stain well and can be brought to a brilliant, lustrous finish.

Seasoning
African blackwood dries very slowly and can take 2–3 years to season fully. Part-seasoned in log or billet form, it is then converted, end-coated and stacked under cover. There can be problems with heart shakes and end splitting.

Durability
The heartwood is very resistant to decay and to preservative treatment. The sapwood is vulnerable to attack from the powder-post beetle.

Typical uses
Woodwind instruments including bagpipe chanters, piano keys, police truncheons, chess pieces, ornamental turnery, inlay work, handles, building construction, joists and framing.

Grows
Eastern Africa
Typical height: 15–20ft (4.5–6m)
Trunk diameter: rarely more than 1ft (0.3m)

⚠ **Possible health risks**
Sneezing, asthma, conjunctivitis, acute dermatitis

BRAZILIAN ROSEWOOD

Dalbergia nigra (Leguminosae)

Also called: Rio rosewood, Bahia rosewood, jacarandá, jacarandá da Bahia, jacarandá do Brasil, jacarandá caviúna, palisander

Description

The heartwood of Brazilian rosewood ranges in colour from chocolate to violet-brown, and often has irregular black and golden-brown streaks. It is typically straight-grained, but can be wavy, and has a medium to coarse texture with a medium lustre. The wood has a gritty feel and is oily to the touch. Brazilian rosewood is a particularly beautiful wood, and much prized.

Typical dry weight: 53lb/ft³ (850kg/m³)

Specific gravity: .85

Properties

The wood is rated high in all strength categories except stiffness, which is low. Consequently, it has a very good steam-bending rating. Due to its hardness it is a difficult wood to work, and has a severe blunting effect on cutters. Depending on the stock being used, planing, boring, moulding and mortising, turning and sanding can range from being easy to difficult. Gluing can be tricky due to the density and oil content of the wood. Pre-boring is advised for nailing and screwing, and with care the wood can be brought to a high polish.

Seasoning

Brazilian rosewood dries slowly and is sometimes prone to checking and splitting, but exhibits little degrade on kilning. It is very stable in use.

Durability

The heartwood is very resistant to fungus and insect attack. Preservative treatment is not normally required because of the uses to which the wood is put.

Typical uses

As one of the world's most prized woods, Brazilian rosewood is used for fine furniture and cabinetmaking, turnery, carving, sculpture, shop and bank fittings; musical instruments, including piano keys, classical guitar bodies and violin bows; shuttles and handles. It is also sliced for decorative figured veneers used in cabinetwork, marquetry and panelling.

▲ Pivot-top table in Brazilian rosewood crossbanded with satinwood (*Zanthoxylum flavum*)

Grows

Brazil

Typical height: 125ft (38m)

Trunk diameter: 3–4ft (1–1.2m)

⚠ **Possible health risks**

The dust can cause dermatitis, irritation to the eyes and respiratory problems

COCOBOLO

Dalbergia retusa (Leguminosae)

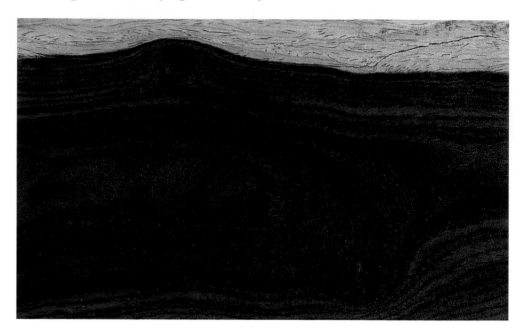

Also called: granadillo, Nicaraguan rosewood, pau preto, caviuna, nambar, cocobolo prieto, palo negro

Grows
Pacific areas of Central America
Typical height: 45–60ft (13–18m)
Trunk diameter: 1ft 6in–2ft (0.5–0.6m)

⚠ **Possible health risks**
Sensitizer; skin irritation from dust; dermatitis, conjunctivitis, nausea, bronchial asthma, nose and throat irritation, wheezing, chest tightness and headache

Description
Cocobolo is a visually beautiful wood. When newly cut, the heartwood displays a range of colours including rich red, with orange and yellow streaks and zones. On exposure to the air it darkens to deep red or orange-red with markings of black and purple. It is very hard, dense and heavy, and has straight grain, which is sometimes interlocked and can be irregular and variable. It usually has a fine, uniform texture. The clearly defined sapwood is almost white.
Typical dry weight: 68lb/ft³ (1100kg/m³)
Specific gravity: 1.10

Properties
It has a high mechanical strength in all categories, and is heavy, tough and strong. It works reasonably well with machine and hand tools, but cutting edges must be kept sharp. Cocobolo has a moderate blunting effect on cutting tools. The natural oils in the wood make it difficult to glue, but it can be nailed and screwed satisfactorily. Worked surfaces from planing, turning, moulding and mortising come out very smooth and clean. It takes stain and can be brought to an excellent finish.

Seasoning
It dries very slowly, and should be air-dried prior to kilning. It has a strong tendency to split and check while drying. Since the oil content acts as a barrier to water absorption, the wood is very stable in service.

Durability
Cocobolo heartwood is highly durable and very resistant to preservative treatment.

Typical uses
Furniture and cabinetmaking, fine turnery, cutlery handles, police truncheons, chess pieces, wooden jewellery, inlay work and highly decorative veneer.

◀ Bowl in cocobolo heartwood

HONDURAS ROSEWOOD

Dalbergia stevensonii (Leguminosae)

Also called: nogaed, palisandro de Honduras

Description

The heartwood ranges from pinkish-brown to purplish-brown, with irregular lighter and darker bands. The grain is straight to slightly wavy, with a medium to fine texture and low to medium lustre. The sapwood, clearly demarcated from the heartwood, is pale when newly cut, darkening to yellow on exposure. The wood is much prized for its beautiful appearance.
Typical dry weight: 60lb/ft³ (960kg/m³)
Specific gravity: .96

Properties

It is tougher and denser than Brazilian rosewood (*D. nigra*), but it is usually used for products where strength is of relatively minor importance. It is not an easy wood to work with hand tools, but works satisfactorily with machine tools. The wood has a moderate blunting effect on cutting edges and a reduced angle is recommended for planing when the grain is interlocked or wavy. Pre-boring is advised for nailing, and gluing depends on the oil content of the wood being used. It turns very well and can be brought to a good polish.

Seasoning

The wood air-dries very slowly and is prone to splitting, but it can be kilned with little degrade. There is small movement in use.

Durability

The heartwood is highly durable and resistant to preservative treatment, but the sapwood is not at all durable, and is permeable to preservatives.

Typical uses

Fine furniture and cabinetmaking, violin bows, xylophones, classical guitar bodies, fingerboards for guitars, mandolins and banjos, piano keys, organ pipes, panelling, bank and shop fittings, billiard or pool tables and turnery. Honduras rosewood is also sliced for decorative face veneers and used for marquetry.

◀ Bedside table in Honduras rosewood and lacewood (*Platanus hybrida*) burr (burl)

Grows
Belize (formerly British Honduras)
Typical height: 50–100ft (15–30m)
Trunk diameter: 3ft (0.9m)

⚠ **Possible health risks**
Dermatitis and asthma

MACASSAR EBONY

Diospyros celebica (Ebenaceae)

D. ebenum

Syn.: *D. macassar*
Also called: coromandel, calamander wood, Indian ebony, camagon, tendu, temru, timbruni, tunki. *D. tomentosa*, *D. marmorata*, *D. melanoxylon* and *D. ebenum* are similar species with slightly different characteristics

Grows
Sri Lanka, south India, Indonesia and the Philippines
Typical height: 50ft (15m)
Trunk diameter: 1ft 4in (0.4m)

⚠ Possible health risks
The dust can cause acute dermatitis, conjunctivitis and sneezing; possibly a skin sensitizer

Description
The heartwood is black with reddish or brown streaks, which can sometimes be grey-brown, pale brown or yellowish-brown. The grain is usually straight but can be wavy or irregular, and has a fine texture, giving the wood a distinctive metallic lustre.
Typical dry weight: 68lb/ft³ (1090kg/m³)
Specific gravity: 1.09

Properties
Macassar ebony is a very dense, very hard and very heavy wood. The black heart is usually brittle. Because of its hardness and brittleness, Macassar ebony is very difficult to work with both hand and machine tools. Pre-boring is always required for nailing and screwing, and the wood has a fairly severe blunting effect on cutting edges. Gluing is rated as satisfactory to difficult, but the wood turns well and can be brought to a first-class finish.

Seasoning
The wood should be seasoned slowly, and the trees are sometimes girdled for two years prior to felling. Deep, long, fine checks can develop, and fast drying may bring about surface and end checks.

Durability
The heartwood is vulnerable to the forest longhorn beetle, but has a high natural resistance to decay. It is highly resistant to preservative treatment.

Typical uses
Quality cabinetwork, decorative carving, turnery, billiard- or pool-cue butts, inlay, fingerboards and other parts of musical instruments, decorative veneers, tool handles and brush backs.

Laminated side table ▶

AFRICAN EBONY

Diospyros spp., chiefly *D. crassiflora* (Ebenaceae)

Also called: ébène (French), **Ebenholz** (German). May be distinguished by country of origin: **Cameroon, Gabon, Madagascar, Nigerian ebony.** 'Ebony' covers all species of *Diospyros*

D. mespiliformis

Description

The African ebonies are normally only available in short billets of heartwood, of which *D. crassiflora* is the blackest, though even this can have some grey in it. Other ebony species are liable to have black and brown striped heartwood. The wood of all these species is very dense and hard, and the grain ranges from straight to slightly interlocked, with a very fine, even texture.

Typical dry weight: 64lb/ft³ (1030kg/m³)
Specific gravity: 1.03

Properties

This very dense wood has very high crushing and bending strength, with high resistance to shock loads and high stiffness. It has a good steam-bending classification. It has a severe blunting effect on cutting edges, and is hard to work with both hand and machine tools, but scrapes well. Pre-boring is required for nailing and screwing, and the wood glues well. It can be brought to an extremely good finish.

Seasoning

Air-drying is fairly rapid and good, apart from some possible surface checking. The wood is very stable in service.

Durability

Ebony heartwood is a very durable wood; it is highly resistant to preservative treatment, which is generally not required for the uses to which the wood is put.

Typical uses

A prized wood for sculpture and carving, it is also used for fine turnery, cutlery handles, door knobs, piano and organ keys, bagpipe chanters, fingerboards and other parts for stringed instruments, inlay and banding. Traditional uses include parallel rules and cylindrical rulers.

▲ Parallel rules, the smaller one by Harling, London, 1937

Grows
Cameroon, Ghana, Nigeria and Congo
Typical height: 50–60ft (15–18m)
Trunk diameter: 2ft (0.6m)

⚠ Possible health risks

The dust can cause acute dermatitis, skin inflammation, conjunctivitis and sneezing; possible skin sensitizer

PERSIMMON

Diospyros virginiana (Ebenaceae)

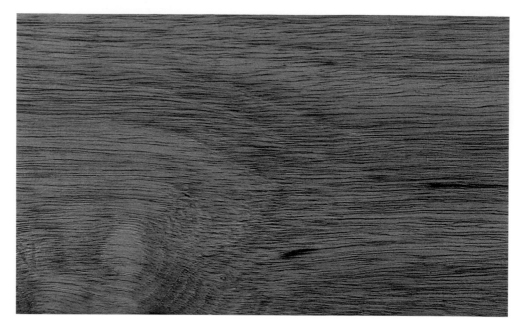

Also called: American ebony, common persimmon, bara-bara, boa-wood, butterwood, possum wood, Virginia date palm, white ebony

Grows

USA
Typical height: 80–120ft
(24–37m)
Trunk diameter: 1–2ft
(0.3–0.6m)

⚠ Possible health risks

The heartwood and dust may cause dermatitis

Description

Persimmon consists mostly of very wide sapwood, with the heartwood as only a small central core. The sapwood is white to creamy-white when newly cut, and darkens to yellowish-brown or greyish-brown on exposure. It is predominantly the sapwood that is sold commercially. The heartwood is black, brown or variegated, and can have streaks of brown or orange-brown. The wood has a fairly close and straight grain, with a fine and even texture.
Typical dry weight: 52lb/ft³ (830kg/m³)
Specific gravity: .83

Properties

The wood is very hard, dense, elastic, tough and wear-resistant, with high crushing and bending strength and medium stiffness. It can be worked with hand tools providing they are kept sharp, and has a moderate blunting effect on cutting edges. Machine-planing requires a reduced cutting angle, but a very smooth finish can be achieved. The wood turns, bores and mortises well, but requires preboring for nailing and screwing. Gluing is problematic, and generally the wood is fairly difficult to work.

Seasoning

Drying can be difficult, with considerable shrinkage. Other typical defects are end and surface checks, and brown chemical staining. There is considerable movement in service.

Durability

The small heartwood is durable and resistant to treatment with preservatives. The sapwood is vulnerable to attack from the powder-post beetle and the persimmon wilt fungus.

Typical uses

Furniture, turnery, musical instruments, domestic flooring, striking-tool handles, textile shuttles, shoe lasts, golf-club heads and decorative veneers.

AYAN

Distemonanthus benthamianus (Leguminosae)

Also called: Nigerian satinwood (UK and USA), **movingui** (UK, France), **ayanran** (Nigeria), **barre, eyen, bonsamdua**

Description

The pale yellow sapwood is not clearly differentiated from the heartwood, which can vary in colour from lemon-yellow to golden-brown, and sometimes has dark streaks. The grain is sometimes wavy and frequently irregular and interlocked, with a medium to fine texture. Quartered surfaces show a very pleasing striped and mottled figure. It has a lustrous surface with a fine and even texture. It can contain silica.

Typical dry weight: 42lb/ft³ (680kg/m³)
Specific gravity: .68

Properties

Ayan is a hard and dense wood with a fairly good steam-bending classification and medium bending strength. It has good compression strength along the grain and high crushing strength, with low stiffness and shock resistance. It can have a severe blunting effect on tools, and a certain resistance to cutting due to silica in the wood. Saw blades can become gummed up. A good finish can be obtained if the surface is pre-filled. Nailing requires pre-boring, and glue holds very well. Screwing properties are satisfactory. It is not suitable for areas such as kitchens, because the yellow dye in the pores is soluble in water, which results in staining.

Seasoning

It dries quite rapidly and must be seasoned carefully, with protection from sunlight and strong winds while drying; otherwise it can twist and check. In service there is little movement, and very good dimensional stability.

Durability

The heartwood is resistant to preservatives and the wood is moderately durable.

Typical uses

Furniture, exterior joinery, window frames, doors, boatbuilding, flooring including gymnasium floors, railway vehicles and plywood. Logs can be sliced for decorative veneers.

Grows
Tropical West Africa
Typical height: 90–125ft (27–38m)
Trunk diameter: 2ft 6in (0.75m)

⚠ **Possible health risks**
Dermatitis

JELUTONG

Dyera costulata and *D. lowii* (Apocynaceae)

Also called: jelutong burkit, jelutong paya

▲ Butterfly carving

Grows
Brunei, Indonesia and Malaysia
Typical height: 200ft (60m)
Trunk diameter: 2–3ft (0.6–0.9m)

⚠ Possible health risks
Possible contact allergy

Description
The heartwood is almost white, but turns to creamy-white or pale straw on exposure. There can be discoloration caused by fungi, which is common in trees tapped for latex. The sapwood is not distinct from the heartwood and is of the same colours. Jelutong is usually straight-grained with a fine and even texture, and slightly lustrous. Latex tubes can be found in clusters 2–3ft (0.6–0.9m) apart, but are usually eliminated in conversion. The latex is used to make chewing gum.
Typical dry weight: 29lb/ft³ (460kg/m³)
Specific gravity: .46

Properties
Jelutong is very light for a hardwood; it is of medium density, has low bending and crushing strength and very low stiffness. It is rated as poor for steam bending. The wood works easily with both hand and machine tools, and has only a slight blunting effect on cutters. Cutting tools must be kept sharp. It screws, sands, nails, glues, planes, polishes and paints well, and varnishes and stains very well.

Seasoning
It dries easily and rapidly with little degrade, but there is a slight tendency towards checking and distortion. There is only small movement in service.

Durability
The wood is non-durable. The heartwood has a low natural resistance to decay, and can suffer from sap stain. It is highly vulnerable to attack by powder-post beetle and termites. Jelutong is permeable and easy to treat with preservatives.

Typical uses
Sculpture and carving, architectural models, patternmaking, picture frames, drawing boards, match splints, battery separators, figured and plain veneer, and craft work. Jelutong is also used as a corestock for laminated boards, plywood and flush doors.

QUEENSLAND WALNUT

Endiandra palmerstonii (Lauraceae)

Also called: Australian walnut, black walnut, oriental wood, walnut bean, Australian laurel

Description

The heartwood ranges in colour from light pinkish-brown to dark brown, with pink, greyish-green, purple-black or black streaks. The grain is interlocked and irregular, and sometimes wavy, with a medium, even texture, and is fairly lustrous. The wood can exhibit very attractive chequered or broken-stripe figure, and is likened to European walnut (*Juglans regia*). The sapwood can be 3–4in (70–100mm) thick and is light brown. Not a true walnut.
Typical dry weight: 42lb/ft³ (680kg/m³)
Specific gravity: .68

Properties

Queensland walnut is a dense and heavy wood, and has very good insulation properties. It has a high crushing strength, medium bending strength, low stiffness, low resistance to shock loads, and a moderate steam-bending rating. The wood has a high silica content, which makes it difficult to work; tungsten-carbide-tipped (TCT) blades are advised for sawing and planing. It has a rapid, severe blunting effect on cutting edges. It turns, nails and screws satisfactorily, glues and paints well, and stains very well. It finishes well and can be highly polished.

Seasoning

It will air-dry quite rapidly, but is prone to end splits. Kiln-drying thin stock can lead to warping, and thicker boards respond better if quartersawn, since this reduces the tendency to split. There is medium movement in use.

Durability

The wood is not durable and can be attacked by wood borers. The heartwood is difficult to treat with preservatives, but the sapwood is permeable.

Typical uses

Cabinetmaking, quality furniture, interior joinery, bank and shop fittings, flooring and insulating boards. Queensland walnut is also cut into decorative veneers for marquetry and panelling, and used as a face veneer for plywood.

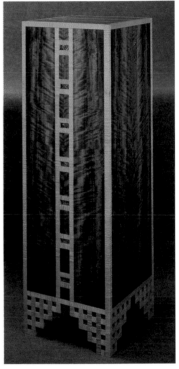

▲ Chest of drawers with details in ripple sycamore (*Acer pseudoplatanus*) and abalone

Grows
Queensland, Australia
Typical height: 120–140ft (37–43m)
Trunk diameter: 6ft (1.8m)

⚠ **Possible health risks**
Not known

GEDU NOHOR

Entandrophragma angolense (Meliaceae)

Also called: abeubegne, dongomanguila, edinam, entandrophragma mahogany, lifaki, tiama, vovo

Description

The heartwood of gedu nohor is a plain, dull red-brown, or sometimes pinkish-brown. When exposed to light, it darkens to a deeper red-brown. Gedu nohor has a moderately crossed or interlocked grain with a fairly uniform medium texture and a dull lustre. The wood can contain copious amounts of gum. The sapwood ranges from cream to pale pink.
Typical dry weight: 34lb/ft³ (540kg/m³)
Specific gravity: .54

Properties

The wood is of medium density, has low resistance to shock loads and low bending strength, medium crushing strength and very low stiffness. Its steam-bending qualities are classified as fairly poor. Gedu nohor works well with hand tools, except that interlocked grain may have a tendency to pick up a lot. There is a moderate blunting effect on cutting edges. The wood nails and screws satisfactorily, and stains, polishes and paints well.

Seasoning

It dries slowly but fairly easily. If dried too fast it can check and split. There is small to medium movement in service.

Durability

The heartwood is moderately resistant to decay, and very resistant to preservative treatment. The sapwood is vulnerable to attack from the powder-post beetle.

Typical uses

Furniture, interior joinery, boatbuilding, shop fittings (store fixtures), office furniture, parquet flooring, coffins and plywood. It is also sliced for decorative veneers, and may be used as a substitute for mahogany.

Grows
West, Central and East Africa
Typical height: 160ft (48m)
Trunk diameter: 4–6ft (1.2–2m)

⚠ **Possible health risks**
Dermatitis

SAPELE

Entandrophragma cylindricum (Meliaceae)

Also called: scented mahogany, sapele mahogany, aboudikro, penkra, sapelewood, sapelli

Description

When newly cut, the heartwood is pink, but this darkens to a red-brown or purple-brown on exposure. The sapwood is clearly defined and is white to pale yellow. The grain is moderately interlocked or wavy, with a moderately fine texture and a high golden lustre. The wood can exhibit an attractive range of figure, with ribbon, bee's-wing and regular stripe on quartersawn stock, and fiddleback, mottle or roe on other cuts.
Typical dry weight: 39lb/ft³ (620kg/m³)
Specific gravity: .62

Properties

Sapele has medium resistance to shock loads, medium bending strength, high crushing strength, low stiffness and poor steam-bending properties. It works well with both hand and machine tools, with a moderate blunting effect on cutting edges. Sapele planes and moulds easily, but interlocked grain can tear if a reduced cutting angle is not used. It bores, routs, carves, nails, screws, stains, varnishes and paints well, and sands very well. The wood glues fairly well, and can be brought to an excellent polished finish.

Seasoning

It dries rapidly and is prone to distortion, although this is less of a problem with quartersawn stock. There is medium movement in use.

Durability

The heartwood is moderately durable and can be attacked by pinhole and marine borers, but is resistant to preservative treatment. The sapwood is vulnerable to the powder-post beetle, and is moderately resistant to preservative treatment.

Typical uses

Furniture and cabinetmaking, musical instruments, office furniture, kitchen cabinets, doors, stairs, window frames, boats, flooring and sports goods. Decorative veneer from choice logs is used for marquetry, panelling and cabinetwork. Sapele is also rotary-cut for plywood.

Grows
West, Central and East Africa
Typical height: 150ft (45m)
Trunk diameter: 4–6ft (1.2–1.8m)

⚠ **Possible health risks**
Skin irritation and sneezing

UTILE
Entandrophragma utile (Meliaceae)

Also called: assié, sipo, abebay, efuodwe, liboyo, kisi-kosi, afau-konkonti

Description
The light brown sapwood is clearly differentiated from the heartwood and can be up to 2in (50mm) thick. When newly cut, the heartwood is pinkish-brown, but it darkens to a deep red-brown on exposure. The grain is typically broadly interlocked, with a medium texture, and lustrous. Quartersawn surfaces can exhibit an irregular wide stripe or ribbon figure.
Typical dry weight: 41lb/ft³ (660kg/m³)
Specific gravity: .66

Properties
Utile is a dense wood with a high crushing strength, medium bending strength, low stiffness and resistance to shock loads, and a poor steam-bending rating. It works well with machine and hand tools, and has a moderate blunting effect on cutters. A reduced cutting angle is advised for planing and moulding interlocked grain on quartersawn stock. Utile saws, glues, turns, routs, mortises, carves, nails, screws and stains well. Once the grain has been filled, the wood can be brought to an excellent polished finish.

Seasoning
If dried at a moderate rate, degrade is minimal, but if it is dried too quickly twisting can occur. It exhibits medium movement in service.

Durability
The heartwood is durable and resistant to decay, whereas the sapwood is vulnerable to attack from the powder-post beetle. The heartwood is highly resistant to preservative treatment.

Typical uses
Furniture and cabinetmaking, turnery, interior and exterior joinery, boatbuilding, musical instruments, counter tops, kitchen cabinets, office furniture, window frames and sports goods. Utile is also sliced for decorative veneers and rotary-cut for plywood.

Grows
West, Central and East Africa
Typical height: 150–200ft (45–60m)
Trunk diameter: 2ft 8in–6ft (0.8–1.8m)

⚠ **Possible health risks**
Irritant to the skin

GUANACASTE

Enterolobium cyclocarpum (Leguminosae)

Also called: conocaste, kelobra, perota, rain tree, jenisero, orejo, timbo, carocaro, eartree

Description
The colour of the heartwood ranges from pale brown to dark walnut-brown, with dark variegated streaks and a greenish hue. Sometimes there may also be a reddish tinge. The sapwood, which is clearly differentiated from the heartwood, is nearly white. The grain is typically interlocked, with a medium to coarse texture and a lustrous surface. The crotchwood of guanacaste is frequently highly figured.
Typical dry weight: 21lb/ft³ (340kg/m³)
Specific gravity: .34

Properties
Guanacaste is classified as low in all strength categories, and has poor bending properties. It is easily worked with machine or hand tools, but chipped and raised grain may be a problem when planing, and if tension wood is present this can result in a woolly finish. The wood has a moderate blunting effect on cutting edges. It nails, screws, glues and polishes well.

Seasoning
The wood dries fairly easily and rapidly, and has a slight tendency to split or warp. It exhibits small movement in service.

Durability
The heartwood is resistant to attack from dry-wood termites and decay fungi, but the wood is highly durable in fresh water. It is permeable for preservative treatment.

Typical uses
Furniture and furniture parts, including office and rustic furniture; interior trim, patternmaking, gunstocks, canoes, water troughs, packing cases, fishing-net floats, corestock. Swirls and crotches are sliced for decorative veneer.

Grows
Mexico, Central America, West Indies, Venezuela, Guyana and Brazil
Typical height: 60–100ft (18–30m)
Trunk diameter: 3–6ft (0.9–1.8m)

⚠ **Possible health risks**
Dust may cause mucous membrane irritation and allergies

The genus *Eucalyptus*

This very large and interesting genus comprises between 700 and 800 species. It is principally native to Australia, but with a small number of native species in New Guinea and Indonesia. Introduced species are now found in many parts of the world, notably California, Brazil, Morocco, Portugal, South Africa and Israel. There is no other continent that is dominated by one genus of tree as Australia is by the eucalyptus. Many eucalypts come under the common name of gum trees, but other names used for various eucalyptus species include stringybark, mallee, box, ironbark and ash.

Probably the first written record of eucalyptus is from Abel Tasman's exploratory voyage in 1642, when a reconnaissance party on what is now Tasmania (named after Tasman) saw some trees that exuded gum, and were unusual in that the lowest branches were 60ft (18m) above the ground. The explorer Dampier, landing in what was to become New South Wales, referred to 'dragon trees', which were of great size and exuded gum. In 1770 Captain James Cook, the British naval explorer, wrote of finding two sorts of gum, and likened them to a 'gum dragon'. A gum-exuding tree that grows on the Canary Islands and Madeira is known as dragon tree (*Dracaena draco*), and this is probably what both explorers had in mind.

The famous botanist Joseph Banks was with Cook on that voyage, and collected many plant specimens. The name *Eucalyptus* was given by the French botanist Charles Louis L'Héritier de Brutelle some years later when he saw Banks's specimens in England. The name means 'well covered', and refers to the distinctive bud cap.

▲ Side table with drawers in jarrah (*E. marginata*) and hard maple (*Acer saccharum* or *A. nigrum*)

Mature eucalypts often have long, willowy leaves and stems, and some species can reach a great height. Arguably the tallest tree ever recorded – taller than the sequoia or coast redwood (*Sequoia sempervirens*), which itself is taller than the giant redwood or wellingtonia (*Sequoiadendron giganteum*) – was a mountain ash (*E. regnans*) that was recorded at 435ft (132.5m) in 1872 at Watts River, Victoria, Australia. The tallest redwood recorded, the Dyerville Giant in California, was 372ft (113.4m) before it fell in 1991.

Different species of eucalyptus can live in a wide variety of environments, from the arid to the very wet. Some are frost-resistant, whilst others will be burnt by frost. Eucalypts are able to regenerate quickly after

◄ Bowl in Tasmanian oak (*E. delegatensis*, *E. obliqua* or *E. regnans*)

▲ Variegated, peeling bark is a feature of many eucalypt species

fresh leaves and branch tops. In traditional Aboriginal medicine, ointments containing eucalyptus oil have been used to heal wounds and treat fungal infections, and infusions of eucalyptus leaves are used to reduce fevers. Eucalyptus oil has antiseptic, antibacterial and expectorant properties, and is often used in cough remedies. In large quantities, however, it is highly toxic. Marsupial herbivores such as koala bears and some possums are relatively tolerant of the toxin, but will select species with low toxicity.

It should be noted that some species previously classified under *Eucalyptus* have since been placed in a new genus, *Corymbia*. These include the two species marketed as spotted gum (now *Corymbia citriodora* and *C. maculata*), and flowering gum (*C. ficifolia*).

a forest fire, and are also very good at scavenging for water at the expense of other plants. Their survival skills are, however, limited by temperature, as most species can only tolerate frosts down to 27 or 23°F (−3 to −5°C), with the hardiest, the snow gum (*E. pauciflora* ssp. *niphophila*), withstanding temperatures down to 0°F (−18°C). As far as human survival in a eucalyptus forest is concerned, it is a good idea not to pitch your tent under a tree, as they have a tendency to drop branches off without warning as they grow.

Some eucalyptus extracts are known to have valuable medicinal properties. For example, the Australian fever tree or blue gum (*E. globulus*), common today in many warmer climes outside Australia, is prized for the eucalyptus oil distilled from the

◄ Ripple bench seat in Tasmanian oak

RED RIVER GUM

Eucalyptus camaldulensis (Myrtaceae)

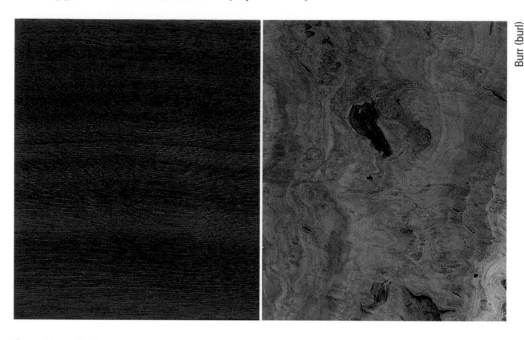

Burr (burl)

Syn.: *E. rostrata*
Also called: Murray red gum, red gum, river gum, river red gum, Queensland blue gum

Grows
Australia; also plantation-grown in Egypt, Israel, Portugal, South Africa and Spain
Typical height: 65ft (20m), but can reach 115ft (35m)
Trunk diameter: 6ft (2m)

⚠ **Possible health risks**
Not known

Description
The heartwood ranges from pink to reddish-brown and is clearly differentiated from the paler sapwood. The grain is interlocked and frequently wavy, and if the wood is quartersawn it can produce a fiddleback or mottled figure. Red River gum has a fine and even texture, but veins of gum can be present.
Typical dry weight: 51lb/ft³ (825kg/m³)
Specific gravity: .82

Properties
The wood is hard and moderately heavy, with very good strength qualities, but is unsuitable for steam bending because of gum exudation. Gum pockets and interlocked grain may make it difficult to work. A reduced cutting angle is advised for machine-planing, and the wood is difficult to bore, sand and mortise. Pre-boring is advised for nailing, and it holds screws well. Gluing can be difficult, and surfaces generally require some pre-treatment. The wood can be brought to a high polish.

Seasoning
It dries well with care, but there can be problems with longitudinal shrinkage and distortion from the gum pockets. It has only small movement in use.

Durability
The heartwood is durable and highly resistant to termites, and also to preservative impregnation. The sapwood is vulnerable to attack from the lyctus borer, and is permeable.

Typical uses
Factory and domestic flooring, mining timbers, heavy construction, piling, shipbuilding, stair rails and treads, sleepers (railroad ties); may also be sliced for decorative panelling and veneering.

Turned bowl ▶

TASMANIAN OAK

Eucalyptus delegatensis, E. obliqua and *E. regnans* (Myrtaceae)

Ripple figure

Burr (burl)

Also called: alpine ash, white-top or gum-top stringybark, woollybutt (*E. delegatensis*); messmate stringybark, brown-top stringybark (*E. obliqua*); mountain ash, stringy gum, swamp gum, Victorian ash (*E. regnans*). All three species are sold as 'Tasmanian oak'

Description

The heartwood is pale biscuit to pale brown with a pinkish hue; the paler, narrow sapwood is indistinct. The grain is typically straight, but can be wavy or interlocked, with a coarse, open, even texture, and the growth rings are frequently clearly visible. Hard gum veins are often present. The wood is neither a true oak nor ash.
Typical dry weight: 39–49lb/ft³ (620–780kg/m³), depending on species
Specific gravity: .62–.78

Properties

The wood has a high crushing strength, with medium shock resistance, bending and stiffness ratings. *E. obliqua* has moderate steam-bending qualities, whereas the other two species are rated as poor. Tasmanian oak can be worked satisfactorily with both hand and machine tools, with a moderate blunting effect on cutting edges, which must be kept sharp. The wood planes fairly well, and moulds, turns, bores, carves and routs satisfactorily. It glues, sands, stains and polishes well. Pre-boring is advised for nailing.

Seasoning

It dries readily and fairly rapidly, but can degrade if care is not taken, with distortion, surface checking, internal checking and collapse. There is medium movement in use.

Durability

The heartwood is moderately durable, and the sapwood is vulnerable to attack from the powder-post beetle. The sapwood is permeable for preservative treatment but the heartwood is resistant.

Typical uses

Furniture, exterior and interior joinery, handles, panelling, domestic flooring, cooperage, boxes, vehicle building, pulp, cladding (siding), weatherboards and plywood. The wood is also sliced for decorative veneer.

◀ Turned box in *E. regnans* burr (burl)

Grows
South-eastern Australia and Tasmania
Typical height: 200–300ft (60–90m)
Trunk diameter: 3–7ft (1–2m)

⚠ **Possible health risks**
Dermatitis, asthma, sneezing. Irritant to eyes, nose and throat

KARRI

Eucalyptus diversicolor (Myrtaceae)

No other names

Description

The heartwood is a uniform reddish-brown, the sapwood paler. Karri has an interlocked grain that produces a striped figure when the wood is quartersawn. It has an even and moderately coarse texture. The wood, though not the tree itself, is very similar in appearance to jarrah (*E. marginata*).

Typical dry weight: 55lb/ft³ (880kg/m³)
Specific gravity: .88

Properties

Karri is rated high in all the strength categories, but only moderate for steam bending. It is difficult to work with hand tools. Machining is also fairly difficult, because the interlocked grain has a moderate to severe blunting effect on cutting edges. Pre-boring is invariably required for nailing and screwing. The wood can be difficult to turn, bore and sand, and a reduced cutter angle is advisable for machine-planing. It glues satisfactorily, and the surface can be brought to a very good finish once the grain has been filled.

Seasoning

The wood is very difficult to dry; partial air-drying is advised before kilning. It can check severely on tangential surfaces, along with deep checking in thick stock. Thin stock is inclined to warp. It moves considerably in service.

Durability

The heartwood is durable, and resistant both to decay and to preservative treatment. The sapwood is resistant to powder-post beetle, and is permeable for preservative treatment.

Typical uses

Heavy furniture, wall panelling, joists, rafters, beams, railway sleepers (railroad ties), poles, mine timbers and above-water dock and harbour work. Karri is also sliced for decorative cabinet and panelling veneers, and rotary-cut for plywood.

Grows
South-west Australia; also cultivated in South Africa
Typical height: 150–200ft (45–60m)
Trunk diameter: 6–10ft (1.8–3m)

⚠ **Possible health risks**
Not known

ROSE GUM

Eucalyptus grandis (Myrtaceae)

Also called: flooded gum, scrub gum

Description

The heartwood can vary in colour from pale pink to red-brown. The sapwood, which is not always clearly differentiated from the heartwood, is typically paler. It has a uniform but moderately coarse-textured grain, which is usually straight or slightly interlocked. There is no pronounced figure.

Typical dry weight: 50lb/ft³ (800kg/m³)
Specific Gravity: .80

Properties

Rose gum is of moderate hardness. It machines and turns well to a good smooth finish, and it takes fixings with no difficulty. It glues satisfactorily, and readily accepts paint, stain and polish.

Seasoning

It dries satisfactorily using both kiln and air drying, but care needs taking in the early part of the seasoning period to avoid surface checking and collapse.

Durability

Rose gum is moderately resistant to decay when exposed to the weather above ground with free air circulation. It is not recommended for below-ground use. The sapwood is not vulnerable to lyctid borer attack.

Typical uses

Quality furniture, joinery, turnery, carving, boatbuilding, house framing, internal and external flooring, fascias, bargeboards, cladding (siding), oars, dowelling, fruit cases and structural plywood.

Grows
New South Wales and Queensland, Australia. Also plantation-grown in Brazil, South Africa and Malaysia
Typical height: 140–170ft (45–55m)
Trunk diameter: 3–6ft (1–2m)

⚠ **Possible health risks**
Not known

JARRAH

Eucalyptus marginata (Myrtaceae)

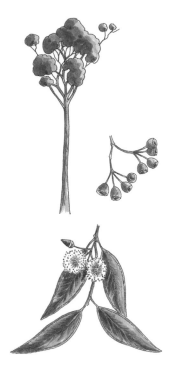

Burr (burl)

Also called: Swan River mahogany

▲ Square turned platter in jarrah burr (burl)

Description

The heartwood is a rich brownish-red, sometimes marked by short, dark brown radial flecks on the end grain and boat-shaped flecks on flatsawn surfaces. It often has black streaks, and occasionally bark inclusions. There is a moderate to high degree of colour variation, and the wood changes to a rich mahogany-red on exposure. The grain is often interlocked or wavy, with a moderately coarse, even texture. Gum pockets and veins are commonly present. The clearly defined sapwood is usually pale yellow, but can darken with age. Jarrah is very similar in appearance to karri (*E. diversicolor*).
Typical dry weight: 50lb/ft³ (800kg/m³)
Specific gravity: .80

Properties

This dense, heavy, hard wood has medium bending and high crushing strength. It is satisfactory for steam bending. Jarrah is fairly difficult to work with hand tools, and when machined it has a moderate blunting effect on cutting edges. The planer blade angle should be reduced to prevent tear-out on irregular-grained and figured stock. Pre-boring is recommended for nailing and screwing. Jarrah glues and turns well, and polishes very well.

Seasoning

It needs careful drying, with partial air-drying before kilning. Broad stock may warp or check in drying, and collapse can occur. Movement in service is medium.

Durability

The heartwood is extremely durable and resistant to termites and marine borers; it is also noted for being fire-resistant. It has high resistance to preservative treatment, whereas the sapwood is permeable.

Typical uses

Furniture, tool handles, flooring including parquet, shipbuilding and marine work, railway sleepers (railroad ties), shingles and weatherboards, joists and rafters, chemical vats, decks. Selected logs are also sliced for decorative veneers and panelling. Jarrah burr (burl) is prized by woodturners for artistic work.

TALLOWWOOD

Eucalyptus microcorys (Myrtaceae)

Also called: Australian tallowwood

Description

The heartwood varies from pale to dark yellow-brown, with a quite distinct near-white sapwood. The grain is interlocking and moderately coarse. As its name indicates, tallowwood has a waxy feel and can be quite slippery to handle. The waxy or oily content gives the wood a distinctive lustre. There is an absence of conspicuous figure and growth rings, and the wood is usually free of gum veins.
Typical dry weight: 62lb/ft³ (1000kg/m³)
Specific Gravity: 1.00

Properties

Tallowwood is a dense, heavy, hard, strong wood, but is reasonable to work because of its natural greasiness, though it can have a severe blunting effect on tools. It both machines and turns well, and takes fixings with no difficulty, but care is advised when nailing to avoid splitting. Due to the greasy characteristics of the wood, gluing can be difficult; washing surfaces with a 10% sodium hydroxide solution prior to gluing is said to aid adhesion. The wood will readily accept paint, polish and stain, but knowledge of the particular finishes for this unusual wood is important. It can be finished to a reasonably high polish.

Seasoning

It seasons satisfactorily with both kiln and air drying, with good resistance to surface checking. It is normally stable in service.

Durability

The wood is extremely durable and resistant to decay when in contact with the ground, and in damp, poorly ventilated areas. Bridges made from tallowwood have an extremely long life due to the extractive content of the wood. The sapwood can be susceptible to lyctid borer attack. The sapwood readily accepts preservative treatment, but penetration of the heartwood is negligible.

Typical uses

Joinery, outdoor furniture, turnery, boatbuilding, flooring, decking, cladding, fencing, tool handles, croquet mallets, poles, piles, bridge timber and plywood.

Grows
Coastal New South Wales and Queensland, Australia
Typical height: 80–185ft (25–60m)
Trunk diameter: 3–6ft (1–2m)

⚠ **Possible health risks**
Not known

BLACKBUTT

Eucalyptus pilularis (Myrtaceae)

Also called: pink blackbutt. Related to **Western Australian blackbutt** or **yarri** (*E. patens*), **New England blackbutt** (*E. andrewsii*) (this is Australian, not American) and **Dundas blackbutt** (*E. dundasii*)

Description

The heartwood is pale brown, sometimes with a faint pinkish tinge, especially when freshly cut. The sapwood can be almost indistinguishable from the heartwood, but is paler in colour. Blackbutt grain is usually straight, but can be interlocked. It has a medium, even texture but frequently includes gum veins. Sometimes it can have a greasy feel and appearance.
Typical dry weight: 58lb/ft³ (930kg/m³)
Specific gravity: .93

Properties

Blackbutt is a hard, dense wood that has high crushing, stiffness and bending strength, but poor steam-bending properties. The wood has a moderate blunting effect on cutters, and pre-boring is advised for nailing and screwing, as blackbutt splits easily. Gluing can be problematic, but is more effective on freshly finished surfaces. It stains and polishes reasonably well, but painting can sometimes give poor results due to surface checking and staining caused by high extractive content.

Seasoning

Air-drying is advised before kilning, but it can be either air- or kiln-dried effectively. The juvenile wood near the pith has a slight tendency to collapse, and the wood is prone to checking as it dries.

Durability

When clear of the ground the wood is highly durable, and it is moderately decay-resistant in the ground. The sapwood is not susceptible to lyctid borer attack. The heartwood is virtually impenetrable to preservative treatment, but the sapwood readily accepts impregnation.

Typical uses

Quality furniture, outdoor furniture, internal joinery, turnery, boatbuilding, parquetry, internal and external flooring, external cladding (siding), timber framing and other structural uses, fencing, vehicle building. It is also used to make structural plywood and hardboard.

AUSTRALIAN RED MAHOGANY

Eucalyptus resinifera (Myrtaceae)

Also called: red mahogany eucalyptus, red mahogany, red stringybark, red messmate

Description
The sapwood, which is clearly demarcated from the heartwood, is pale cream in colour. The heartwood ranges from red to dark red, with a slightly interlocked grain and a medium to coarse, even texture. The interlocked grain can give rise to an attractive ripple figure. The tree is not a true mahogany.
Typical dry weight: 60lb/ft³ (960kg/m³)
Specific gravity: .96

Properties
The wood is stiff, very hard, tough and strong. It works well with machine and hand tools, and has a moderate blunting effect on cutting edges. Planing may require a reduced cutter angle to minimize tear-out, and nailing can cause splitting, so pre-boring is advisable. Red mahogany sands, stains, paints and polishes well, and glues reasonably well.

Seasoning
Red mahogany dries slowly and without any serious degrade. It is reasonably stable in service.

Durability
The heartwood is durable, but the sapwood is vulnerable to attack from the lyctus borer. The sapwood is permeable for preservative treatment, but the heartwood is extremely resistant.

Typical uses
Furniture, turnery, interior and exterior flooring, boatbuilding, panelling, heavy construction, house framing, vehicle bodies, cladding (siding), railway sleepers (railroad ties) and structural plywood.

Grows
Eastern Australia
Typical height: 150ft (45m)
Trunk diameter: 3–5ft (1–1.5m)

⚠ **Possible health risks**
Not known

SYDNEY BLUE GUM

Eucalyptus saligna (Myrtaceae)

Also called: blue gum

Description

The heartwood is usually pink to dark red, though with some regrowth timber it can be pale straw with pink highlights. The sapwood, which is distinct from the heartwood, is usually paler. The wood will darken over time, with the colours becoming slightly muted. Although it is usually straight, the grain can be interlocked and produce nice figure. It has a moderately coarse, even texture, and gum veins are common.
Typical dry weight: 56lb/ft³ (900kg/m³)
Specific gravity: .90

Properties

Sydney blue gum is hard, heavy, tough and strong, with reasonable steam-bending properties. However, it is comparatively easy to work with both hand and machine tools. It glues, screws and nails well. The wood takes most finishes well, and can be brought to a high polish.

Seasoning

It is difficult to dry and can be prone to surface checking. The wood is moderately stable in service.

Durability

The softwood can be subject to attack from the lyctus borer; the heartwood is moderately durable.

Typical uses

Cabinetmaking, flooring, panelling, boatbuilding, general construction and structural plywood.

Grows

New South Wales and southern Queensland, Australia. Introduced to USA, New Zealand, South Africa, parts of Asia and Hawaii
Typical height: 160ft (50m)
Trunk diameter: 6ft (2m)

⚠ **Possible health risks**

Contact dermatitis; nose and throat irritation

The genus *Fagus*
Beeches

◀ Young beech trees often retain their leaves through the autumn and winter

▲ Miniature green man, shown actual size

▲ Neoclassical side table in spalted beech

The *Fagus* genus comprises only about ten species, found in North America, Europe and Asia. The European beech (*F. sylvatica*) is often grown as an ornamental shade tree, but is also very widely used in utilitarian furniture and joinery, as is the broadly similar American beech (*F. grandifolia*).

Beech trees can reach 100ft (30m) when fully grown, and sometimes much taller. They can live for up to 300 years, and even 400 if they are pollarded.

Beech is one of the strongest native timbers in northern temperate regions, but because of its short grain structure it lacks the tensile strength of woods like ash (*Fraxinus* spp.).

It is, however, dense and hard. Beech can be problematic to season, as it is prone to splitting and distortion because of the considerable shrinkage that takes place during drying. Because it is a good turning wood and steam-bends well, it has long been used for handles for non-striking tools, for furniture making, sports equipment and kitchen utensils. Charcoal made from beech is apparently very good for making gunpowder.

The southern beeches, found in Australia, New Zealand and South America, belong to a different but related genus, *Nothofagus*.

◀ Bentwood chair designed by Michael Thonet (1796–1871)

AMERICAN BEECH

Fagus grandifolia (Fagaceae)

Also called: beech

Description

The sapwood is very thin and almost white, whereas the heartwood can be whitish with a reddish tinge, or light to reddish brown. American beech is of a coarser quality than the European species (*F. sylvatica*), and a little heavier. It has straight grain, which is sometimes interlocked, and a fine, even texture, with clearly defined rays giving a characteristic fleck on quartersawn surfaces. The wood has a silvery sheen.

Typical dry weight: 46lb/ft³ (740kg/m³)
Specific gravity: .74

Properties

American beech has excellent steam bending properties, medium stiffness, high crushing strength and medium resistance to shock loads. An excellent turnery wood, it works well with both hand and machine tools, but it does have a tendency to bind when being sawn, and to burn when drilled or crosscut. American beech glues and nails well, takes stain and polish well, and can be brought to a good finish.

Seasoning

Care is needed in drying, because the wood dries rapidly and tends to split, warp and surface-check. During seasoning there can be a large amount of shrinkage and the wood can discolour. There is moderate movement in service, which can be dependent on humidity.

Durability

American beech is perishable, and permeable for preservation treatment. It is vulnerable to attack from the longhorn and common furniture beetles.

Typical uses

Furniture and cabinetmaking, turnery, interior joinery, flooring, brush backs, domestic woodware, vehicle bodies, cooperage, tools, handles, food containers and veneers.

Grows

Eastern Canada and USA
Typical height: 150ft (45m)
Trunk diameter: 4ft (1.2m)

⚠ Possible health risks

Dermatitis, eye irritation, decrease in lung function, rare incidence of nasal cancer

EUROPEAN BEECH
Fagus sylvatica (Fagaceae)

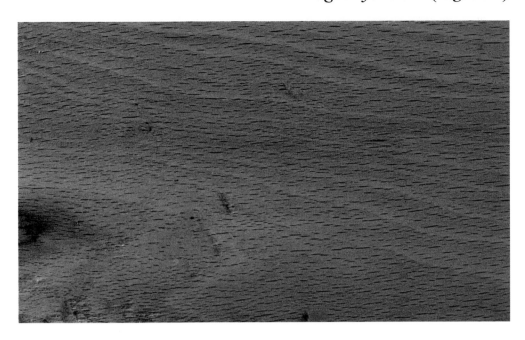

Also called: English, Danish, French, Romanian beech, depending on country of origin; **hêtre** (French), **Buche, Rotbuche** (German), **beuk** (Dutch)

Description
The sapwood is hard to differentiate from the heartwood. The colour varies from whitish to very pale brown, and may darken to a pale pinkish-brown. It can turn to a deeper reddish-brown with steaming. Sometimes the wood has a dark red heart or darker veining. It has a straight grain with fine, even texture and a characteristic fleck, and quartersawn wood may display an attractive broad ray figure on radial surfaces.
Typical dry weight: 45lb/ft³ (720kg/m³)
Specific gravity: .72

Properties
European beech is very suitable for steam-bending. It has medium stiffness and high crushing strength. When poorly seasoned, beech is liable to bind on saws, burn on crosscutting, and cause planing problems. Otherwise, it has medium resistance to hand tools, with moderate blunting of cutters. For nailing, pre-boring is necessary. Beech glues easily, stains and dyes well and takes an excellent finish. It is a very good turnery wood.

Seasoning
It dries fairly rapidly, but can warp, check, split and shrink. Care is needed in both air- and kiln-drying.

Durability
Beech is perishable and can be vulnerable to the common furniture beetle and the death-watch beetle. Longhorn beetle can attack the sapwood.

Typical uses
Solid and laminated furniture such as desks, benches and chairs (including bentwood furniture), quality joinery, kitchenware, tools, tool handles and workbenches, turnery, musical instruments, toys, bobbins, domestic flooring, decorative veneers and plywood.

▲ 19th-century moulding planes, showing ray figure on quartersawn surfaces

Grows
Throughout central Europe and UK; also western Asia
Typical height: 100ft (30m)
Trunk diameter: 4ft (1.2m)

⚠ Possible health risks
Dermatitis, eye irritation, decrease in lung function, rare incidence of nasal cancer

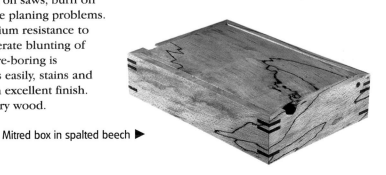

Mitred box in spalted beech ▶

QUEENSLAND MAPLE

Flindersia brayleyana and *F. pimenteliana* (Rutaceae)

F. brayleyana, radial surface

F. pimenteliana

Also called: Australian maple, flindersia, maple silkwood, silkwood

Description

The heartwood is a pinkish-brown which darkens to a medium brown on exposure. The grain can sometimes be straight, but is more usually interlocked and can be wavy or curly, producing an interesting range of figuring. The wood has a medium, uniform texture and a natural silky lustre. It is not a true maple.
Typical dry weight: 34lb/ft³ (550kg/m³), but can be heavier.
Specific gravity: .55

Properties

The wood has low resistance to shock loads and low stiffness, with medium crushing and bending strengths. It is not suitable for steam bending. It works well with both hand and machine tools, and has a moderate blunting effect on cutting edges. A reduced cutting angle is recommended for planing interlocked grain. Queensland maple turns, glues, sands, screws and nails well. It can be fumed with ammonia to deepen the colour, and can be polished to an excellent finish.

Seasoning

It is difficult to dry as it tends to distort, has high shrinkage, and wide boards can collapse or cup. There is medium movement in use.

Durability

The heartwood has a natural moderate resistance to decay and insect attack, and is resistant to preservative treatment.

Typical uses

The wood is prized in Australia for cabinetmaking and fine interior joinery. It is also used for turnery, boatbuilding, oars, rifle stocks, building, office furniture and plywood. Character logs are sliced for decorative veneers, which may have bird's-eye, striped, ripple, block mottle or fiddleback figuring.

Grows

Northern Queensland, Australia; Papua New Guinea
Typical height: 100ft (30m) or more
Trunk diameter: 3–4ft (0.9–1.2m) or more

⚠ **Possible health risks**

Dermatitis

SILVER ASH

Flindersia schottiana, F. bourjotiana, F. pubescens (Rutaceae)

F. bourjotiana

Also called: bumpy ash, cudgerie, southern silver ash, dumpy ash (*F. schottiana*); Queensland silver ash (*F. bourjotiana*); northern silver ash (*F. pubescens*)

Description

These three *Flindersia* species are all sold commercially as 'silver ash' and all have similar properties. The heartwood ranges from near-white to pale yellow, and can sometimes be greyish-silver; the sapwood is not clearly differentiated from the heartwood. Silver ash has a mainly straight grain, but it can be shallowly interlocked or wavy, with an even, medium texture and a natural lustre. There is usually little or no figure. It is not a true ash.

Typical dry weight: 35lb/ft³ (560kg/m³)
Specific gravity: .56

Properties

It is a tough and elastic wood, with low resistance to shock loads and low stiffness, medium crushing and bending strength, and a very good steam-bending classification. The wood works well with both hand and machine tools, and has only a slight blunting effect on cutting edges. Quartersawn surfaces need a reduced cutting angle when being planed or moulded by machine, to avoid pick-up. Silver ash screws, nails and glues well, and can be brought to a good finish and a high polish.

Seasoning

Silver ash is slow-drying and prone to slight warping, but generally air- and kiln-dries fairly well, with little degrade. It exhibits only small movement in use.

Durability

The heartwood is durable above ground, and is very resistant to preservative treatment, but the sapwood, which is vulnerable to attack by the lyctus borer, is treatable.

Typical uses

Furniture, turnery, carving, interior trim, joinery, musical instruments, boatbuilding, sporting goods, flooring and food containers. It is sliced for decorative veneers and rotary-cut for plywood.

Grows
New South Wales and Queensland, Australia; Papua New Guinea
Typical height: 115ft (35m)
Trunk diameter: 3ft (1m)

⚠ **Possible health risks**
Not known

The genus *Fraxinus*
Ashes

▲ Hollow form in *F. excelsior* with ripple figure

The *Fraxinus* genus contains about 70 species that are native to Central and North America, Europe and Asia. A typical ash tree can live for 200 years, and they can survive much longer. The European or common ash (*F. excelsior*) can grow to heights of between 60 and 115ft (18–35m) after about 45 years.

Due to its strength, high shock resistance and straight grain, ash is often used for the handles of striking tools, baseball bats and other sports equipment, furniture and interior joinery. In the past great use was made of ash as a material for wheel rims, oars, gates and walking sticks. It is said that a proper shepherd's crook should be made of ash. Interestingly, the Old English name for a spear was *æsc* (pronounced 'ash'); these would be made from young ash saplings, known as 'ground ash'.

Before the development of light metal alloys, ash was used – and still is in some cases – to construct the frames of carriages, and later those of motor vehicles and aircraft, because of its toughness and relatively light weight. Ash, along with Sitka spruce (*Picea sitchensis*), Douglas fir (*Pseudotsuga menziesii*) and birch (*Betula* spp.), was used in the construction of the famous lightweight de Havilland Mosquito bomber of World War II. The British Morgan sports car still features a hand-built ash body frame.

Ash is a wood I like to work with, not only because of its strength, but also for the sake of its light colour, subtle figure and distinct grain.

▲ Common or European ash (*F. excelsior*)

▶ Cabinet in *F. excelsior* with panels of quartersawn French oak (*Quercus petraea*)

AMERICAN ASH

Fraxinus americana and related species (Oleaceae)

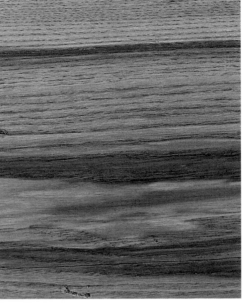

Olive figure

Also called: *F. americana*: white ash (USA), **Canadian ash** (UK); ***F. pennsylvanica*: green ash** (USA), **red ash** (Canada); ***F. nigra*: black ash, brown ash** (USA)

Description

Although similar in structure and properties, the three species of American ash vary in colour. The black and brown ash are slightly darker, with a greyish-brown colour, than the other varieties, which tend to be a lighter grey-brown tinged with red. The wood is normally straight-grained and coarse, with an even texture, and lustrous. The narrow heartwood is almost white.

Typical dry weight: *F. americana* and *F. pennsylvanica* 41lb/ft³ (660kg/m³), *F. nigra* 35lb/ft³ (560kg/m³)

Specific gravity: *F. americana* and *F. pennsylvanica* .66, *F. nigra* .56

Properties

Bending properties vary, but are normally very good. The wood is elastic, tough and strong relative to its weight, and has good stiffness and hardness. Shock resistance is very good. It works well with machine and hand tools but has a moderate blunting effect. The harder species need pre-boring for nailing and screwing. It polishes, stains and glues well.

Seasoning

American ash dries fairly rapidly with little degrade, but grey-brown stains and surface checks can occur. There is little movement in service.

Durability

American ash is perishable and non-durable, with permeable sapwood. It is vulnerable to attack from the common furniture and powder-post beetles. It takes preservative treatment well.

Typical uses

American ash is used for quality furniture, interior joinery, boatbuilding and built-in kitchens. Other uses include sports equipment such as oars, paddles, bats and cues, and handles for workshop and garden tools. It is also a good source of decorative veneers.

▲ Wardrobe in American ash

Grows
Canada and USA
Typical height: 80–120ft (25–36m)
Trunk diameter: 2–5ft (0.6–1.5m)

⚠ **Possible health risks**
Decrease in lung function, rhinitis, asthma

EUROPEAN ASH
Fraxinus excelsior (Oleaceae)

Also called: common ash; frêne (French), **gemeine Esche** (German), **gewone es** (Dutch). Usually distinguished by country of origin: **English, Polish, French,** etc.

Description
The sapwood is not clearly distinct from the heartwood. The colour is generally creamy to light tan, sometimes with a dark brown to black-streaked heartwood, which resembles olivewood (*Olea europaea*) and is referred to as **olive ash**. Ash is tough, heavy, straight-grained and flexible, coarse but even in texture.
Typical dry weight: 44lb/ft³ (710kg/m³)
Specific gravity: .71

Properties
Ash is an excellent wood for steam bending, It has medium resistance to crushing and shock loads, and low stiffness. It is tough and resilient, with good elasticity. Ash works well with both hand and machine tools, but can have a moderate blunting effect on cutters. Pre-boring is necessary for nailing and screwing. It saws, stains and finishes well.

Seasoning
Since it dries fairly rapidly, care is needed to avoid splitting and checking. European ash is moderately stable in service.

Durability
The wood is perishable and non-durable, vulnerable to attack from the powder-post and common furniture beetles. Trees can be attacked by forest longhorn beetles.

Typical uses
Furniture and cabinetmaking, turnery, tool handles; sports equipment such as racquets, bats, polo-mallet heads and cricket stumps; oars, boatbuilding, panelling and decorative veneers. It was traditionally used for coachbuilding and wheelwrighting. Olive-ash figure is prized for decorative work.

Grows
Europe, North Africa, western Asia
Typical height: 80–120ft (25–35m)
Trunk diameter: 2–5ft (0.6–1.5m)

⚠ Possible health risks
Decrease in lung function, rhinitis, asthma

Pike carving ▶

JAPANESE ASH

Fraxinus mandschurica (Oleaceae)

Also called: tamo

Description
The colour of the heartwood varies from straw to light brown. The wood is typically straight-grained, but can sometimes be curly or wavy, which produces an attractive and unusual 'peanut' figure, and sometimes also leaf, mottle, fiddleback, swirl and burr (burl) figure. Some logs are half figured and half plain. Like the other ash species, Japanese ash has a coarse texture.
Typical dry weight: 43lb/ft³ (690kg/m³)
Specific gravity: .69

Properties
It has medium crushing strength and resistance to shock loads, low stiffness and very good steam-bending qualities. Japanese ash works well with both machine and hand tools, and has a moderate blunting effect on cutting edges. Provided the cutters are kept sharp, it planes well. Pre-boring is recommended for nailing and screwing. Japanese ash glues well, stains satisfactorily and can be brought to a highly polished finish.

Seasoning
The wood dries fairly rapidly with little degrade, and exhibits medium movement in service.

Durability
It is perishable, with little resistance to decay fungi and termites. The sapwood is permeable for preservative treatment, and the heartwood is moderately resistant.

Typical uses
Furniture and cabinetmaking, flooring, interior joinery and handles. Choice ash is used for sporting goods such as skis, cues, racquets and bats, and selected logs are sliced for high-quality veneers used in cabinetwork and panelling.

Grows
Japan, South-East Asia
Typical height: 45ft (15m)
Trunk diameter: 1–2ft (0.3–0.6m)

⚠ **Possible health risks**
Can affect lung function

RAMIN

Gonystylus macrophyllum and *G. bancanus* (Gonystylaceae)

G. bancanus

Also called: ramin telur, melawis, lanutan-bagyo

Description

Both heartwood and sapwood are a pale straw or creamy-brown, with a straight to shallowly interlocked grain. Ramin has a moderately fine and even texture and is quite plain in appearance, lacking figure or lustre.

Typical dry weight: 41lb/ft³ (660kg/m³)
Specific gravity: .66

Properties

Ramin is moderately hard and heavy. It has low resistance to shock loads, medium stiffness, high crushing and bending strengths, and a poor steam-bending rating. Ramin works reasonably well with both hand and machine tools, and has a moderate blunting effect on cutting edges. It planes fairly well, may split on nailing if not pre-bored, but glues, stains, varnishes and paints well. Ramin can be polished satisfactorily provided the grain is filled first.

Seasoning

It seasons readily with little degrade, but to prevent staining from mould growth it should be dipped in preservative immediately after conversion. The wood may suffer surface checking, end splitting and slight distortion while drying. There is large movement in use.

Durability

It has little or no resistance to rot. The sapwood is vulnerable to attack from dry-wood termites and powder-post beetles. Ramin is permeable and responds well to preservative treatment.

Typical uses

Furniture, carving, turnery, flooring, interior joinery, shop fittings (store fixtures), toys, picture-frame mouldings, dowelling, plywood and decorative veneer.

Grows
Malaysia, Sarawak and South-East Asia
Typical height: 80ft (24m)
Trunk diameter: 2ft (0.6m)

⚠ **Possible health risks**
Breathing difficulties, coughing, shivering, sweating and tiredness. Sharp bark fibres can cause skin irritation and dermatitis

AGBA

Gossweilerodendron balsamiferum (Leguminosae)

Also called: Nigerian cedar, tola, tola branca, n'tola, white tola, egba, emongi

Description

The heartwood is yellowish to pinky-brown when first cut, but darkens to a brick red on exposure to light and air. The grain is normally straight or slightly wavy, but may sometimes be interlocked. The wood has a fine, even texture and is highly lustrous, with some similarities to mahogany (*Swietenia macrophylla*). A broad striped figure can sometimes be found on quartersawn surfaces. Resin pockets are fairly frequent.
Typical dry weight: 32lb/ft³ (520kg/m³)
Specific gravity: .52

Properties

Bending strength and resistance to shock loads are low. Agba has medium crushing strength and very low stiffness. In large logs there may be extensive areas of brittleheart. The wood has only a slight blunting effect on tools, but gum build-up on cutters may be a problem. It nails satisfactorily and screws and glues well. Agba stains well once the grain has been filled, and is capable of being polished to a shiny finish. Agba is unsuitable for contact with food, because of the odour from the resin.

Seasoning

There is a slight tendency to warp and check, but generally it dries fairly easily. It can exude gum or oleoresin. It is stable after seasoning.

Durability

The sapwood is vulnerable to common furniture beetle, but the heartwood is durable. Preservative penetration of the sapwood is adequate, but the heartwood is resistant to preservative treatment.

Typical uses

Furniture, interior and exterior joinery, turnery, boatbuilding, domestic flooring, truck floors, coffins and marine plywood. Some selected wood is made into decorative veneers.

Grows
West African rainforests
Typical height: 200ft (60m)
Trunk diameter: 6ft 6in (2m)
or more

⚠ **Possible health risks**
Dermatitis

MARACAIBO BOXWOOD

Gossypiospermum praecox (Flacourtiaceae)

Syn.: *Casearia praecox*
Also called: zapatero, palo blanco, agracejo. Also distinguished by country of origin:
Colombian, Venezuelan, West Indian boxwood

Description
The heartwood is not distinct from the sapwood, and can range in colour from almost white to lemon-yellow. It is normally straight-grained, with a very fine, compact, uniform, almost featureless texture, and is highly lustrous. It is not a true boxwood.
Typical dry weight: 53lb/ft³ (850kg/m³)
Specific gravity: .85

Properties
Because of the type of goods the wood is used for, and the small size of the stock, strength properties are not available, but it is said to steam-bend well. Although a very dense wood, it works satisfactorily with both machine and hand tools. It has a moderate blunting effect on cutting edges. Maracaibo boxwood turns and carves easily, glues well, and can be taken to a very smooth and polished finish.

Seasoning
The wood is slow-drying and fairly difficult to air-dry. It can suffer from splitting and surface checking, and can acquire blue staining if stored in humid conditions. It is advisable to halve stock lengthwise or dimension it before drying. There is only small movement in service.

Durability
The wood is fairly durable, but has poor resistance to attack from termites and decay fungi. The sapwood is vulnerable to attack from the common furniture beetle. The heartwood is resistant to preservative treatment.

Typical uses
Engraving, carving, woodwind instruments, piano keys, bobbins, chess pieces, shuttles, knife handles, stringing and bandings, and inlay. It is also used as decorative veneer for cabinetmaking.

Grows
Venezuela, Colombia,
Dominican Republic
Typical height: 30ft (10m) max.
Trunk diameter: 8–16in
(0.2–0.4m)

⚠ **Possible health risks**
Not known

LIGNUM VITAE

Guaiacum officinale and related species (Zygophyllaceae)

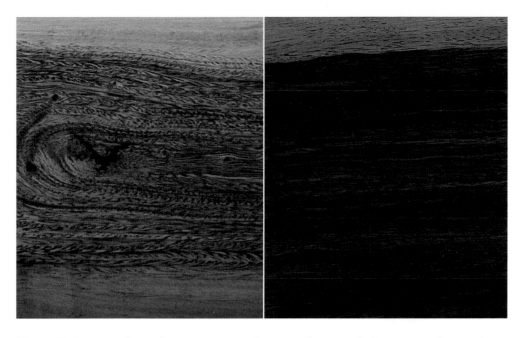

Also called: guayacán, palo santo, guayacán negro, ironwood. *G. sanctum* is now the most important commercial species, as *G. officinale* is in short supply

Description

The heartwood can be dark greenish-brown or nearly black. It has a strongly interlocked, irregular grain, with a very fine texture. Since about 30% of the weight of the wood is guaiac gum, lignum vitae has an oily or waxy feel to it. The sapwood is clearly demarcated from the heartwood, and is pale yellow or cream.
Typical dry weight: 77lb/ft³ (1230kg/m³)
Specific gravity: 1.23

Properties

Lignum vitae has very high strength properties, and the heartwood is exceptionally hard, dense and heavy; sapwood is decidedly less hard. The wood is unsuitable for bending. It is a very difficult wood to work with hand tools, and very hard to saw and machine. It has a tendency to ride on the cutters when being machine-planed, and has a moderate blunting effect on cutting tools. Gluing and sanding are liable to be difficult because of the oil content, but lignum vitae can be brought to a good polished finish.

Seasoning

The wood is rather difficult to season; it requires a lot of care in the process, and end coating is recommended. Shakes and end splits are typical defects. It has moderate dimensional stability.

Durability

The heartwood has high natural resistance to decay and does not normally require preservative treatment. Green wood can, however, be attacked by the longhorn beetle.

Typical uses

Lignum vitae is used for ships' propeller bushes and bearings, since it has three times the life of bronze or steel as a result of its natural self-lubricating qualities. It is also used for other machinery parts, pulley sheaves, naval architecture, wheels, textile equipment, mallet heads and bowling balls or 'woods'.

▲ Woodworking mallets, the right-hand one dated 1921

Grows
Central America, Caribbean, Venezuela, Colombia
Typical height: 20ft (6m)
Trunk diameter: 1ft (0.3m)

⚠ **Possible health risks**
Dermatitis

GUAREA
Guarea cedrata (Meliaceae)

Also called: bosasa, white guarea, obobo nofua, scented guarea, bossé. *G. thompsonii* is also sold as guarea, and has similar properties

Grows
Tropical West Africa and
Uganda
Typical height: 160ft (48m)
Trunk diameter: 5ft (1.5m)

⚠ **Possible health risks**
Skin and mucous membrane
irritation, dermatitis, asthma, nausea,
headaches and visual disturbances

Description
The heartwood is a pale pinkish-brown
when newly cut, but darkens with time.
The sapwood is paler. Guarea generally
has a straight grain, which can sometimes
be curly or wavy. When the wood is plain-
cut, a small, attractive zigzag figure is
sometimes visible. It has a fine texture
and contains medium levels of silica.
Typical dry weight: 36lb/ft³ (580kg/m³)
Specific gravity: .58

Properties
The wood is of medium density, has low
resistance to shock loads and a good
steam-bending classification. It is very
resistant to abrasion and has a medium
blunting effect on cutting edges. Guarea
has good nailing and screwing properties,
and works fairly well with hand tools.
Finished surfaces can be woolly if care is
not taken. It can be finished well, but
there may be problems with gum
exudation when polishing is carried out
in warm conditions. Gluing is not
normally a problem, but resin deposits
can affect this.

Seasoning
It dries fairly rapidly with little degrade,
but has a slight warping and splitting
tendency. Movement in service is minimal.

Durability
The heartwood is durable and highly
resistant to preservative treatment,
whereas the sapwood is permeable.

Typical uses
Furniture and furniture parts, quality
joinery, shop fittings (store fixtures),
boatbuilding, rifle butts, marine piling in
certain waters, decorative veneers
and marine plywood.

BUBINGA

Guibourtia demeusei and related species (Leguminosae)

Also called: African rosewood, akume, essingang, buvenga, ovang, waka, okweni; veneers are marketed as **kevasingo**

Description

The heartwood is a medium red-brown, with lighter red to purple veining. The sapwood is usually greyish-white, ivory, or streaked ivory-white, and sometimes brownish-white. Typically, the grain is straight or interlocked and there are distinct annual rings. Fine pores, which may contain a reddish gum, can be found throughout. The texture is fairly coarse but even, and can be highly lustrous.
Typical dry weight: 55lb/ft³ (880kg/m³)
Specific gravity: .88

Properties

There can be problems with gum exudation, and steam-bending qualities are poor. It works well with both hand and machine tools, though irregular grain may pick up during planing or moulding, so a low cutting angle should be used. It has a moderate to severe blunting effect, because it contains silica. Nailing and screwing require pre-boring, and gum pockets may make gluing difficult. It takes stain easily, and can be sanded and polished to an excellent finish.

Seasoning

It seasons well with little degrade, but gum can cause problems. Slow seasoning is advised to prevent distortion and checking. It is stable in service.

Durability

Bubinga is moderately resistant to marine borers and vulnerable to the common furniture beetle. The heartwood is resistant to preservative treatment, the sapwood moderately so.

Typical uses

Its main use is for sliced decorative veneers for panelling and cabinets, especially in the rotary-cut form known as **kevasingo**. It is also prized for turnery. Other uses include boatbuilding, furniture, flooring, decorative items, brush backs and knife handles.

◀ Display stand

Grows
Central and west central tropical Africa
Typical height: 70ft (21m) max.
Trunk diameter: 4ft (1.2m)

⚠ **Possible health risks**
Dermatitis and possible skin lesions

OVANGKOL

Guibourtia ehie (Leguminosae)

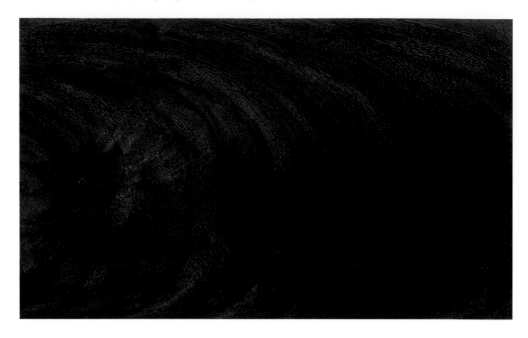

Also called: ovèngkol, amazakoué, anokye, ehie, hyeduanini

Description

The heartwood of ovangkol ranges from yellow-brown to chocolate-brown, with grey to almost black stripes. The grain varies from straight to interlocked, with a moderately coarse texture, and can sometimes show an attractive figuring. The yellow-white sapwood is about 4in (100mm) thick and is clearly demarcated from the heartwood.
Typical dry weight: 50lb/ft³ (800kg/m³)
Specific gravity: .80

Properties

Apart from a poor steam-bending rating, ovangkol is classified as medium in all strength properties. It works fairly easily with hand tools, but the silica content of the wood does have a moderate blunting effect on cutting edges. Although it planes cleanly, quartersawn stock should be planed with a reduced cutting angle. The wood glues, screws, nails and stains well, and can be brought to an excellent polished finish. Iron staining is liable to occur if the wood is used in contact with ferrous metals.

Seasoning

Ovangkol usually seasons rapidly and well with little degrade, but is difficult to kiln-dry. It has medium movement in service.

Durability

The heartwood is moderately durable and usually resistant to termites, and is difficult to treat with preservatives. The sapwood is permeable and easy to treat.

Typical uses

Cabinetmaking, quality joinery, turnery, domestic flooring, tool handles, panelling and shopfitting. It is also sliced for decorative veneers.

Grows

Gabon, Ghana, Ivory Coast, Nigeria
Typical height: 100–150ft (30–45m)
Trunk diameter: 2–3ft (0.6–0.9m)

⚠ **Possible health risks**

Not known

MENGKULANG

Heritiera javanica and related species (Sterculiaceae)

Also called: kembang, choboch, huynh, chopwoch, dongtchem

Description
The heartwood ranges from almost white when newly cut, to pale orange-brown, bluish-pink, red, red-brown or a deep golden-brown. It can have dark streaks on longitudinal surfaces, and red flecks from quite large rays on quartered surfaces. The grain can vary from straight to very interlocked, which will sometimes give a fiddleback or ray figure. It is often lustrous, and has a fairly coarse and even texture with a greasy feel to the surface. The sapwood is pale and not always clearly differentiated from the heartwood.
Typical dry weight: 45lb/ft³ (720kg/m³)
Specific gravity: .72

Properties
This dense, heavy wood has medium stiffness, bending strength and resistance to shock loads. It has high crushing strength, but is not suitable for steam bending. Small deposits of silica, along with the irregular grain, produce a strong blunting effect on cutting edges. Tungsten-carbide-tipped (TCT) blades are advised for sawing, and planing, turning,

mortising and moulding are all difficult. It is difficult to work with hand tools, and needs pre-boring for nails and screws. The wood glues satisfactorily, and stains, paints and polishes well after filling.

Seasoning
It dries well and quickly with little degrade, but can be subject to surface checking and sometimes to warping and twisting. There is only small movement in service.

Durability
The wood is not durable and has little resistance to decay. It is vulnerable to attack from marine borers and termites. The sapwood is moderately resistant to preservative treatment, and the heartwood is very difficult to treat.

Typical uses
Furniture, interior joinery, kitchen cabinets, panelling, flooring including parquet, boatbuilding, construction, railway sleepers (railroad ties) and mine timbers. It is also rotary-cut for plywood and sliced for decorative veneer.

Grows
Burma (Myanmar), Indonesia, Malaysia, Philippines
Typical height: 100–150ft (30–45m)
Trunk diameter: 2–4ft (0.6–1.2m)

⚠ **Possible health risks**
Not known

COURBARIL

Hymenaea courbaril (Leguminosae)

Also called: locust, West Indian locust, jutaby, jatobá, alga, algarrobo, copal, jatai vermelho

Description

The sapwood is clearly differentiated from the heartwood and is white, grey or pinkish in colour. Newly cut heartwood can vary in colour from salmon-pink to orange-brown, but darkens to a russet to reddish-brown on exposure, and is often marked with dark streaks. The grain is predominantly interlocked and has a medium to coarse texture.

Typical dry weight: 56lb/ft³ (910kg/m³)
Specific gravity: .91

Properties

Courbaril has good steam-bending properties, and is very hard, tough and strong. Because of its hardness, working courbaril is moderately difficult. It has a moderate blunting effect on cutting edges, and since the grain tends to be interlocked a reduced cutting angle is advised for a good finish. It nails badly and pre-boring is required for screwing. Gluing properties are fair; it stains well, and can be brought to a satisfactory finish, but not to a high polish.

Seasoning

It dries at a moderate to fast speed, resulting in a possibility of case hardening, surface checking and warping. Slower drying can reduce these defects. There is little movement in service.

Durability

The heartwood is moderately durable and very resistant to dry-wood termites. It is also very resistant to preservative treatment, whereas the sapwood will take preservative adequately.

Typical uses

Furniture and cabinetmaking, turnery, boatbuilding, kitchen cupboards, tool handles, sports equipment, factory flooring, parquet flooring and railway sleepers (railroad ties).

Grows
West Indies, South and Central America
Typical height: 100ft (30m)
Trunk diameter: 2–4ft (0.6–1.2m)

⚠ **Possible health risks**
Irritant to the skin

HOLLY

Ilex spp. (Aquifoliaceae)

Also called: European holly (*I. aquifolium*), American holly (*I. opaca*), houx (French),
Ilex (German). There are a great many species of holly worldwide

Description

The very wide sapwood is usually whiter than the heartwood, which ranges from very white to ivory-white in colour. Holly has a very close, irregular grain with a very fine, even texture. It is normally without any figure.
Typical dry weight: 50lb/ft³ (800kg/m³)
Specific gravity: .80

Properties

The wood is tough, heavy and hard in all categories. It is not normally used for steam bending, because of the small sections available. The irregular grain makes sawing and planing difficult. Cutting edges must be very sharp and used at a reduced angle. The wood has a moderate blunting effect on tools. It turns, carves, sands, glues, screws, stains and polishes well.

Seasoning

It is better cut in the winter, so that the white wood does not discolour. It is not easy to season, and will end-split and distort if dried in the round. It dries better if cut into small stock and dried slowly while weighted down. There can be large movement in service.

Durability

The wood has little or no resistance to insect attack and decay-causing fungi. It is permeable for preservative treatment, but this is not normally necessary because of the uses to which holly is put.

Typical uses

Fine turnery, carving, inlay lines, engraving, handles, piano and organ keys, and marquetry inlay. Holly is often used as an alternative to boxwood (*Buxus sempervirens*), and dyed black as a substitute for ebony (*Diospyros* spp.).

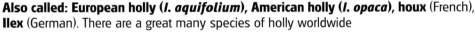

Teardrop box ▶

▲ Cabinet: drawers in holly, carcass in satinwood (*Zanthoxylum flavum*)

Grows

Europe and western Asia
(*I. aquifolium*), USA (*I. opaca*)
Typical height: 40–70ft
(12–21m)
Trunk diameter: 1–2ft
(0.3–0.6m)

⚠ Possible health risks

Not known

MERBAU

Intsia bijuga and *I. palembanica* (Leguminosae)

Syn. for *I. palembanica*: *I. bakeri*
Also called: hintzy, ipil, mirabow, kubok, lumpho, zolt, kwila, vesi

Description
The heartwood is yellowish to orange-brown when newly cut, but matures to brown or dark red-brown; there can be moderate to high colour variation. The grain can be straight, wavy or interlocked, and may form a ribbon figure on radial surfaces. Merbau has a moderately coarse but even texture with an oily feel to it. The surface can often be lustrous, but vessel cavities may contain yellow deposits that can dye cloth. The sapwood is clearly demarcated from the heartwood and is whitish-grey to yellowish-brown.
Typical dry weight: 56lb/ft³ (900kg/m³)
Specific gravity: .90

Properties
It is moderately heavy and hard, with medium stiffness, bending strength and resistance to shock loads. The wood has moderate steam-bending properties, but high crushing strength. It works well with hand tools, but has a severe blunting effect. Tungsten-carbide-tipped (TCT) blades are advised for sawing, which can be difficult because of the gum content. A reduced angle is recommended for planing, to reduce tear-out and pick-up on quartersawn stock. It turns, bores, mortises, glues, stains, varnishes and paints well. It needs pre-boring for nailing and screwing, and sands satisfactorily.

Seasoning
The wood seasons well with little degrade. Sealing is recommended to prevent end checking. Movement in service is small.

Durability
The heartwood is durable and very resistant to preservative treatment. The sapwood is vulnerable to insect attack, but permeable to preservatives.

Typical uses
Furniture, quality joinery, office furniture, kitchen cabinets, boatbuilding, flooring including parquet, striking-tool handles, heavy construction and railway sleepers (railroad ties). Interestingly figured logs are sliced for decorative veneer.

BUTTERNUT

Juglans cinerea (Juglandaceae)

Also called: white walnut, oilnut, nogal, nogal blanco, nuez meca

Description

The heartwood is light brown, frequently interspersed with red tones or dark brown streaks. The sapwood is usually about 1in (25mm) wide, and ranges from white to a light greyish-brown. Butternut is typically straight-grained, with a medium to coarse, but soft, texture and a satiny lustre.

Typical dry weight: 28lb/ft³ (450kg/m³)
Specific gravity: .45

Properties

The wood is weak in terms of stiffness, and moderately weak in bending. It can be worked easily with both machine and hand tools, and it planes well provided the cutting edges are sharp. Butternut screws, glues and nails well. It also takes stains well, and can be polished to an excellent finish.

Seasoning

Butternut dries slowly with minimal shrinkage or degrade, and should be thoroughly air-dried prior to kilning. It is fairly stable in service.

Durability

Butternut has little or no resistance to decay and is vulnerable to attack from the common furniture beetle. The sapwood is permeable for preservative treatment, and the heartwood is moderately resistant.

Typical uses

Quality joinery, domestic and office furniture, boatbuilding, crates and boxes, interior construction and panelling. Butternut is an excellent carving wood. It is also sliced as a decorative veneer.

Grows
Canada and USA
Typical height:
40–70ft (12–21m)
Trunk diameter:
1–2ft (0.3–0.6m)

⚠ **Possible health risks**
Irritation to skin and eyes

AMERICAN WALNUT
Juglans nigra (Juglandaceae)

Also called: American black walnut, eastern black walnut, gunwood, walnut, Virginia walnut

▲ Pedestal desk detail

Description
The heartwood can be light greyish-brown, dark chocolate or purplish-black. The sapwood is whitish- to yellowish-brown, unless stained or steamed to match the heartwood. The slightly open grain is typically straight, but can be curly or wavy. The texture is usually coarse, but develops a lustrous patina in time. Burrs (burls), stumpwood and crotches produce notable mottled, curly and wavy figure.
Typical dry weight: 40lb/ft³ (640kg/m³)
Specific gravity: .64

Properties
This hard, tough wood has moderate crushing and bending strength, low stiffness, and steam-bends well. It works well with machine and hand tools, with a moderate blunting effect. It generally planes well, but irregular grain can be tricky. It turns, carves, mortises, nails, screws, sands and paints well. Gluing is satisfactory. It stains and polishes easily to a high finish.

Chess box ▶

Seasoning
The wood dries slowly and care must be taken to avoid degrade. This can include checking, iron staining, ring failure, honeycombing and collapse. There is small movement in use.

Durability
American walnut heartwood is highly durable, resistant to decay and to preservative treatment. The sapwood is permeable for treatment, and can be vulnerable to the powder-post beetle.

Typical uses
A prized cabinetmaking wood, it is also the chosen wood in the US for gunstocks and rifle butts. It is also used for quality furniture, architectural work, flooring, boatbuilding, musical instruments, turnery, carving, office furniture, kitchen cabinets, sporting goods and umbrella handles. It is sliced for decorative veneers and is an important wood for making plywood. The tree also produces edible nuts.

EUROPEAN WALNUT

Juglans regia (Juglandaceae)

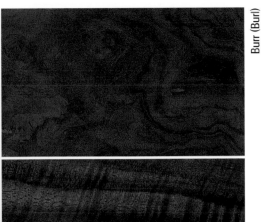

Burr (Burl)

Ripple figure

Also called: noyer (French), **Nussbaum** (German). Usually differentiated according to origin: **Persian, French, Black Sea,** etc.

Description

The heartwood varies in colour, but is typically greyish-brown with irregular dark streaks. The sapwood is paler and clearly distinct from the heartwood. European walnut is normally straight-grained, but can be wavy. It has a coarse texture. A clearly defined central core will sometimes produce beautifully figured wood. Walnut crotch, burr (burl) and stumpwood figure can be very attractive.

Typical dry weight: 40lb/ft³ (640kg/m³)

Specific gravity: .64

Properties

It has a high crushing strength, medium resistance to shock loads, medium bending strength, low stiffness, and very good steam-bending qualities. It works well with both machine and hand tools, and has a moderate blunting effect on cutting edges. The wood planes well and finishes cleanly. It turns, carves, nails, screws and sands well, and moulds, bores, routs, mortises and glues satisfactorily. Walnut stains very well, but ultraviolet light inhibitors in the finish are advised to prevent colour fade. The wood can be brought to an excellent polished finish.

Seasoning

The wood dries well but slowly. Honeycombing can occur in thicker stock if the drying is too fast. It exhibits medium movement in service.

Durability

The heartwood has moderate durability, whereas the sapwood is vulnerable to attack from the common furniture and powder-post beetles. The sapwood is permeable for preservative treatment, but the heartwood is resistant.

Typical uses

Walnut is prized for cabinetwork and for gunstocks and rifle butts. It is used for quality furniture, office and bank fittings, turnery, sports goods, carving, and interior trim in luxury cars. Figured wood is sliced into veneers for cabinetwork, marquetry and panelling. The tree also produces edible nuts.

▲ Life-size wren carving

Grows
Europe, Turkey, south-west Asia
Typical height: 100ft (30m)
Trunk diameter:
2–3ft (0.6–0.9m), but can be broader

⚠ **Possible health risks**
Dermatitis; irritation to nose, eyes and throat; possible nasal cancer

VIRGINIAN PENCIL CEDAR
Juniperus virginiana (Cupressaceae)

Also called: pencil cedar, eastern red cedar, juniper, red cedar, savin

Description
The heartwood is light red, rose-red or purplish, but ages to a dull red or reddish-brown. It can contain small knots. The narrow sapwood is off-white to light cream. It has fine, even, straight grain with a fine texture, and a typical cedary scent, though not classed as a true cedar.
Typical dry weight: 33lb/ft³ (530kg/m³)
Specific gravity: .53

Properties
It has low resistance to shock loads and low stiffness, with medium crushing and bending strength. Its steam-bending classification is poor. It has only a little blunting effect on cutters, and works well with both hand and machine tools. Knotty decorative stock needs very sharp cutters to obtain a good finish. It glues and stains well, and takes a high polish. Splitting is possible when nailing.

Seasoning
Seasoning is not difficult, but to avoid end splitting and fine surface checking it should be fairly slow.

Durability
The wood is durable, with a naturally high resistance to decay and insect attack.

Typical uses
Pencils, cigar boxes, coffins, shipbuilding, blanket chests, furniture, foundation posts. Decorative panelling and veneers are made from selected logs. Essential oils are distilled from shavings and chips.

Grows
Canada and USA
Typical height: 40–60ft
(12–18m)
Trunk diameter: 1–2ft
(0.3–0.6m)

⚠ Possible health risks
May cause dermatitis and respiratory problems

AFRICAN MAHOGANY

Khaya ivorensis and related species (Meliaceae)

Also called: akuk, bandoro, bisselon, eri kiree, ogwango, undianunu, n'gollon, zaminguila, oganwo, acajou. Also distinguished by country of origin: **Nigerian, Benin, Senegal,** etc. The term 'African mahogany' also includes other *Khaya* species: ***K. anthotheca, K. grandifoliola, K. senegalensis*** and ***K. nyasica***

Description

The wood is usually light pinkish-brown when freshly cut, darkening on exposure to a deep reddish colour, often with a purple cast. The grain can be straight, but is typically interlocked, showing a striped or roey figure on quartersawn surfaces. Crotch and swirl figures are often present. The texture is variable, often moderately coarse, with a high, golden lustre. The sapwood, not always distinct from the heartwood, is creamy-white to yellowish.
Typical dry weight: 33lb/ft³ (530kg/m³)
Specific gravity: .53

Properties

It has medium crushing strength, low bending strength, very low stiffness and resistance to shock loads. It is generally easy to work with hand tools. Interlocked grain can cause woolliness and tearing when planing, and there is a moderate blunting effect on cutters. It turns, sands, bores, glues and nails satisfactorily, but non-ferrous fastenings are recommended to avoid iron staining. It stains and polishes very well.

Seasoning

The wood dries rapidly with little degrade, though if tension wood is present, serious distortion can occur. There is only small movement in service.

Durability

Forest longhorn and buprestid beetles may attack logs and trees. The heartwood has moderate resistance to decay; the sapwood is vulnerable to the common furniture and powder-post beetles. The heartwood is highly resistant to preservatives, the sapwood moderately so.

Typical uses

Furniture and cabinetmaking, interior joinery, bank, office and shop fittings, boatbuilding. It is also sliced for veneers and rotary-cut for plywood.

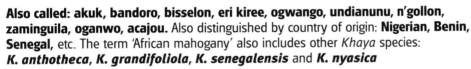

Grows
Tropical areas of West, Central and East Africa
Typical height: 110–140ft (33–43m)
Trunk diameter: 6ft (1.8m)

⚠ **Possible health risks**
Dermatitis, especially of the face, forearms and backs of hands; respiratory problems, rhinitis and nasal cancer

◀ Turned box

REWAREWA

Knightia excelsa (Proteaceae)

Also called: New Zealand honeysuckle

Description

Rewarewa has a deep red heartwood with a strong ray figure. It is a lustrous wood with irregular grain and a fine texture. Since the logs are frequently crooked, the grain can be distorted. Flatsawn boards may show a speckled ray figure, and quartersawn stock sometimes reveals strong figuring from the conspicuous red-brown rays.

Typical dry weight: 735kg/m³ (46lb/ft³)
Specific Gravity: .73

Properties

The wood is hard and strong, with high resistance to shock loads, high stiffness and crushing strength, and medium bending strength. It is not suitable for steam bending. Rewarewa works well with both hand and machine tools, and has a medium blunting effect on cutting edges. Gluing is satisfactory, and pre-boring is required for nailing. It holds screws well. Oil and varnish finishes are not recommended, because they detract from the interesting grain. The wood can be taken to an excellent finish with care.

Seasoning

It is a difficult wood to dry. There can be problems with blackheart, causing collapse, shrinkage and distortion. There is considerable movement in use.

Durability

Rewarewa is not durable. The heartwood is resistant to preservative treatment, but the sapwood is permeable.

Typical uses

Fine furniture and cabinetmaking, interior trim, internal joinery, ornamental turnery, bowls, handles, inlay and flooring. Choice logs are sliced for decorative veneer used in marquetry, cabinetwork and panelling. Treated wood is used for railway sleepers (railroad ties), decking, gates and piling. It is also rotary-cut for plywood facing.

Grows
New Zealand
Typical height: 100ft (30m)
Trunk diameter: 3ft (1m) max.

⚠ **Possible health risks**
Not known

LABURNUM

Laburnum anagyroides (Leguminosae)

Also called: golden chain, aubour (French), **Goldregen** (German)

Description

Freshly cut heartwood is bright yellow with a greenish tint, darkening on exposure to golden-brown and then to deep brown. The narrow, almost white sapwood is distinct from the heartwood. It is generally straight-grained, with a fairly fine texture and a lustrous surface. It has a growth-ring figure when flatsawn, and a decorative fleck when quartersawn. It is usually sold in small billets.

Typical dry weight: 52lb/ft³ (820kg/m³)
Specific gravity: .82

Properties

It is hard and dense, but works well with hand and machine tools. It turns well, and can be sliced into fine veneers, particularly cross-grain to make laburnum 'oysters'. It takes a good finish. Since it is normally used in small sections, the other strength categories are not relevant.

Seasoning

It should be seasoned slowly to avoid end checking and splitting, but does dry readily. There is little movement in service.

Durability

Laburnum is durable, but the sapwood can be vulnerable to insect attack.

Typical uses

It is excellent for turning and is used for parts of musical instruments, knife handles and decorative work. It is also sliced for veneers and inlay, including the distinctive cross-grain sections known as 'oysters'.

◄ Squirrel walking stick

Grows
Central and southern Europe
Typical height: 20–30ft (6–9m)
Max trunk diameter: 1ft (0.3m)

⚠ **Possible health risks**
The seeds are highly toxic to animals and humans

HUON PINE

Lagarostrobos franklinii (Podocarpaceae)

Syn.: *Dacrydium franklinii*
Also called: white pine, Macquarie pine

Description

The pale, narrow sapwood is not easily distinguished from the heartwood, which ranges from light cream to golden- or yellowish-brown. The wood is usually straight-grained, with a fine and even texture, has closely spaced growth rings, and can exhibit an attractive bird's-eye figure. It is not a true pine.

Typical dry weight: 32lb/ft³ (520kg/m³)
Specific gravity: .52

Properties

Huon pine has low resistance to shock loads and low stiffness, medium crushing strength and good bending properties. It is easily worked with machine and hand tools, and has only a slight blunting effect on cutters. Pre-boring is advisable for nailing and screwing, and gluing is satisfactory. It can be brought to a high polish, and generally finishes well.

Seasoning

Huon pine dries readily. There is a slight tendency to surface checking.

Durability

It is a highly durable wood, mainly due to the presence of methyl eugenol oil, and resists insect attack. It is permeable for preservative treatment.

Typical uses

The supply of Huon pine is controlled and limited. It is regarded as one of the best of all boatbuilding woods, and is also used for cabinetmaking, quality joinery and decorative veneers.

Grows

Tasmania
Typical height: 65–100ft (20–30m)
Trunk diameter: 3ft 3in (1m)

⚠ **Possible health risks**

Not known

EUROPEAN LARCH

Larix decidua (Pinaceae)

Syn.: *L. europaea*
Also called: mélèze (French), **Lärche** (German), **Europese lork** (Dutch)

Description

The heartwood is pale red to brick-red and has clearly marked growth rings, with a clear distinction between earlywood and latewood. It usually contains hard knots that may loosen after seasoning. The wood is typically straight-grained, but some trees develop spiral grain. It has a fine, uniform texture.
Typical dry weight: 37lb/ft³ (590kg/m³)
Specific gravity: .59

Properties

It has low stiffness, medium resistance to shock loads and crushing, a medium bending rating and moderate suitability for steam bending. It works fairly easily with hand tools, but the hard knots can cause severe blunting. It works well generally with machine tools, but loose knots can be a problem, and the hardness of the knots may cause uneven blunting of cutters. Pre-boring is required for nailing and screwing. It stains, varnishes and paints well. It is regarded as tough by comparison with other conifers.

Seasoning

The wood seasons fairly rapidly, but can have a tendency to distort. Knots may loosen and split in the drying process. Resin can be a problem if the wood is not seasoned correctly. It has high dimensional stability when seasoned.

Durability

Although more durable than most conifers, larch is still only moderately durable, and remains vulnerable to insect attack. The heartwood responds poorly to preservative treatment, and the sapwood is moderately resistant to it.

Typical uses

Door and window frames, flooring including parquet, staircases, boat and ship building, poles, piling, posts, fencing and shingles. It is also sliced to make decorative veneers.

Grows
Europe, including UK; also New Zealand
Typical height: 70ft (21m)
Trunk diameter: 2ft (0.6m)

⚠ **Possible health risks**
Nettle rash, dermatitis (possibly from bark lichens), respiratory irritation

JAPANESE LARCH
Larix kaempferi (Pinaceae)

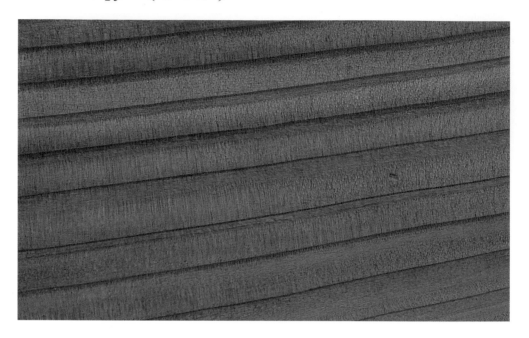

Syn.: *L. leptolepis*
Also called: red larch, kara-matsu

Description
The heartwood of Japanese larch is reddish-brown, and the growth rings are clearly defined. The wood is resinous and straight-grained, and has a fine to medium texture.
Typical dry weight: 33lb/ft³5 (30kg/m³)
Specific gravity: .53

Properties
Japanese larch has medium compression strength, and is of average weight and density. Although it has a fairly high bending strength, its steam-bending qualities are rated as poor. When properly seasoned, its characteristics are similar to those of European larch (*L. decidua*). The wood can be worked reasonably easily with hand tools, but knots can be a problem. When planing, very sharp cutters are recommended in order to prevent tearing and crumbling in the soft earlywood areas. Japanese larch turns, bores, routs, moulds, carves, varnishes and paints well. Pre-boring is advisable for nailing.

Seasoning
If dried rapidly it will warp, check and split. Slow kiln-drying is recommended. There is very small movement in service.

Durability
Japanese larch has a moderate natural resistance to decay, but is vulnerable to attack from the pinhole borer beetle.

Typical uses
Furniture including office and rustic, domestic flooring, framing, boat and ship building, bridge building and construction.

Grows
Japan; also Europe, including UK
Typical height: 70ft (20m)
Trunk diameter: 1–2ft (0.3–0.6m)

⚠ **Possible health risks**
Not known

WESTERN LARCH

Larix occidentalis (Pinaceae)

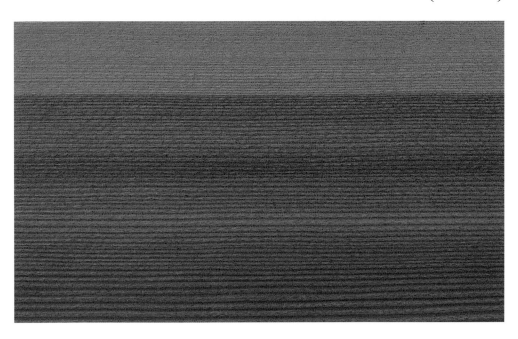

Also called: tamarack, western tamarack, hackmatack, Montana larch, mountain larch.
It is often sold as **Douglas fir-larch**, and may also be sold interchangeably with Douglas fir
(*Pseudotsuga menziesii*)

Description

Western larch has a narrow near-white to pale straw sapwood, contrasting with a reddish to russet-brown heartwood. It is typically straight-grained, with a coarse texture and very narrow growth rings. The wood is slightly resinous, with a marked oily appearance, and feels greasy to the touch. Knots are common, but tend to be tight and small. The wood can be prone to ring shake.
Typical dry weight: 30lb/ft³ (480kg/m³)
Specific gravity: .48

Properties

Western larch is one of the stronger, heavier and harder softwoods. It exhibits high stiffness, crushing and bending strength. It works quite well, but stringy grain can sometimes cause problems during planing. The wood moulds, turns, mortises, routs and bores well, and it takes glue very well. Pre-boring is advised for screwing, and when nailing either pre-bored holes or blunt-pointed nails are recommended, as the wood splits easily. The surface needs to be primed well before painting.

Seasoning

The wood seasons well, but there is usually high shrinkage, and warping and checking can be a problem. Additionally, there can be ring shakes and resin exudation. It is stable in service.

Durability

The heartwood is moderately resistant to decay, but needs preservative treatment in decay hazard situations.

Typical uses

It is predominantly used in the construction industry, and also for framing, windows, panelling, flooring, boxes, pallets, casks, laminated beams, and telegraph poles. It is made into veneer, corestock and plywood.

Grows
Western Canada and USA
Typical height: 80–150ft
(24–46m)
Trunk diameter: 1ft 6in–3ft
(0.5–0.9m)

⚠ **Possible health risks**
Working with pinelike woods in general can cause allergic bronchial asthma, rhinitis and dermatitis

PUKATEA

Laurelia novae-zelandiae (Atherospermataceae)

No other names

Description
The heartwood of pukatea is a dull, uniform greyish-brown, frequently with a greenish hue and sometimes with streaks. It has a generally straight grain, with a fine, even texture and a cloudy silver lustre. The growth rings in pukatea are clearly defined, and the medullary rays can produce an attractive flecked figure on quartersawn surfaces.
Typical dry weight: 27lb/ft³ (430kg/m³)
Specific gravity: .43

Properties
The wood is moderately strong for its density, and it has been aptly described as a lightweight hardwood. Pukatea is very soft, and can be planed and machined easily to give a good finish, provided the wood is properly dry. It saws, nails and screws easily, and accepts paints and finishes well.

Seasoning
The wood air-dries well, with little degrade, but if incipient decay is present it is prone to spreading.

Durability
The heartwood is durable above ground, but has low decay resistance below ground. The sapwood has little resistance to decay. Both heartwood and sapwood are fairly easy to treat with preservatives.

Typical uses
Boatbuilding, building construction, flooring, framing, weatherboards and clogs. This was once the traditional wood for Maori canoes.

Grows
New Zealand
Typical height: 100ft (30m)
Trunk diameter: 2–3ft (0.6–0.9m), but sometimes greater

⚠ **Possible health risks**
Not known

AMERICAN SWEET GUM

Liquidambar styraciflua (Hamamelidaceae)

Also called: American red gum, sweet gum, red gum, bilsted red gum, liquidambar, sap gum, satin walnut, hazel pine

Description

The heartwood is reddish-brown, frequently variegated with dark streaks, and is usually highly figured, whereas the contrasting sapwood is pinkish-white and often has blue sap stains. The wood typically has an irregular grain, with a fine, uniform texture and a satin lustre. Quartersawn stock will often show a pleasing mottled figure. The heartwood is sold as **red gum** (**satin walnut** in the UK), and the sapwood as **sap gum** (**hazel pine** in the UK).
Typical dry weight: 35lb/ft³ (560kg/m³)
Specific gravity: .56

Properties

Red gum is rated as having medium strength in all categories, except for a very poor steam-bending classification. The wood works readily with both hand and machine tools, and has only a slight blunting effect on cutting edges. Red gum screws, nails, glues, sands, stains and polishes well, and can be brought to an excellent finish.

Seasoning

It dries rapidly and has a distinct tendency to twist and warp; shrinkage and splitting can be high if the drying is not carried out with care. The wood shows moderate movement in use.

Durability

The wood is not durable, and is vulnerable to insect attack. The sapwood is permeable for preservative treatment, but the heartwood is moderately resistant.

Typical uses

Furniture and cabinetmaking, interior joinery, turnery, doors, interior trim, panelling, flooring, dry cooperage, boxes, railway sleepers (railroad ties) and pulpwood. It is also sliced for decorative veneers and rotary-cut for plywood.

Grows
USA and Central America
Typical height: 100–150ft (30–45m)
Trunk diameter: 3–4ft (0.9–1.2m)

⚠ **Possible health risks**
Dermatitis

AMERICAN WHITEWOOD
Liriodendron tulipifera (Magnoliaceae)

Also called: American tulipwood, canary whitewood, canary wood, canoe wood, poplar, saddletree, tulipwood, tulip tree, white poplar, whitewood, yellow poplar.
Not related to Brazilian tulipwood (*Dalbergia frutescens*), or to spruce (*Picea abies*), a softwood also known as 'whitewood'

Description

American whitewood has a wide, creamy-white, streaked sapwood. The heartwood is pale olive-green to brown, or light yellow to tan or greenish-brown, often with streaks of blue, purple, dark green and black. When newly cut the wood is light yellow to brown, but it changes to a greenish colour on exposure to light. It is usually straight-grained with a fine and even texture, and can sometimes have an attractive blister figure.
Typical dry weight: 31lb/ft³ (510kg/m³)
Specific gravity: .51

Properties

It has low resistance to shock loads, low bending strength and low stiffness, with medium crushing strength and steam-bending properties. The wood is easy to work with both hand and machine tools. It bores, mortises, planes, stains, paints, polishes and varnishes well. It does not mould or sand well, but is very good for turning and carving, and has excellent gluing properties. Nailing is easy, but holding properties are only moderate.

Seasoning

The wood air-dries with little degrade and kiln-dries very well, normally without degrade. If it is dried too slowly, sapwood stains and mould can develop. It exhibits small movement in service.

Durability

It is non-durable, and vulnerable to decay-causing fungi and insects. The sapwood is susceptible to the common furniture beetle, but accepts preservative treatment; the heartwood is difficult to treat.

Typical uses

Furniture, interior joinery, carving and sculpture, patternmaking, doors, dry cooperage, pallets, boxes, corestock, plywood and pulp. Choice logs are sliced into veneers for use in marquetry and cabinetwork.

Grows
Eastern Canada and eastern USA
Typical height: 80–120ft (24–37m)
Trunk diameter: 2–3ft (0.6–0.9m)

⚠ **Possible health risks**
Dermatitis, allergic reactions

MANGEAO

Litsea calicaris (Lauraceae)

Also called: tangeao

Description

The heartwood of mangeao ranges from silvery-cream to pale brown, with darker vessel lines showing on flatsawn surfaces. The wood is straight-grained with a fine, even texture and a dull lustre, and can sometimes have a very attractive figure.

Typical dry weight: 40lb/ft³ (640kg/ft³)
Specific gravity: .64

Properties

Mangeao is strong and tough, with high resistance to shock loads, medium crushing and bending strengths, low stiffness and a very good steam-bending classification. It works easily with both hand and machine tools, with just a slight blunting effect on cutting edges, and sharp tools are required to get a clean finish. It planes, sands, glues, nails, screws and turns well, and takes well to stains and polishes.

Seasoning

Mangeao generally dries well without degrade, and exhibits only small movement in use.

Durability

The wood is durable and unaffected by insect and fungal attack. The sapwood is permeable for preservative treatment.

Typical uses

Turnery, boatbuilding, sporting goods, handles, heavy-duty flooring, vehicle bodies, gates, rifle stocks, decking, mine timbers and railway sleepers (railroad ties). It is also used for plywood and highly decorative veneers.

Grows
New Zealand
Typical height: 100–140ft (30–43m)
Trunk diameter: 3ft (1m)

⚠ **Possible health risks**
Not known

BOLLYWOOD

Litsea glutinosa, L. leefeana and *L. reticulata* (Lauraceae)

L. reticulata

Also called: bollygum, bolly beech, brown beech, brown bollywood, soft bollygum, Queensland sycamore

Description

The heartwood ranges from pale straw to pale brown, and may sometimes have pinkish, yellow or grey tones. The narrow sapwood is of a similar colour or sometimes paler. The grain is typically straight, but can sometimes be interlocked, and the wood has a moderately coarse and even texture.
Typical dry weight: 32lb/ft³ (510kg/m³)
Specific gravity: .51

Properties

Bollywood is of a medium density and works easily with machine and hand tools, with a small blunting effect. When interlocked grain is present, a reduced planer angle is advised. It normally gives a smooth finished surface, and nails, glues and screws well. It stains, paints and polishes readily.

Seasoning

Drying is generally good with little degrade, and the wood is moderately stable in service.

Durability

The heartwood has moderate durability, but the sapwood is vulnerable to attack by lyctus borer. The sapwood is permeable for preservative treatment, but the heartwood is resistant.

Typical uses

Furniture, joinery, turnery, carving, boatbuilding and oars, roller and venetian blinds, cooperage, patternmaking, picture frames and plywood.

Grows
New South Wales and Queensland, Australia
Typical height: 80–130ft (25–40m)
Trunk diameter: 5ft (1.5m)

⚠ **Possible health risks**
Skin irritation

EKKI

Lophira alata (Ochnaceae)

Also called: aba, akoura, azobé, bakundu, bongossi, eba, kaku, hendui, red ironwood

Description

The pale pink sapwood is distinct from the heartwood, which is dark red or deep chocolate-brown, and can have purple highlights. White deposits in the pores add to the interesting pattern of the wood. The grain is normally interlocked and the texture uneven and coarse.
Typical dry weight: 64lb/ft³ (1025kg/m³)
Specific gravity: 1.02

Properties

Ekki is extremely heavy and dense. It has high stiffness and resistance to shock loads, and very high crushing and bending strength. Steam-bending qualities are poor. It has a severe blunting effect on cutters and is very difficult to work with hand tools, but can be worked by machine. It requires pre-boring for screwing and nailing, and it stains and glues satisfactorily.

Seasoning

It is very slow-drying and can be subject to severe splitting, surface checking, end splitting and distortion. It gives poor stability in service.

Durability

The heartwood is highly durable and decay-resistant, and is very resistant to preservative treatment. Ekki weathers well and is resistant to acids.

Typical uses

Flooring including parquet, heavy construction, decking, bridge building, marine construction, truck bodies and railway sleepers (railroad ties).

Grows
Tropical West Africa
Typical height: 160ft (50m)
Trunk diameter: 5ft (1.5m)

⚠ **Possible health risks**
Dermatitis and itching

AFRICAN WALNUT
Lovoa trichilioides (Meliaceae)

Also called: Benin walnut, Nigerian golden walnut, Ghana walnut, alona wood, bibolo, congowood, eyan, lovoa, nivero noy, noyer d'Afrique, dibétou (France)

Description
The buff or pale brown sapwood is separated from the heartwood by a narrow transition zone. The heartwood is bronze or golden-brown, streaked with black gum lines. The grain is typically interlocked but can be straight, and has a uniform fine texture, with distinct growth rings and a lustrous surface. Quartersawn surfaces can show a very attractive ribbon figure with alternating areas of dark and light wood. It is not a true walnut.
Typical dry weight: 35lb/ft³ (560kg/m³)
Specific gravity: .56

Properties
It has medium crushing strength, low bending strength and resistance to shock loads, very low stiffness, and moderate steam-bending qualities. It works well by hand or machine, with a slight blunting effect on tool edges. Planing is generally good, but interlocked grain can cause tear-out, so a reduced cutting angle is advisable. Pre-boring is advised for nailing and screwing. It turns, moulds, routs, bores and glues well, and stains satisfactorily. Filling is recommended before painting or polishing.

Seasoning
African walnut dries easily and fairly rapidly with little degrade. There may be some distortion, and existing shakes may extend during seasoning. Heart shakes are fairly common, and can cause splitting. There is small movement in service.

Durability
The heartwood is moderately durable and resistant to decay, but vulnerable to dry-wood termites. The sapwood can be attacked by powder-post beetles. The heartwood is very resistant to preservative treatment, the sapwood moderately so.

Typical uses
Quality furniture and cabinetmaking, turnery, decorative joinery, kitchen cabinets, office furniture, domestic flooring, billiard and pool tables, gun and rifle stocks, and decorative veneers.

Grows
Tropical West Africa
Typical height: 150ft (45m)
Trunk diameter: 4ft (1.2m)

⚠ **Possible health risks**
Irritation to the mucous membranes and alimentary tract, nasal cancer

JACARANDÁ PARDO

Machaerium villosum (Leguminosae)

Also called: jacarandá amarello, jacarandá do cerrado, jacarandá escuro, jacarandá do mato, jacarandá paulista, jacarandá pedra, jacarandá roxo

Description
The heartwood of jacarandá pardo is between pinkish-brown and violet-brown. It has straight but undulating grain with a coarse texture, and tends to be fibrous. It is rather similar in appearance to Brazilian rosewood (*Dalbergia nigra*), but is less highly figured and slightly lighter in colour.
Typical dry weight: 53lb/ft³ (850kg/m³)
Specific gravity: .85

Properties
Jacarandá pardo has high strength properties in all categories apart from steam bending, which is rated as moderate. It is quite difficult to work, and has a severe blunting effect on cutting edges. A reduced cutting angle of 20° is advised when planing or moulding quartersawn material, in order to prevent grain pick-up.

Seasoning
The wood air-dries slowly and can be prone to checking.

Durability
Jacarandá pardo is highly durable and very resistant to attack from decay fungi; it is also resistant to preservative treatment.

Typical uses
Furniture and cabinetmaking, interior trim, musical instruments, cutlery handles, marquetry and decorative veneers.

Grows
Brazil
Typical height: 50–100ft (15–30m)
Trunk diameter: 1–2ft (0.3–0.6m)

⚠ **Possible health risks**
Contact dermatitis and allergic symptoms

OSAGE-ORANGE

Maclura pomifera (Moraceae)

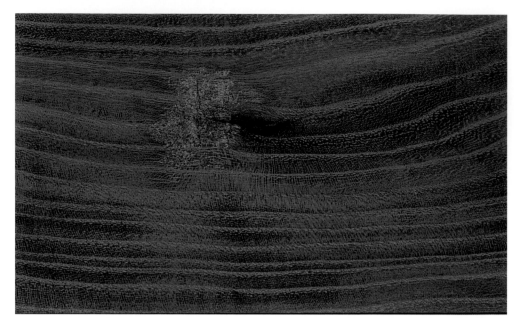

Also called: bow wood, bodare, bodark, bois d'arc, hedge, hedge apple, horse apple, naranjo chino, mock-orange, Osage

Description

When freshly cut, the colour of the heartwood varies from greenish-yellow or golden-yellow to bright orange. It darkens to a russet-brown on exposure, with darker reddish streaks. The sapwood of Osage-orange is light yellow and is clearly differentiated from the heartwood. The wood has a straight, close grain and a somewhat coarse texture.
Typical dry weight: 48lb/ft³ (760kg/m³)
Specific gravity: .76

Properties

Osage-orange is a tough, heavy, very hard and resilient wood, and rates highly in all strength categories. It is a particularly difficult wood to work because of its hardness, and tools need sharpening frequently. The wood accepts nails only with difficulty, but it screws, glues and finishes well.

Seasoning

The wood seasons well, and shows high stability in service.

Durability

It is highly resistant to decay, being the most durable of all North American woods. When used for posts or stakes it can last indefinitely.

Typical uses

Turnery, posts, stakes, insulator pins, tobacco pipes, machinery parts, railway sleepers (railroad ties) and dyestuffs. In the past it was also used for wheel hubs and rims, and by Native Americans for archery bows.

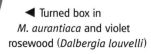

◀ Turned box in *M. aurantiaca* and violet rosewood (*Dalbergia louvelli*)

Grows
USA
Typical height: 50ft (15m)
Trunk diameter: 2ft (0.6m)

⚠ **Possible health risks**
Sap may cause dermatitis

MAGNOLIA

Magnolia grandiflora (Magnoliaceae)

Also called: evergreen magnolia, southern magnolia, cucumber wood, black lin, bat tree, mountain magnolia, sweet magnolia, big laurel, bullbay

Description

The heartwood is straw to greenish-beige in colour, and often has dark purple streaks caused by mineral deposits. There are also fine, light-coloured lines. It is straight-grained, with a uniformly fine, closed texture and a satiny lustre. The sapwood is yellowish-white.
Typical dry weight: 35lb/ft³ (560kg/m³)
Specific gravity: .56

Properties

Magnolia is a medium-density wood, with moderate qualities of stiffness and hardness, and good shock resistance. It has a low bending strength, but a good steam-bending rating. The wood is easy to work with both machine and hand tools. It planes to a smooth surface easily, and turns very well. It has only a small blunting effect on cutting edges. Magnolia bores and routs well, but sanding, moulding and mortising are not so easy. The wood is excellent for staining, polishing, painting and varnishing, but pre-boring is advised for nails and screws.

Seasoning

Air-drying can bring about excessive tangential shrinkage, with a tendency to warp and check. The wood responds well to kiln-drying, with little degrade. There is small movement in service.

Durability

Magnolia has little resistance to decay, and the sapwood is vulnerable to attack from the common furniture beetle. The heartwood is moderately resistant to preservative treatment, but the sapwood is permeable.

Typical uses

Furniture including office furniture, interior joinery, turnery, mouldings, kitchen cabinets, louvres and blinds (shades), dowels, casks, crates, foundry moulds and pulp. Selected wood is sliced for decorative veneers, which are often used for panelling.

Grows
USA; also cultivated in UK
Typical height: 60–80ft
(18–24m)
Trunk diameter: 2–3ft
(0.6–0.9m)

⚠ **Possible health risks**
Not known

APPLE

Malus sylvestris (Rosaceae)

Syn.: *M. pumila, Pyrus malus*
Also called: pommier (French), **Apfel** (German). The wood of **crab apple** (various *Malus* spp.) is very similar

Description

The heartwood is pinkish-buff and somewhat brittle. It is generally straight-grained with a fine, even texture, but can have spiral or distorted grain. The grain is not as fine as in pear (*Pyrus communis*).
Typical dry weight: 43lb/ft³ (700kg/m³)
Specific gravity: .70

Properties

Apple does not bend well because of its brittleness. It is of moderate strength, dense and heavy, and has a moderate blunting effect. Straightforward to work with both hand and machine tools, it saws well and can be brought to a very good finish. Apple finishes cleanly but care must be taken to avoid tear-out on irregular-grained wood. It takes stain well.

Seasoning

Apple can be difficult to season. It dries slowly and may distort during air-drying. It can be kiln-dried successfully with little degrade. Movement in service is small.

Durability

The wood is non-durable and easily permeable for preservative treatment.

Typical uses

Turnery, carving, tool parts such as masons' mallet heads and saw handles; also decorative veneers.

Natural-edge bowl ▶

Grows

Europe and south-west Asia
Typical height: 25–35ft (8–10m)
Trunk diameter: 1–2ft (0.3–0.6m)

⚠ Possible health risks

Not known

MANSONIA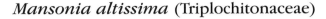

Mansonia altissima (Triplochitonaceae)

Also called: aprono, bété, koul, ofun

Description

Mansonia heartwood ranges in colour from yellowish-brown to dark greyish-brown or light mauve. It can also be purplish, with lighter or darker bands. The wood is usually straight-grained, with a medium to fine, even texture, and the surface has a low to medium lustre. The sapwood, which is sharply differentiated from the heartwood, is usually white.
Typical dry weight: 37lb/ft³ (590kg/m³)
Specific gravity: .59

Properties

Mansonia has high bending and crushing strength, low stiffness and medium resistance to shock loads. It is a hard, dense and heavy wood. It steam-bends well provided the wood is knot-free, and is easy to work with both hand and machine tools. Mansonia has a slight to medium blunting effect on cutting edges. The wood saws, planes, turns, moulds, routs, carves, glues, screws, nails and sands well. It also responds well to stains and polishes.

Seasoning

The wood dries fairly rapidly and well, but knots can split, and existing splits and shakes may extend. There is medium movement in service.

Durability

The heartwood is durable and very resistant both to preservative treatment and to insect attack; it can, however, be vulnerable to pinhole borers. The sapwood is permeable.

Typical uses

Mansonia is frequently used as a substitute for American black walnut (*Juglans nigra*). Its uses include high-quality furniture and cabinetmaking, turnery; musical instruments including pianos; interior trim and dashboards on cars; boatbuilding, kitchen cabinets, shuttles and truck bodies. The wood is also sliced for decorative veneers, and used in plywood manufacture.

Grows
West Africa
Typical height: 100–120ft
(30–36m)
Trunk diameter: 2–3ft (0.6–1m)

⚠ **Possible health risks**

Splinters go septic. Dust can cause nosebleeds, sneezing, skin irritation, asthma, respiratory problems, headache, nausea, vomiting and cardiac disorders. The bark contains mansonin, a digitalis cardiac poison

RATA
Metrosideros robusta (Myrtaceae)

Also called: northern rata, New Zealand ironwood. Closely related to **mainland pohutukawa (*M. excelsa*)** and **southern rata (*M. umbellata*)**

Description
Rata ranges from reddish-brown to chocolate-brown in colour. It is usually straight-grained, with a fine, even texture, but the grain can sometimes be wavy or interlocked. Because of the manner in which the tree grows, it can produce distorted wood that yields a particularly pleasing figure.
Typical dry weight: 50lb/ft³ (800kg/m³), but varies quite widely
Specific gravity: .80

Properties
Rata is an extremely tough, strong, heavy and hard wood. It has high stiffness and high crushing and bending strengths, with medium resistance to shock loads and moderate bending properties. It has a high resistance to cutting, and a moderate blunting effect on cutting edges. When planing by machine, a much reduced angle is recommended to prevent grain pick-up. The wood stains and polishes satisfactorily and glues easily, but nailing and screwing can be difficult.

Seasoning
It is difficult to dry, and there can be high shrinkage. It is advisable to air-dry rata partly before kiln-drying. There is large movement in use.

Durability
The heartwood is highly durable and highly resistant to preservative treatment. The sapwood is permeable, but invulnerable to attack from the powder-post beetle.

Typical uses
Furniture, decorative turnery, sports goods, house construction, bridges, machine beds, shipbuilding and railway sleepers (railroad ties). It is also sliced for decorative veneers.

Grows
New Zealand
Typical height: 80ft (25m)
Trunk diameter: 8ft (2.5m)

⚠ **Possible health risks**
Dust irritation to the nose and eyes

ZEBRANO

Microberlinia brazzavillensis and *M. bisulcata* (Leguminosae)

Also called: African zebrawood, allen ele, zingana, ele, amouk, okwen

Description
The sapwood is normally whitish in colour, whereas the heartwood is a light golden-yellow or pale brown, with narrow darker streaks or veins that range from dark brown to near-black. These give the wood the zebra-stripe pattern from which it gets its name. The grain is typically interlocked or wavy, with a medium to coarse texture and a high lustre. The interlocked grain, which is alternately hard and soft, can produce an attractive ribbon figure.
Typical dry weight: 46lb/ft³ (740kg/m³)
Specific gravity: .74

Properties
Zebrano is a hard, dense and heavy wood with high strength properties and very high stiffness. It is not suitable for steam bending. It works well with hand tools and in most machining operations. Planing can be tricky, since interlocked grain can tear badly, so sanding is advised for a final finish. The wood routs, bores, moulds and mortises well, and gluing is satisfactory if care is taken. Pre-boring is advised for nailing and screwing. If a clear filler is used, the wood can be brought to an excellent polished finish.

Seasoning
Zebrano is difficult to dry. There can be problems with splitting, distortion and surface checking if insufficient care is taken. It exhibits small movement in use.

Durability
The heartwood is not durable and is subject to insect attack; it is resistant to preservative treatment, but the sapwood is permeable.

Typical uses
The principal use for zebrano is as a decorative veneer, which is usually sliced from quartersawn stock to minimize buckling. This is used in cabinetwork, as inlay, crossbandings, panelling and marquetry. The wood is also used for furniture, decorative turnery, sculpture, brush backs, handles, boatbuilding and decorative plywood.

▲ Turned box in zebrano and holly (*Ilex aquifolium*)

Grows
West Africa, particularly Cameroon, Congo and Gabon
Typical height: 150ft (45m)
Trunk diameter: 4–5ft (1.2m–1.5m)

⚠ **Possible health risks**
Irritant to the eyes and skin; asthma, breathing difficulties; sensitizer

IROKO
Milicia excelsa and *M. regia* (Moraceae)

Syn.: *Chlorophora excelsa, C. regia*
Also called: kambala, lusanga, mokongo, moreira, rokko, tule, intule, odum

▲ Carved bowl

Grows
East and West Africa
Typical height: 160ft (50m)
Trunk diameter: 10ft (3m)

⚠ **Possible health risks**
Dermatitis, furunculosis, asthma, nettle rash, oedema of eyelids, respiratory problems, sneezing and giddiness

Description
The yellowish-white sapwood is clearly differentiated from the heartwood, which is golden-orange to brown. Large deposits of calcium carbonate with darker wood around them are usually present. Yellow bands of soft tissue form a zigzag pattern, and lighter vessel lines can be seen on flatsawn surfaces. The grain is moderately interlocked, with a fairly coarse and even texture, and the wood is mildly lustrous. Iroko is often used as a substitute for teak (*Tectona grandis*).
Typical dry weight: 40lb/ft³ (640kg/m³)
Specific gravity: .64

Properties
Iroko has low resistance to shock loads and low stiffness. It has medium crushing and bending strength, medium density and a moderate steam-bending rating. It works satisfactorily with hand tools, but can have a moderate to severe blunting effect on cutting edges. When planing, turning and moulding, the results are generally good. Interlocked grain can cause tearing, and the mineral deposits can blunt cutters rapidly. It glues, nails and stains well, and screws, varnishes and paints satisfactorily. Iroko can be brought to a highly lustrous finish after filling.

Seasoning
The wood dries well and fairly rapidly, with little degrade. There can be slight checking and distortion. It moves very little in service.

Durability
Although the heartwood has a high natural resistance to decay, it is vulnerable to attack from dry-wood insects, and the sapwood can be attacked by the powder-post beetle. The heartwood is highly resistant to preservative treatment, which is not, however, normally required.

Typical uses
Furniture, interior and exterior joinery, carving, mouldings; boatbuilding, shipbuilding, piles and other marine work; laboratory benches, factory and parquet flooring. Also plywood, wall panelling and decorative veneer.

WENGÉ

Millettia laurentii (Leguminosae)

Also called: awoung, bokonge, dikela, mibotu, nson-so, palissandre du Congo, tshikalakala

Description
The sapwood is whitish or pale yellow and is clearly demarcated from the heartwood, which is dark brown with fine, close, near-black veins and white lines. This patterning gives the wood a very attractive appearance. The grain is fairly straight, with a medium to coarse texture and a low lustre.
Typical dry weight: 55lb/ft³ (880kg/m³)
Specific gravity: .88

Properties
Wengé is a heavy and dense wood which is highly resistant to abrasion. It has a high resistance to shock loads and a high bending strength, low stiffness, medium crushing strength and a low steam-bending rating. The wood works well with both machine and hand tools, and has a moderate to medium blunting effect on cutting edges. Pre-boring is required for nailing, and gluing and polishing can be difficult because of the resin cells in the wood. Sawing is slow, but it planes fairly easily. It is a good wood for turning, and sands satisfactorily. Once the grain has been filled, a satisfactory surface finish can be achieved.

Seasoning
The wood seasons slowly and is fairly difficult to dry. It is highly prone to surface checking and there is a slight tendency to distort. Wengé exhibits small movement in use.

Durability
It is a durable wood and resistant to fungi and termites. The sapwood is permeable for preservative treatment, but the heartwood is highly resistant.

Typical uses
Furniture, turnery, carving, exterior and interior joinery, violin bows, block and strip flooring, boatbuilding and construction work. Decorative veneers are used for cabinetwork and marquetry.

▲ Chest of drawers in wengé and quilted maple (*Acer* sp.) with malachite drawer pulls

Grows
Congo, Cameroon, Gabon, Tanzania and Mozambique
Typical height: 50-60ft (15–18m)
Trunk diameter: 2ft 6in–3ft (0.75–1m)

⚠ Possible health risks
Dermatitis, giddiness, drowsiness, visual problems, stomach cramps; splinters go septic. Irritation of the eyes, skin and respiratory system

◀ Turned bowl

PANGA PANGA

Millettia stuhlmannii (Leguminosae)

Also called: partridgewood, jambiré, messara

Description

The heartwood is chocolate-brown with alternating dark- and light-coloured bands running through it; or it can be dark brown to near-black with bands of white tissue. The sapwood is clearly demarcated from the heartwood, and is pale yellow. Panga panga usually has a straight grain, with a coarse and variable texture. The wood often displays a partridge-feather figure. It is very similar to wengé (*M. laurentii*).
Typical dry weight: 50lb/ft³ (800kg/m³)
Specific gravity: .80

Properties

The wood is dense and heavy, with very high tensile strength, high bending strength and shock resistance, and medium stiffness and crushing strength. It is very resistant to abrasion and has a low steam-bending rating. Panga panga is a hard wood to work, and has a moderate to severe blunting effect on cutting edges. A reduced cutting angle is advised for moulding and planing, and it is difficult to saw. It turns and polishes very well, but most other processes are difficult. Pre-boring is necessary for nailing and screwing. Gluing can be affected by the resin content of the wood.

Seasoning

It dries slowly with minimal degrade, but care is needed to avoid surface checking. It is stable in service.

Durability

The heartwood is very durable and resistant to fungal attack and insects; it is highly resistant to preservative treatment. The sapwood is moderately permeable.

Typical uses

Domestic and office furniture, interior and exterior joinery, musical instruments, boatbuilding, flooring, panelling and decorative veneer.

Grows
East Africa
Typical height: 60ft (18m)
Trunk diameter: 1ft 8in–2ft (0.5–0.6m)

⚠ **Possible health risks**
Not known

ABURA

Mitragyna ciliata (now *Hallea ledermannii*) (Rubiaceae)

Also called: bahia, eliom (Cameroon), **elomom** (Gabon), **subaha** (Ghana), **baya, m'boy, vuku**

Description

The bulk of the tree is orange-brown to pink sapwood. The heartwood, which is sometimes spongy, is reddish-brown with darker streaks. Usually straight-grained, it can have interlocking and spiral grain also; the grain is generally fine and even. Gum veins can show as dark streaks.
Typical dry weight: 35lb/ft³ (560kg/m³)
Specific gravity: .56

Properties

Abura is of medium density, with low bending strength and very low stiffness. It has medium crushing strength and low shock resistance. It works well but can have a moderate to severe blunting action on edge tools. Pre-boring for nailing is advised, and it holds nails, glues and screws well. It stains well and takes an excellent finish.

Seasoning

Abura air- and kiln-dries well, provided shakes are cut out in conversion. There is little movement in service, and it is stable.

Durability

Abura is vulnerable to attack from common furniture beetle and powder-post beetle. The heartwood is not resistant to decay, and offers little resistance to preservative treatment.

Typical uses

It is used for furniture, cabinetwork, interior joinery and mouldings, flooring, patternmaking and vehicle bodywork; due to its acid resistance it is also used for battery boxes and laboratory equipment. Certain logs can be sliced for veneer, and it is also used for plywood.

Grows
Tropical West Africa
Typical height: 100ft (30m)
Trunk diameter:
3–5ft (1.0–1.5m)

⚠ **Possible health risks**
Vomiting, nausea, eye irritation, giddiness; short, sharp splinters can be hard to remove

OPEPE

Nauclea diderrichii (Rubiaceae)

Syn.: *Sarcocephalus diderrichii*
Also called: akondoc, aloma, badi, bilinga, engolo, kusia, kusiaba, linzi, n'gulu, maza, opepi

Grows
Equatorial West Africa
Typical height: 160ft (50m)
Trunk diameter: 5ft (1.5m)

⚠ Possible health risks
Dermatitis, mucous membrane irritation, giddiness, visual problems, nosebleeds and blood spitting

Description
The sapwood is about 2in (50mm) thick and creamy-white, pink, pale yellow or grey in colour. It is clearly demarcated from the heartwood. The heartwood is golden-yellow when newly cut, and matures on exposure to an orange-brown with a coppery lustre. The grain is typically interlocked or irregular, with a coarse to medium texture and a medium to high lustre. Opepe is an attractive wood and can feature ribbon or rope figure on quartersawn surfaces.
Typical dry weight: 46lb/ft³ (740kg/m³)
Specific gravity: .74

Properties
Opepe has medium stiffness and bending strength, low resistance to shock loads, a high crushing strength and poor steam-bending qualities. It works fairly well with hand and machine tools, with a medium blunting effect on cutting edges. The wood planes fairly easily, but a reduced planing angle is advised for quartersawn stock to prevent tear-out. It moulds, mortises and varnishes fairly well, and turns and sands fairly easily. Opepe glues satisfactorily and requires pre-boring for nailing and screwing. A high finish can be obtained after filling.

Seasoning
Quartersawn wood dries well; flatsawn stock can suffer from checking, splitting and distortion. Movement in use is small.

Durability
The heartwood is very durable, but the sapwood is vulnerable to attack from the powder-post beetle. The sapwood is permeable for preservative treatment, and the heartwood fairly treatable.

Typical uses
Domestic and office furniture, exterior joinery, turnery, shop fittings (store fixtures), boatbuilding, domestic flooring, vehicle bodies, and veneers for panelling and decorative work. It is also used for exterior construction, jetties, docks, piling and other marine work.

TASMANIAN MYRTLE
Nothofagus cunninghamii (Fagaceae)

Also called: Tasmanian beech, Australian nothofagus, myrtle beech, mountain beech

Description
The heartwood is pink to reddish-brown, and there is a zone of intermediate colour between the heartwood and the narrow white sapwood. Typically, the grain is straight or slightly interlocked; sometimes it is slightly wavy, which can give some figure on quartersawn stock. The wood has a fine, even texture and is normally lustrous. It is not a true myrtle or beech.
Typical dry weight: 45lb/ft^3 (720kg/m^3)
Specific gravity: .72

Properties
Tasmanian myrtle is a dense, moderately hard wood with medium stiffness and bending strength, low resistance to shock loads and high crushing strength; it steam-bends very well. The wood works well with hand and machine tools, with a moderate blunting effect on cutting edges; crosscutting and boring can cause burning. Otherwise, it planes, bores, routs, moulds, mortises, carves, sands, stains and polishes well, and has good nail- and screw-holding properties. Gluing is satisfactory.

Seasoning
The wood can be tricky to dry. The outer, lighter wood dries readily, but the real heartwood has to be dried very carefully; otherwise there can be surface checking, internal honeycombing and collapse. There is only small movement in use.

Durability
The heartwood is not durable, and has very little resistance to decay if in contact with the ground. The sapwood is vulnerable to attack from lyctus borer and powder-post beetles. The heartwood is resistant to preservative treatment, and the sapwood is permeable.

Typical uses
Furniture and cabinetmaking, joinery, flooring, kitchen cabinets, brush backs, tool handles, interior trim, food containers, vehicle bodies and plywood. It is also sliced for decorative veneer.

Grows
Tasmania and Victoria, Australia
Typical height: 100–130ft (30–40m) or higher
Trunk diameter: 3–5ft (0.9–1.5m)

⚠ **Possible health risks**
Irritation to the mucous membranes

RED BEECH

Nothofagus fusca (Fagaceae)

Also called: silver beech (see next entry)

Description

The heartwood ranges in colour from a pale pink to a deep red, while the sapwood is a pale creamy-white. Red beech is usually straight-grained but can be curly occasionally, and has a fine, even texture. It is not a true beech.
Typical dry weight: 41lb/ft³ (670kg/m³)
Specific gravity: .67

Properties

As a rule, red beech exhibits medium stiffness and resistance to shock loads, medium crushing and bending strength, and has a good steam-bending classification; but these ratings may sometimes be considerably lower, depending on the geographical origin of the timber. The wood can be worked easily with both machine and hand tools, but a reduced cutting angle is recommended when machine-planing quartersawn stock with irregular grain. Red beech has only a slight to moderate blunting effect on cutting edges. The wood glues and stains well, and can be brought to a good finish.

Seasoning

It is difficult to season, because it dries slowly and unevenly, and is prone to warp and check. If kilned from green, it can suffer collapse and honeycombing. There is only small movement in use.

Durability

The heartwood is very durable, but vulnerable to attack from the powder-post and common furniture beetles. The heartwood is very resistant to preservative treatment, but the sapwood is permeable.

Typical uses

Furniture and cabinetmaking, turnery, boatbuilding, flooring, decking, tool handles, bobbins, bridges and vehicle bodywork. It is also sliced for decorative veneers and rotary-cut for plywood.

SILVER BEECH

Nothofagus menziesii and *N. truncata* (Fagaceae)

Also called: Southland beech (*N. menziesii*); hard beech, clinker beech (*N. truncata*)

Description

These *Nothofagus* species are sold commercially as 'silver beech' and have similar properties, but differ in weight. Red beech (*N. fusca*) is sometimes also sold under the same name. The heartwood ranges from white through salmon-pink to pinkish-brown, and the sapwood is white. There is a zone between the sapwood and heartwood, which is generally regarded as sapwood. The wood is typically straight-grained, but can be curly, and has a fine and even texture. They are not true beeches.
Typical dry weight: from 29lb/ft³ (475kg/m³) to 48lb/ft³ (770kg/m³) according to species
Specific gravity: .47 to .77

Properties

Silver beech has low resistance to shock loads and low stiffness, medium crushing and bending strengths, and a good steam-bending rating. The wood works well with hand and machine tools, but a reduced cutting angle is advised when planing quartersawn stock. Hard beech (*N. truncata*) can have a moderately severe blunting effect on cutting edges, due to its silica content. Both species screw, nail, glue and stain well, and can be brought to a very good polished finish.

Seasoning

Silver beech dries relatively easily; there can be problems with end splitting, but generally distortion is slight. Thicker stock can present problems with retained moisture. Movement in service is small.

Durability

With the exception of hard beech, the wood is not durable, and is vulnerable to attack from the common furniture and powder-post beetles.

Typical uses

Furniture, joinery, turnery, boatbuilding, dowelling, strip flooring, rifle stocks, looms, brushware, woodenware, tool handles, food containers, bridge timbers and vehicle bodywork. It is also sliced for plain veneer and rotary-cut for plywood.

Grows
New Zealand
Typical height: 100ft (30m)
Trunk diameter: 2–5ft
(0.6–1.5m)

⚠ **Possible health risks**
Not known

BLACKGUM
Nyssa sylvatica (Nyssaceae)

Also called: black gum, black tupelo, bowl gum, pepperidge, sour gum, swamp black gum, swamp tupelo, tupelo, tupelo gum, wild pear tree, yellow gum. It is one of five *Nyssa* species found in the USA

Grows
Eastern and south-eastern USA
Typical height: up to 100ft (30m)
Trunk diameter: 2–4ft (0.6–1.2m)

⚠ **Possible health risks**
Not known

Description
The heartwood ranges from pale creamy-grey-brown or yellowish tan to a soft brown. The sapwood is wide and lighter in colour, sometimes a creamy buff-brown. It has close, interlocked grain with a uniform texture. When quartersawn it shows a characteristic figure. It has no particular odour or taste.
Typical dry weight: 31lb/ft³ (500kg/m³)
Specific gravity: .50

Properties
Blackgum is tough, moderately hard and heavy, with low steam-bending, stiffness and shock-resistance properties. It can be difficult to work because of the interlocking grain, but can be brought to a smooth, shiny finish. It is notoriously difficult to split with hand tools, and requires pre-drilling for screwing or nailing. Gluing is rated as just satisfactory. Finishing oils can darken the wood considerably.

Seasoning
The wood needs great care to avoid warping and twisting whilst drying.

Durability
Blackgum has low decay resistance.

Typical uses
Inexpensive furniture, furniture components, boxes, crates, baskets, cooperage, food containers, industrial flooring, rollers, gunstocks, railway sleepers (railroad crossties), pulp.

BALSA

Ochroma pyramidale (Bombacaceae)

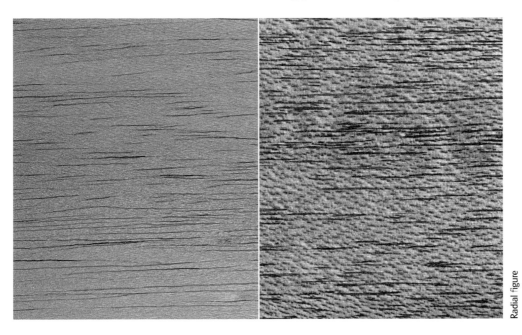

Radial figure

Syn.: O. lagopus
Also called: guano, cuano (Puerto Rico and Honduras), **lanero** (Cuba), **topa** (Peru), **polak** (Belize and Nicaragua), **tami** (Bolivia), **catillo** (Nicaragua)

Description

The sapwood is the commercial part of the tree, and is white to oatmeal in colour. It can have a pink or yellow tinge. The core heartwood is pale brown in large logs. Balsa has a medium texture with straight grain and can be lustrous. Its dry weight can vary from as little as $2\frac{1}{2}$lb/ft³ to 21lb/ft³ (40–340kg/m³).
Typical dry weight: 10lb/ft³ (160kg/m³)
Specific gravity: .16

Properties

Balsa is the weakest, softest and lightest of all commercial woods, with a very poor steam-bending rating. It is very buoyant (*balsa* means 'raft' in Spanish), and has very good heat, sound and vibration insulative properties. Although strong in relation to its weight, it cannot be bent without buckling. It is very easy to work with thin, sharp tools, but does not hold nails and screws well, so it is better to use glue. It can be stained, painted and polished, but is very absorbent.

Seasoning

Balsa contains 200–400% moisture in its green state. It is a very problematic wood to dry, and should be converted soon after felling. Kiln-drying is preferable to air-drying, to minimize splitting and distortion; but poor kilning can cause browning (or 'toasting') and case hardening. The wood is stable in service.

Durability

Balsa is perishable and vulnerable to insect attack. It is, however, permeable for preservative treatment.

Typical uses

Balsa is prized for its lightness in model making. It is much used as an insulating material in refrigerated ships and cold storage. It is also used for its buoyancy in buoys, life jackets (life preservers), floats and rafts. It is used as corestock in lightweight metal-faced sandwich sheets for the aircraft industry.

◀ Maquette of a cabinetmaker's tool chest

Grows
Ecuador, West Indies, central and tropical South America; also India and Indonesia
Typical height: 80ft (24m)
Trunk diameter: 2ft 6in (0.75m)

⚠ **Possible health risks**
Not known

STINKWOOD

Ocotea bullata (Lauraceae)

Also called: Cape olive, Cape laurel, stinkhout, umnukane

Description

The heartwood varies from bright yellow through yellowish-brown or green and chocolate or reddish-brown to near-black. The sapwood gradually merges into the heartwood. Its grain ranges from straight to interlocked or spiral, with a moderately fine, uniform texture and a high natural lustre. Because of its narrow medullary rays it can exhibit a fine ribbon figure. The lighter the colour, the lighter the weight. Stinkwood gets its name from the unpleasant smell it gives off when newly cut, but this fades on drying.
Typical dry weight: 42–50lb/ft³ (680–800kg/m³)
Specific gravity: .68 to .80

Properties

The wood is hard and strong, with high resistance to shock loads, and medium bending, crushing and stiffness properties. It is not suitable for steam bending. It is generally easily worked, but this depends on the density of the particular wood being used. Stinkwood has a severe blunting effect on cutting edges, and pre-boring is advised for nailing and screwing. It glues well. Scraping and sanding are necessary to achieve a smooth surface, after which the wood can be polished to a high finish.

Seasoning

The darker wood dries very slowly and is difficult to season. Thicker stock tends to honeycomb and shrink unevenly. Lighter wood dries fairly rapidly with little degrade.

Durability

The wood is not durable and is vulnerable to attack from termites, but is resistant to fungal infection. The sapwood is permeable to preservative treatment, but the heartwood is resistant.

Typical uses

The wood is highly prized for cabinetry and furniture, turnery, light flooring, vehicle bodies, ladders and tool handles. Choice logs are also sliced to make decorative veneers.

EUROPEAN OLIVE

Olea europaea (Oleaceae)

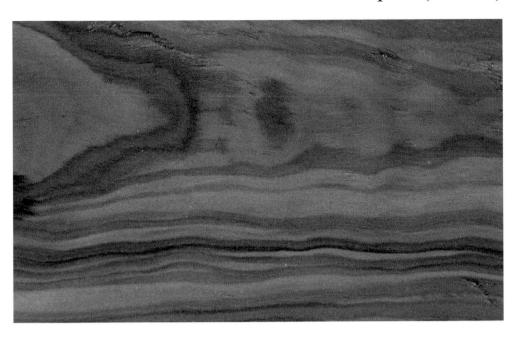

Also called: olivier (French). Related to East African olive (*O. hochstetteri*), which is a much larger tree

Description

This is a very attractive wood. The heartwood is normally tan, pale brown or yellowish-brown, and can be streaked with black, grey or brown. The sapwood, which is clearly demarcated from the heartwood, is gold or creamy-yellow and often striped. The close grain is shallowly interlocked, and it has a fine and even texture. The annual rings are clearly visible, and there can be slight figuring on tangential surfaces. Olive is not usually available in large sections, due to the stumpy and gnarled nature of the tree. The wood is essentially a by-product of the olive-oil industry.

Typical dry weight: 50lb/ft³ (800kg/m³)
Specific gravity: .80

Properties

Olive is hard, strong and heavy. The wood has good wearing properties and resistance to abrasion. Because of its interlocked grain and twisty nature it does not respond particularly well to hand tools, and it has a moderate blunting effect on cutters.

Olive does, however, plane, mortise and turn well. Because of its natural waxy lustre it polishes to an excellent finish.

Seasoning

Olive dries very slowly and is liable to check and warp.

Durability

It is moderately durable and has some resistance to fungi, but little defence against termite attack. The heartwood is resistant to preservative treatment, but the sapwood is permeable.

Typical uses

Because of its limited size, European olive is used for novelties, decorative turnery, decorative boxes, furniture, handles, and in the form of veneer and inlay.

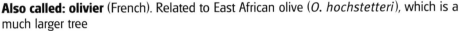

▲ Soprano recorder

Grows

Mediterranean region, Middle East and North Africa
Typical height: 25ft (8m) max.
Trunk diameter: 1ft (0.3m), but can reach 3ft (0.9m)

⚠ Possible health risks

The dust can be an irritant to the eyes, skin and respiratory system

◀ Turned box

EAST AFRICAN OLIVE

Olea hochstetteri and *O. welwitschii* (Oleaceae)

Also called: olive, loliondo, olivewood, ironwood, musharagi, olmasi

Grows

Cameroon, Congo, Ethiopia, Guinea, Ivory Coast, Kenya, Sierra Leone, Sudan, Tanzania, Uganda, Zambia
Typical height: 24–30m (80–100ft)
Trunk diameter: 0.6–0.9m (2–3ft)

⚠ Possible health risks

The dust can be an irritant to the skin, eyes, nose and lungs

Description

The heartwood is generally pale brown, but has irregular markings and streaks ranging from brown and grey to black, which can give the wood a marbled look. The grain is typically straight, but sometimes shallowly interlocked, with a fine and even texture. The sapwood is pale yellow.
Typical dry weight: 55lb/ft³ (890kg/m³)
Specific gravity: .89

Properties

It is a hard and strong wood with a high density, and is very resistant to wear. The wood is rated high in strength for crushing, stiffness, bending and resistance to shock loads, and moderate for steam bending. It is a difficult wood to work with hand tools, and the interlocked grain can make it difficult to machine also, with a moderate blunting effect on cutting edges. Machine-planing should be done with a reduced cutting angle, and there can be problems with vibration, and with chattering when moulding. Pre-boring is advised for nailing and screwing. It sands, carves and varnishes well, and stains and polishes very well. Turning properties are very good indeed.

Seasoning

The wood dries slowly; it tends to check and split, and can honeycomb if dried too quickly. Kiln-drying is advised. It moves considerably in service.

Durability

The heartwood has little natural resistance to decay fungi, and is also vulnerable to attack from white ants and termites. The sapwood is permeable for preservative treatment, but the heartwood is quite resistant to it.

Typical uses

Furniture, turnery, sculpture; durable, decorative and parquet flooring; shop fittings (store fixtures), kitchen cabinets, office furniture, panelling and tool handles. It is also sliced to make decorative veneers.

DESERT IRONWOOD

Olneya tesota (Fabaceae)

Also called: Arizona ironwood, palo-de-hierro (Spanish), **palo-de-fierro, palo fierro** (Portuguese), **tesota**

Description

As its name implies, this beautiful wood is very hard, heavy and dense. The heartwood can range from a rich honey-coloured golden-orange to an almost purplish black, mottled with a golden orange-red. The sapwood is narrow and creamy-white. Unfortunately, the wood tends to darken to a uniform deep brown on exposure to light. It has a very fine, dense grain and is also quite brittle. It is often obtained in smallish bough or trunk sections that may contain splits or wormholes. The tree can live for up to 1500 years.
Typical dry weight: 54lb/ft³ (860kg/m³)
Specific Gravity: .86

Properties

As the wood is extremely dense and fine-grained it is hard to work, but can be carved and turned in fine detail. With patience and very fine abrasive (up to 1000 grit), it can be brought to a superbly high finish. Extremely sharp tools are required to work desert ironwood, and it is advisable to pre-drill before inserting

screws. When properly seasoned, its pores shrink and consequently close up, thus sealing in its own natural oils. This can make the application of stains and oils very difficult, but this drawback is offset by the natural colour and lustre of the wood.

Seasoning

This is a difficult wood to season, liable to cracking and checking, which is not always visible on the surface. Once seasoned it is extremely stable and does not move or warp.

Durability

Desert ironwood is a highly durable timber, and almost impervious to preservative treatment.

Typical uses

Furniture, carvings, decorative turning, knife handles, police batons. It is the traditional material for Seri Native American carvings that reflect the wildlife of the Arizona Sonora Desert. The wood is also used as a source of charcoal.

Grows
Sonoran Desert region of Arizona (USA) and Mexico
Typical height: up to 30ft (10m)
Trunk diameter: 2ft (0.6m)

⚠ Possible health risks

Irritant. The extremely fine dust is unpleasant and is reported to cause sneezing and rhinitis

WHITE PEROBA

Paratecoma peroba (Bignoniaceae)

Also called: ipé peroba, peroba branca, peroba de campos, peroba manchada, golden peroba, peroba amarella

Grows
Brazil
Typical height: 90–130ft
(27–40m)
Trunk diameter: 5ft (1.5m)

⚠ Possible health risks
The dust may cause dermatitis, nasal irritation and asthma; splinters may become septic

Description
The heartwood can vary in colour, but is generally light olive with a reddish, greenish or yellowish cast, and may often contain faint variegated streaks. The grain is typically interlocked or wavy, with a fine, uniform texture. White peroba is fairly lustrous. The sapwood is clearly differentiated from the heartwood by its white or yellowish colour.
Typical dry weight: 47lb/ft³ (750kg/m³)
Specific gravity: .75

Properties
White peroba is hard, heavy and wear-resistant, with low stiffness and resistance to shock loads, high crushing strength and medium bending strength. It is classified as moderate for steam bending. The wood is usually easy to work and has only a slight blunting effect on cutting edges. It planes, turns, moulds, bores, routs and mortises well, and responds well to sanding. It takes glue and screws readily. White peroba can be stained and polished to a very fine finish.

Seasoning
It dries rapidly and well. There can be slight splitting, and variable grain may cause twisting. There is medium movement in service.

Durability
The heartwood is highly durable and resistant to decay, and is also resistant to preservative treatment.

Typical uses
Furniture and cabinetmaking, quality interior and exterior joinery, heavy-duty flooring including parquet, decks, shipbuilding, food containers and vehicle bodies. It is also sliced into decorative veneers for marquetry and panelling.

PAULOWNIA

Paulownia fortunei, P. tomentosa and related species
(Scrophulariaceae)

Also called: kiri, Chinese empress tree, dragon tree, princess tree, foxglove tree

Description

Paulownia is an incredibly fast-growing wood and is often referred to as a 'soft hardwood'. In recent years it has become an important plantation-grown timber. The wood is light honey to blond in colour with a gradual transition from heartwood to the lighter sapwood. It is soft and straight-grained, has distinct growth rings, a very fine lustrous sheen, and is odourless. Plantation-grown wood is usually free of knots. The wood is prized for its texture, and by musical instrument makers for its tone.
Typical dry weight: 20lb/ft³ (320kg/m³)
Specific Gravity: .32

Properties

The wood has a very high strength to weight ratio, but is comparatively soft for a hardwood. Due to its softness, low silica content and low level of resin, it works easily with both machine and hand tools. It nails and screws well, with a very low tendency to split. However, it does not hold nails strongly, so gluing is advised in conjunction. The wood glues very well, with a fast cure time. It sands to a fine finish and accepts oils, stains and paint well. Sanding sealer is advised as a base

for clear finishes. Paulownia can bruise quite easily, so care has to be taken during processing. It has high sound and heat insulation properties and is much more fire-resistant than most timbers.

Seasoning

The wood can be air-dried in 30–60 days, and kiln-dried in 30–60 hours. There is very little degrade, but care has to be taken at avoid sap stain and surface bruising. There is only small movement in service.

Durability

It is resistant to rotting and decay provided it is not in contact with the ground. It is also resistant to insect attack, including termites.

Typical uses

Fine furniture, internal and external joinery, carvings, musical instruments, toys, boatbuilding, blind slats, interior cladding, coffins, vehicle framing, paper, corestock, plywood, and fine veneer. Used in Japan for centuries for ceremonial furniture, musical instruments, decorative mouldings, laminated structural beams and clogs.

Grows
Indigenous to China, Taiwan, Cambodia, Laos and Vietnam. Also grown in Japan and Korea for 1000 years. Now plantation-grown in Australia, Canada, New Zealand, South and Central America, USA
Typical height: 130ft (40m), but plantation-grown trees are shorter
Trunk diameter: 6ft (2m) maximum when fully mature

⚠ **Possible health risks**
Not known

PURPLEHEART

Peltogyne porphyrocardia and related species (Leguminosae)

Also called: amarante, guarabu, morado, nazareno, pau roxo, saka, tananeo, violetwood

Description
Newly cut heartwood is bright purple, turning a deep purplish-brown on exposure. There may be colour variation between boards, and minerals may cause uneven colour. The grain is usually straight, but can be roey, wavy or irregular, with a medium to fine texture and a high lustre. The off-white sapwood is distinct from the heartwood.
Typical dry weight: 54lb/ft³ (860kg/m³)
Specific gravity: .86

◀ Turned box in *P. venosa*

Properties
It is hard, dense and heavy, with high crushing, stiffness and bending strengths, a moderate steam-bending rating and medium resistance to shock loads. It is difficult to work by hand, and machining is moderately difficult. The blunting effect on cutters is moderate to severe. Slow feed rates and a reduced cutting angle are advised. Dull cutters will heat the wood and cause resin to exude. It glues, waxes, stains and polishes well, turns very well, but is not easy to sand. Pre-boring is advised for nailing or screwing. Spirit finishes tend to remove the purple colour; lacquer retains it.

Seasoning
It generally dries fairly rapidly with only slight warping and splitting. Moisture in the centre of thicker stock may be a problem. Movement in service is small.

Durability
The heartwood is highly durable and very resistant to decay fungi and dry-wood termites; the sapwood is vulnerable to the powder-post beetle. The heartwood is highly resistant to preservative treatment, but the sapwood is permeable.

Typical uses
Quality furniture, turnery, inlay and marquetry, boatbuilding, billiard- or pool-cue butts, handles and shafts, flooring, heavy exterior construction, bridge building, cladding (siding), vats, piling and decorative veneer.

Grows
Central America and northern South America
Typical height: 100–150ft (30–45m)
Trunk diameter: 2–4ft (0.6–1.2m)

⚠ **Possible health risks**
Dust can cause nasal irritation and nausea

AFRORMOSIA

Pericopsis elata (Leguminosae)

Syn.: *Afrormosia elata*
Also called: assamela (France and Ivory Coast), **mohole** (Netherlands), **ejen** (Cameroon), **ayin, egbi** (Nigeria), **kokrodua** (Ghana), **ole, olel pardo, tento**

Description

The heartwood darkens on exposure from deep orange-brown or brown to brownish-yellow with darker streaks. The sapwood is creamy-brown. The grain varies from straight to slightly interlocked, and has a ropelike figure when cut radially; the texture is medium to fine. An attractive mottled figure is revealed on quartersawn surfaces.

Typical dry weight: 43lb/ft³ (690kg/m³)
Specific gravity: .69

Properties

This heavy, dense wood has medium stiffness and resistance to shock loads. It has high bending and crushing strength, but can distort during steaming. Interlocking grain can affect machining, and it has a moderate blunting effect on cutting tools. It works well with normal tools, but a low cutting angle is advised for planing. Pre-boring for screws and nails is recommended. It glues well and takes an excellent finish.

Seasoning

It dries fairly slowly, but seasons reasonably well with little degrade. There is little movement in service.

Durability

Afrormosia is highly durable, resistant to fungi and termites. Due to its high tannin content, it can stain on contact with ferrous metals. The heartwood is very resistant to preservative treatment.

Typical uses

Afrormosia was originally used as a substitute for teak (*Tectona grandis*). Now it is used for furniture and cabinetmaking, boatbuilding, parquet flooring, stairs, shop fittings (store fixtures) and marine piling. It is also used in veneer form for wall panelling, furniture and doors.

▲ Dining table

Grows
West Africa
Typical height: 150ft (45m)
Trunk diameter: 3ft (1m)

⚠ **Possible health risks**
Skin and eye irritation; splinters become septic; can affect the nervous system; may cause rhinitis and asthma

IMBUIA

Phoebe (now *Ocotea*) *porosa* (Lauraceae)

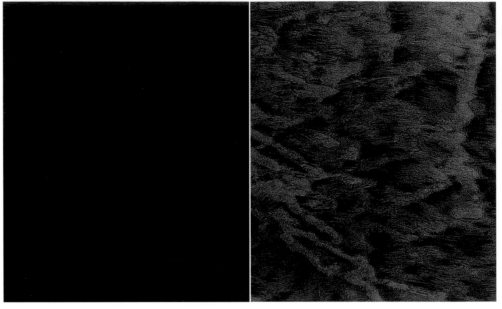

Figured

Also called: amarela, Brazilian walnut, canella imbuia, embuia

Description

The heartwood ranges from yellow-olive to chocolate brown, with variegated stripes and streaks. There can be considerable colour variation. The grain is usually straight, but can frequently be curly or wavy, producing a fine ribbon figure. The wood can be burry (burled), and may have cluster burrs, or be quilted or bubbly in appearance. It has a medium to fine texture and a high natural lustre. Imbuia has been compared to American walnut (*Juglans nigra*) in appearance.
Typical dry weight: 41lb/ft³ (660kg/m³)
Specific gravity: .66

Properties

Imbuia is a fairly hard, heavy and dense wood. It has low to medium strength in all categories, and a very low steam-bending classification. It works well with both hand and machine tools, but the grain is liable to pick up during planing unless a reduced cutting angle is used. The wood nails, screws and glues well, and it can be stained and polished to a high finish.

Seasoning

It dries rapidly and tends to warp unless care is taken. Thicker stock is inclined to develop honeycomb and collapse. There is medium to small movement in service.

Durability

The heartwood is durable, resistant to decay and to most wood-boring insects, and is moderately resistant to preservative treatment. The sapwood is permeable.

Typical uses

In Brazil it is highly regarded for furniture and cabinetmaking, panelling and shop fittings (store fixtures). It is also used for gunstocks, domestic flooring, kitchen cabinets, office furniture, sporting goods and good-quality decorative veneers.

Grows
Southern Brazil
Typical height: 130ft (40m)
Trunk diameter: 6ft (1.8m)

⚠ **Possible health risks**
The sawdust can be an irritant to the nose, eyes and skin

Turned box in imbuia with insert of maple burr (*Acer* sp.) ▶

CELERY-TOP PINE

Phyllocladus aspleniifolius (Podocarpaceae)

No other names

Description
The heartwood varies from pale yellow to pale brown, and the narrow sapwood is typically the same colour and not clearly differentiated from the heartwood. It has a straight grain with a fine, even texture and distinct, closely spaced growth rings. It is not a true pine.
Typical dry weight: 40lb/ft³ (640kg/m³)
Specific gravity: .64

Properties
Celery-top pine is tough and strong, with medium to high strength in all categories, except for bending, which is rated only moderate. It works easily with both machine and hand tools, although compression wood can sometimes cause difficulties. It glues, nails, screws, stains and varnishes well, and can be brought to a reasonably fine finish. It also has good chemical- and acid-resisting properties.

Seasoning
Celery-top pine dries well with little degrade, and exhibits moderate movement in service.

Durability
It is moderately durable, and both sapwood and heartwood are treatable with preservatives.

Typical uses
Office and other furniture, joinery, turnery, carving, boatbuilding, flooring, acid and chemical vats, and fencing. Choice logs are also sliced for veneers.

Grows
Tasmania
Typical height: 100ft (30m)
Trunk diameter: 3ft (1m)

⚠ **Possible health risks**
Not known

SPRUCE
Picea abies (Pinaceae)

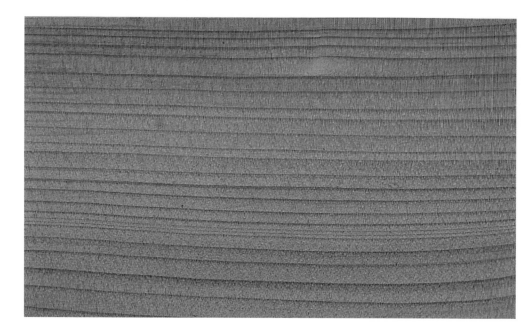

Also called: Baltic whitewood, common spruce, Norway spruce, fir, whitewood, Baltic white pine, white deal, Swiss pine, épicéa (French), **Fichte** (German); also according to origin: **Norway spruce, Russian spruce,** etc.

▲ Lute, showing flower grain

Grows
Europe, including western Russia; also Canada and USA
Typical height: 80–120ft (24–36m)
Trunk diameter: 2–4ft (0.6m–1.2m)

⚠ Possible health risks
Respiratory problems, irritation to nose and throat, allergic bronchial asthma

Description
Spruce ranges from near-white to a pale yellow-brown, with very little distinction between sapwood and heartwood. It is typically straight-grained, with a fine texture and a natural lustre. The contrast between the lighter earlywood and darker latewood makes the growth rings clearly visible. Quartersawn surfaces occasionally show an attractive ripple figure known as 'flower grain' or *Haselfichte*.
Typical dry weight: 29lb/ft³ (470kg/m³)
Specific gravity: .47

Properties
The wood has low resistance to shock loads and low stiffness, medium crushing and bending strength, and very poor steam-bending properties. It works easily and well with both machine and hand tools and has only a slight blunting effect, but hard knots can damage cutting edges. Spruce planes, turns, saws, bores, moulds, glues, sands, nails, screws, varnishes, paints and stains well.

Seasoning
It dries rapidly and well, but care must be taken to minimize degrade. The wood can be prone to check and split, knots may loosen and split, and spiral-grained stock may distort. Movement in use is medium.

Durability
The wood is not durable, with little resistance to attack from decay-causing fungi, longhorn and pinhole borers, and wood wasps. The sapwood is vulnerable to attack from the common furniture beetle. The heartwood is resistant to preservative treatment.

Typical uses
Apart from Christmas trees, spruce is used for carpentry, interior construction and joinery, boxes and crates, domestic flooring, pit props, pulp and paper, ladder stringers, veneer and plywood. Selected timber (known as 'Swiss pine') is quartersawn to make soundboards for stringed musical instruments.

SITKA SPRUCE

Picea sitchensis (Pinaceae)

Also called: silver spruce, tideland spruce, Menzies spruce, coast spruce, yellow spruce

Description

The creamy-white to light yellow sapwood merges into the heartwood, which is pinkish or light pinkish-yellow to pale brown with a purplish hue. On exposure the colour darkens to a silvery-brown with a faint touch of red. The grain is typically straight, but occasionally spiral, and is often dimpled on tangential surfaces. It has an even, medium to fine texture and a natural lustre. The annual rings are clearly defined, and the wood is not resinous.
Typical dry weight: 27lb/ft³ (430kg/m³)
Specific gravity: .43

Properties

Sitka spruce has a high strength to weight ratio, with medium ratings for bending, crushing, resistance to shock loads, and stiffness, and a very good steam-bending rating. Provided sharp tools are used, it works well by hand or machine, with very little blunting effect on cutting edges. It finishes cleanly and planes, saws, moulds, bores, mortises and sands very well. It nails, screws and glues excellently, and stains, varnishes and polishes well.

Seasoning

The wood both air- and kiln-dries readily, but if larger stock is dried too quickly twisting and cupping can occur. Checks, splits and raised grain are other problems that can arise in young-growth wood. It is moderately stable in use.

Durability

It is not durable, and is vulnerable to attack from pinhole borer and jewel beetles. The heartwood is moderately resistant to preservative treatment.

Typical uses

Depending on the grade, Sitka spruce has a great many uses. It is used for joists, rafters, studding, pallets, beams, decking, formwork, ladder sides, interior joinery, cooperage, boatbuilding, oars and masts. It is used as corestock for plywood, and sliced to make laminates for glider and aircraft building. It is widely used as pulp for paper, and, in contrast, selected quartersawn wood is used to make soundboards for stringed instruments.

Grows
Western Canada and USA
Typical height: 125–175ft
(38–54m)
Trunk diameter: 3–6ft
(0.9–1.8m)

⚠ **Possible health risks**
Respiratory irritation, allergic bronchial asthma, rhinitis and dermatitis

The genus *Pinus*
Pines

The genus *Pinus* is made up of trees and shrubs that are evergreen, monoecious (having male and female flowers on the same plant), and have a high resin content. It is the most economically important genus of conifers, and its products include timber, wood pulp, plywood, poles, turpentine, resin, pine nuts and Christmas trees.

There are 90 to 100 species of pine that can be found in temperate regions, and the mountain areas of tropical regions, in the northern hemisphere. The only species that naturally occurs in the southern hemisphere is Merkus pine (*P. merkusii*), which grows in Sumatra; though other pines have been planted in the southern hemisphere, most notably loblolly pine (*P. taeda*).

Although all pines are classified as softwoods, botanists distinguish between 'soft' and 'hard' pines. Soft pines are also called white pines, and typically have needles in bundles of five; whereas hard pines, also referred to as yellow pines, have needles in bundles of two or three.

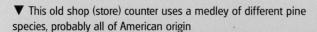

Various species of pine, along with other conifers, have long been used as Christmas trees. The origins of the use of Christmas trees are said to go back as far as the eighth century, when a British monk, St Boniface, was apparently preaching about the Nativity to a group of Germanic Druids. To convince his audience that a particular oak tree was not sacred and untouchable, he chopped it down, and as it fell it crushed every shrub in its path except for a fir sapling. St Boniface then used this symbolism of survival as a miracle, and to win converts, referred to the fir as the tree of the Christ child. By the sixteenth century the decoration of Christmas trees, both indoors and out, had become common. Martin Luther, the sixteenth-century Protestant reformer, is said to have added lighted candles to his family Christmas tree, or Christ tree. When the British queen Victoria married her German husband Albert in 1840, the German custom of Christmas trees became popular in England also.

▲ Pine is often the material of choice for inexpensive interior joinery

▼ This old shop (store) counter uses a medley of different pine species, probably all of American origin

▼ A 19th-century house door undergoing restoration. Pine can be very durable when painted

It is said that Pennsylvania Germans introduced the Christmas tree to the United States in the 1820s. Today, something in excess of 35 million Christmas trees are harvested annually in the USA alone.

What is said to be the oldest tree in the world – Methuselah, a bristlecone pine (*P. aristata*), still growing in Inyo National Forest, California – is calculated to be over 4,700 years old. There was an even older tree of this species at Wheeler Peak on the borders of Utah and Nevada, but it was killed by an overenthusiastic researcher in 1964. As his coring tool had broken he was apparently given permission by the US Forestry Service to cut it down so that he could count the rings – so he killed what was probably the oldest living thing on earth, which turned out to be 4,862 years old.

LODGEPOLE PINE
Pinus contorta (Pinaceae)

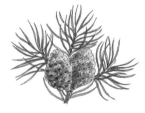

Also called: knotty black pine, spruce pine, Rocky Mountain lodgepole pine, black pine, pin tordu

Description

The sapwood is narrow, near-white to yellow and not very distinct from the heartwood. The latter is light yellow to pale yellowish-brown, only slightly darker than the sapwood. Small knots are quite common. It has a typically straight but uneven grain and a medium to fine texture. The growth rings are distinct, and flatsawn wood often has a dimpled effect.
Typical dry weight: 24lb/ft³ (390kg/m³)
Specific gravity: .39

Properties

The wood has moderate weight and density, medium bending strength and low compression strength. It works well by hand and machine. It planes to an excellent, clean finish if the cutters are very sharp, and moulds, mortises, glues, bores, nails and screws very well. Turning, painting, staining and polishing are good.

Seasoning

It dries quite rapidly and there is little degrade, with just minimal warping and checking. There is little movement in use.

Durability

Lodgepole pine has low durability and is vulnerable to attack from insects, and to decay. The sapwood is permeable for preservative treatment, but the heartwood is moderately difficult to treat.

Typical uses

Rustic furniture, flooring, framing, boxes and crates, corral rails, posts and poles, cabin logs, shingles, railway sleepers (railroad ties), heavy construction, wood pulp, plywood, hardboard and particleboard.

Grows

Canada, USA, Mexico; also UK and New Zealand
Typical height: 20–80ft (6–24m)
Trunk diameter: 1–3ft (0.3–0.9m)

⚠ **Possible health risks**

Working with pine woods in general can cause decrease in lung function, allergic bronchial asthma, rhinitis and dermatitis

SUGAR PINE

Pinus lambertiana (Pinaceae)

Also called: big pine, California sugar pine, gigantic pine, great sugar pine, shade pine

Description

The heartwood of sugar pine ranges from a pale brown to a light reddish-brown, while the sapwood varies from near-white to pale yellowish-white. Sugar pine typically has a straight and even grain with a fairly coarse and very uniform texture, and dark brown resin canals which are particularly distinctive.

Typical dry weight: 22lb/ft³ (360kg/m³)
Specific gravity: .36

Properties

Sugar pine is light and soft, with low strength overall, low stiffness and crushing strength, and low resistance to shock loads. It works well with both hand and machine tools, and has only a slight blunting effect on cutting edges. Because of its uniform texture and low density it is exceptionally easy to work. The wood moulds, turns, nails and sands well, and is excellent for gluing, mortising, screwing and planing. Staining, painting and polishing are all satisfactory, though resin in the wood may react unfavourably with some finishes.

Seasoning

The wood dries readily without difficulty, with only minor checking and warping. There can be problems with brown stains in wet wood. It has high dimensional stability in service.

Durability

The heartwood has little natural resistance to decay, and is fairly resistant to preservative treatment.

Typical uses

Doors, frames, domestic flooring, piano keys, organ pipes, rafters, shingles, boxes and crates, foundry patterns, building and construction, panelling and plywood.

Grows
USA
Typical height: 100–160ft
(30–50m)
Trunk diameter: 3–6ft
(0.9–1.8m)

⚠ Possible health risks

Working with pine woods in general can cause decrease in lung function, allergic bronchial asthma, rhinitis and dermatitis

WESTERN WHITE PINE
Pinus monticola (Pinaceae)

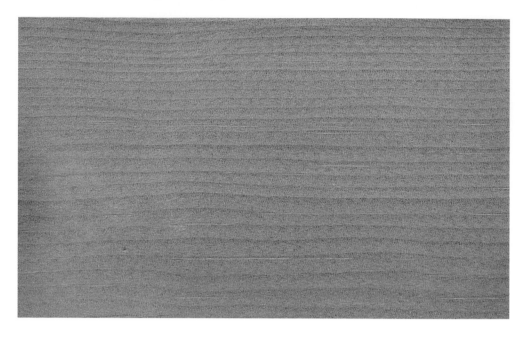

Also called: Idaho white pine, mountain pine, white pine, silver pine

Grows
Western Canada and western USA
Typical height: 100ft (30m), but can be much taller
Trunk diameter: 3ft (0.9m) or larger

⚠ Possible health risks
Working with pine woods in general can cause decrease in lung function, allergic bronchial asthma, rhinitis and dermatitis

Description
The sapwood is near-white to yellowish-white, and the heartwood is pale yellow to reddish-brown, with resin ducts forming fine brown lines on longitudinal surfaces. There is little distinction between earlywood and latewood zones. The wood is straight-grained with an even, uniform texture, but tends to be rather knotty.
Typical dry weight: 26lb/ft³ (420kg/m³)
Specific gravity: .42

Properties
Western white pine is soft and light, and is rated as moderate for shock resistance and stiffness. It is moderately weak in bending, and weak in compression. It works well with both machine and hand tools, and has only a small blunting effect on cutting edges. Clean, smooth surfaces can be achieved when planing and moulding, and it turns, bores and mortises very well. Sanding, staining, varnishing and painting qualities are good, and it is rated as excellent for nailing, screwing and gluing.

Seasoning
It dries readily and well, with only a little checking and warping. There is small movement in service.

Durability
The wood is not durable and can be vulnerable to insect attack. The sapwood is permeable for preservative treatment but the heartwood is moderately resistant.

Typical uses
Furniture, interior joinery, windows, doors, shelving, trim, drawing boards, boat and ship building, flooring, woodware, matches, packing cases, roofing, pulp, particleboard and plywood. Interesting pieces are also sliced into decorative veneers for panelling.

LONGLEAF AND SLASH PINE

Pinus palustris and P. elliottii (Pinaceae)

Also called: Florida pine, Florida longleaf pine, Florida yellow pine, Georgia yellow pine, heart pine, pitch pine, spruce pine (*P. palustris*); slash pine, yellow slash pine (*P. elliottii*). Often sold together with loblolly pine (*P. taeda*) and shortleaf pine (*P. echinata*) as **southern pine** or **southern yellow pine**

Description

The sapwood varies in width, and is whitish to yellowish, orange-white or pale yellow. The heartwood is light yellow, orange or reddish-brown, and is resinous. The marked contrast between earlywood and latewood is clearly shown in the growth rings. The grain is straight and uneven with a medium texture. It is the heaviest of the commercial softwoods. Heavier stock is sold as 'pitch pine', and lighter stock as 'southern pine'.
Typical dry weight: 41lb/ft³ (670kg/m³)
Specific gravity: .67

Properties

It has high crushing, stiffness and bending strengths, and medium resistance to shock loads. The resin content makes it unsuitable for steam bending. The wood responds fairly well to being worked with either hand and machine tools. It has a moderate blunting effect on cutting edges, and the resin can clog cutters and saws. It planes, moulds, bores and turns fairly well, and glues, screws, sands and nails well. The wood has satisfactory qualities for painting, varnishing, staining and polishing.

Seasoning

These pines dry well with little degrade. There is only small movement in service.

Durability

It has moderate resistance to decay, and can be vulnerable to insect attack. The sapwood is permeable for preservative treatment, but the heartwood is resistant.

Typical uses

Joinery, domestic flooring, railway sleepers (railroad ties), heavy construction, bridges, mine timbers, decking, boxes, crates, pallets, particleboard, fibreboard, plywood, hardboard and pulp. Turpentine and resin are also produced from the wood.

> **Grows**
> Southern USA
> **Typical height:** 80–100ft
> (24–30m)
> **Trunk diameter:** 2ft–2ft 8in
> (0.6–0.8m)

⚠ Possible health risks

Working with pine woods in general can cause decrease in lung function, allergic bronchial asthma, rhinitis and dermatitis

PONDEROSA PINE
Pinus ponderosa (Pinaceae)

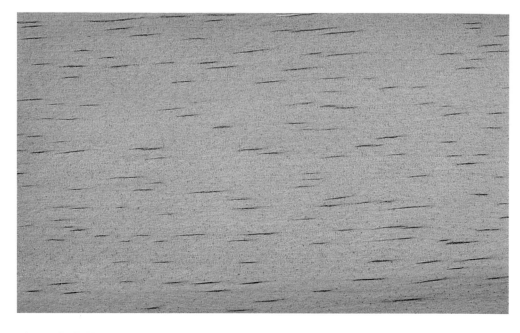

Also called: big pine, bird's-eye pine, knotty pine, western yellow pine, Californian white pine, British Colombia soft pine

Description

Ponderosa pine has a wide, whitish to pale yellow sapwood, with a darker heartwood that is deep yellow to reddish-brown or orange-brown and is much heavier than the sapwood. The grain is typically straight and even, and is often characterized by many knots, which are normally sound, and the dark lines of resin ducts. Bird's-eye figuring can sometimes occur. The wood has a uniform medium texture.

Typical dry weight: 32lb/ft³ (510kg/m³)
Specific gravity: .51

Properties

Ponderosa pine is characterized by medium crushing and bending strength, low resistance to shock loads, low stiffness and a poor steam-bending rating. It works well with both hand and machine tools, and has only a little blunting effect on cutting edges. Resin exudation can, however, sometimes cause problems. The wood saws, nails and screws well, and planes, turns, moulds, bores and glues very well. It finishes well, though it may require treatment of the resin before applying certain finishes.

Seasoning

The wood dries well, but the sapwood can suffer from blue fungal staining. Movement in service is medium.

Durability

It is not durable and has little natural resistance to decay fungi or insects. The sapwood is permeable for preservative treatment, the heartwood moderately so.

Typical uses

The sapwood is used for patternmaking, and the heartwood for domestic and rustic furniture, turnery, window frames, doors, kitchen furniture, building, boxes, packing cases, dowels, cabins and general woodwork. Character logs are sliced to make knotty pine panelling, and rotary-cut for veneers. Suitably treated wood is used for telephone poles, railway sleepers (railroad ties) and posts.

Grows

Canada and USA
Typical height: 60–130ft (18–40m)
Trunk diameter: 2ft 6in–4ft (0.8–1.2m)

⚠ Possible health risks

Working with pine woods in general can cause decrease in lung function, allergic bronchial asthma, rhinitis and dermatitis

RADIATA PINE
Pinus radiata (Pinaceae)

Also called: Monterey pine, insignis pine

Description
The pale-coloured sapwood is wide and distinct from the heartwood, which is usually pinkish-brown. The heartwood is generally straight-grained, but can contain spiral grain. There is little contrast in the growth rings, which leads to a relatively uniform and even texture. Resin ducts show as fine brown lines on longitudinal surfaces, and, depending on its precise origin, the wood can be knotty.
Typical dry weight: 30lb/ft³ (480kg/m³)
Specific gravity: .48

Properties
The wood has medium crushing strength and resistance to shock loads, low bending and stiffness properties, and is unsuitable for steam bending. It works well with machine and hand tools and has little blunting effect on cutters. Thin and sharp cutters are advisable for a clean finish when planing. Although areas around knots can tear, the wood can be planed, turned, moulded and bored cleanly. It nails, screws and stains well, and glues and polishes satisfactorily.

Seasoning
Radiata pine dries easily and rapidly with little degrade. Spiral grain can cause warping in wood from immature trees. There is medium movement in use.

Durability
The heartwood has little natural resistance, and is vulnerable to attack from insects, decay fungi and other wood-destroying organisms. It is permeable for preservative treatment.

Typical uses
Better-quality stock is used for furniture and interior joinery, and may be sliced for decorative veneers. Other uses include general joinery, building and construction, floors, cladding (siding), boxes and crates, cabin building, wood pulp, brush handles, particleboard, corestock and plywood.

Grows
California, Australia, New Zealand, Chile, South Africa
Typical height: 50–100ft (15–30m)
Trunk diameter: 1–3ft (0.3–0.9m)

⚠ **Possible health risks**
Working with pine woods in general can cause decrease in lung function, allergic bronchial asthma, rhinitis and dermatitis

EASTERN WHITE PINE
Pinus strobus (Pinaceae)

Also called: white pine, spruce pine, northern white pine, Quebec pine, Weymouth pine

Description

Yellow pine heartwood ranges in colour from pale yellow to a light reddish-brown; it is sometimes marked by resin ducts that form fine brown lines on longitudinal surfaces. The grain is usually straight and even. The wood has a uniform, medium texture, and the growth rings are inconspicuous.
Typical dry weight: 24lb/ft³ (390kg/m³)
Specific gravity: .39

Properties

Yellow pine is soft and light, and is classified as weak in all the strength categories. It is not suitable for steam bending. It works very readily with both machine and hand tools, and has only a slight blunting effect on cutting edges. Yellow pine planes easily, giving a smooth finish, and moulds, bores, routs, mortises, glues, carves, nails and screws well. It responds well to sanding, and takes paint and varnish well. The wood accepts stain easily and polishes very well. Untreated, it weathers to a light grey.

Seasoning

It air-dries easily and uniformly with low shrinkage, but brown stains and ring failure can occur. Yellow pine is very stable in service.

Durability

The heartwood is not durable, with only moderate resistance to decay organisms. The sapwood is permeable for preservative treatment, but the heartwood is moderately resistant to it.

Typical uses

Furniture, quality joinery, carving, rustic furniture, boatbuilding, musical instruments, light construction, drawing boards, patternmaking, domestic woodware, matches, coffins, cabins, shingles and veneers.

Grows
Eastern Canada and USA
Typical height: 100ft (30m), but can be taller
Trunk diameter: 3–4ft (0.9–1.2m) or larger

⚠ **Possible health risks**
Working with pine woods in general can cause decrease in lung function, allergic bronchial asthma, rhinitis and dermatitis

SCOTS PINE

Pinus sylvestris (Pinaceae)

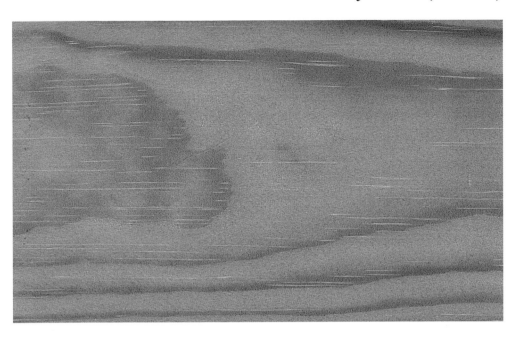

Also called: redwood, red deal, red pine, Baltic redwood, Norway fir, Scots fir, yellow deal, sapin rouge du nord (French), **Föhre, gemeine Kiefer** (German), **grove den** (Dutch); also distinguished by origin: **Finnish, Swedish,** etc.

Description
This widely distributed species varies according to its origin. Typically, the heartwood is pale reddish-brown and clearly distinct from the paler, creamy-white to yellow sapwood. The clear contrast between the light earlywood and the darker latewood results in well-defined annual rings. The wood is resinous and knotty, and its texture may be fine or coarse, depending on origin.
Typical dry weight: 32lb/ft³ (510kg/m³)
Specific gravity: .51

Properties
It has low resistance to shock loads, low stiffness, low to medium bending and crushing strength and a very poor steam-bending rating. The wood works well with both hand and machine tools. It saws, planes, moulds, bores, routs, carves, sands and turns well. Gluing effectiveness can vary according to the resin content, and painting, varnishing, staining and polishing are satisfactory.

Seasoning
The wood dries rapidly and well, but is prone to blue sap stain if precautions are not taken. It exhibits medium movement in use.

Durability
Scots pine is not a durable wood, and is vulnerable to insect attack. The sapwood is permeable for preservative treatment, but the heartwood is moderately resistant.

Typical uses
Quality grades are used for furniture, joinery, turnery and vehicle bodies. Other grades are used for building, railway sleepers (railroad ties), telephone poles and piles. It is also rotary-cut for plywood and sliced for decorative veneers.

> **Grows**
> Europe, including UK, Scandinavia and Russia
> **Typical height:** 70ft (21m)
> **Trunk diameter:** 2ft (0.6m)

⚠ **Possible health risks**
Working with pine woods in general can cause decrease in lung function, allergic bronchial asthma, rhinitis and dermatitis

LOBLOLLY PINE
Pinus taeda (Pinaceae)

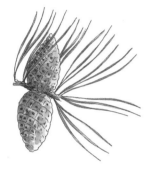

Also called: Arkansas pine, North Carolina pine, oldfield pine, southern yellow pine.
Loblolly pine is one of several pine species that come under the general commercial name of southern yellow pine, all of which are very similar indeed when sawn. The other three key commercial southern yellow pines are **shortleaf pine (*P. echinata*), longleaf pine (*P. palustris*)** and **slash pine (*P. elliottii*)**

Grows
South-eastern USA
Typical height: 80–100ft
(25–30m)
Trunk diameter: 2–3 ft
(0.6–0.9m)

⚠ Possible health risks
Working with pine woods in general can cause decrease in lung function, allergic bronchial asthma, rhinitis and dermatitis

Description
The heartwood is a reddish brown, and the sapwood, which can be narrow or wide, is a yellowish white. Loblolly pine is straight-grained and of coarse texture. This is a resinous wood, and there is a marked contrast between the bands of early and late wood.
Typical dry weight: 33lb/ft3 (540kg/m3)
Specific gravity: .54

Properties
Loblolly pine is rated as moderate for heaviness, hardness, stiffness, strength and shock resistance. It is rated very highly for its strength when compared with other softwoods. It works fairly well with both machine and hand tools, but sometimes resin may gum up cutting edges. It holds screws and nails well, but pre-drilling is required sometimes to prevent splitting. There can be problems with resin bleed-out, but it normally varnishes, paints and stains easily. It is highly resistant to wear.

Seasoning
There is moderately large shrinkage during seasoning, but the wood is reasonably stable once dried.

Durability
It is moderately decay-resistant and takes preservative treatment, including pressure-treating, easily.

Typical uses
Furniture, boatbuilding and woodenware. It is also used for construction work such as roof trusses, beams, posts and joists; for crates, cooperage and pallets; and for other applications requiring good wearing properties, such as patios, marinas and boardwalks. Other uses include pulp and structural-grade plywood. Turpentine, resin, pitch and tar are also products of the yellow pines.

EUROPEAN PLANE

Platanus hybrida (Platanaceae)

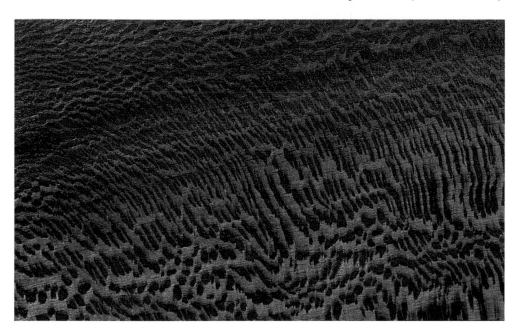

Syn.: *P. x acerifolia, P. x hispanica*
Also called: London plane, platane (French and German). Also by origin: **English, French,**
etc. Related species: ***P. orientalis*** in south-east Europe, Iran and Turkey; ***P. occidentalis***
(American plane), known in the USA as **buttonwood** or, confusingly, **sycamore**

Description
The heartwood is a light reddish-brown.
On quartersawn stock the many and very
clear rays give a distinctive and attractive
fleck figuring, known as **lacewood** – a term
used for the quartersawn wood only.
Plane is straight-grained with a fine to
medium texture.
Typical dry weight: 39lb/ft³ (620kg/m³)
Specific gravity: .62

Properties
Plane has low stiffness, a medium rating
in all other strength categories, and a very
good steam-bending classification. It
works well with both machine and hand
tools, and has a moderate blunting
effect on cutters. When planing
quartersawn stock, cutting
edges need to be kept very
sharp to prevent the rays
from flaking, but otherwise
it planes well. However, it
can bind during sawing.
Plane is an excellent turnery
wood, and screws, nails,
glues and stains well. Boring

and mortising qualities are satisfactory,
and the wood can be brought to an
excellent polished finish.

Seasoning
Plane dries fairly rapidly, but care is
needed to prevent degrade, as the wood
has a tendency to split and distort. There
is small movement in service.

Durability
The heartwood has little resistance to
decay, and the sapwood is vulnerable to
the common furniture beetle. The wood
is permeable for preservative treatment.

Typical uses
Fine furniture, cabinetmaking,
carving, turnery, cigar boxes,
inlay, panelling and veneer,
especially as lacewood.
In veneer form it is
sometimes treated
chemically to form
harewood, which leaves the
flecks in their original colour
but turns the background grey.

▲ Bed with harewood panels

> **Grows**
> Europe
> **Typical height:** 100ft (30m)
> **Trunk diameter:** 3–4ft
> (0.9–1.2m)

⚠ **Possible health risks**
Not known

◀ Lacewood bowl

VINHÁTICO

Plathymenia reticulata (Leguminosae)

Also called: Brazilian mahogany, amarello, candela, yellow wood, gold wood, vinhático castanho, tatare, jaruma

Description

The yellowish-white sapwood is clearly differentiated from the heartwood, which is a pronounced orange-brown colour with darker streaks. On exposure, the wood darkens to a rich reddish-brown. The grain ranges from straight, through roey to wavy, with a moderately fine and even texture and a silky sheen.
Typical dry weight: 37lb/ft³ (600kg/m³)
Specific gravity: .60

Properties

Vinhático has a high crushing strength, low stiffness and resistance to shock loads, medium bending strength and a moderate steam-bending classification. The wood works well with both machine and hand tools, and a clean finish can easily be obtained, but sharp, thin-edged tools are required to avoid tearing, especially when sawing. The wood planes, bores, mortises, glues, nails and screws well, and can be polished to a high finish once the grain has been filled. It is not recommended for turnery.

Seasoning

It dries well with very little degrade, and exhibits small movement in service.

Durability

Vinhático is moderately durable, and reasonably resistant to attack by wood-destroying insects and fungi. The sapwood is permeable for preservative treatment, but the heartwood is moderately resistant.

Typical uses

Furniture and cabinetmaking, quality joinery, domestic flooring, vehicle bodywork; ship and boat building, including traditional dugout canoes in Brazil. It is peeled for plywood and sliced for decorative veneers.

Grows
Brazil; also Argentina and Colombia
Typical height: 125ft (38m)
Trunk diameter: 3ft (0.9m)

⚠ **Possible health risks**
Not known

MACACAUBA

Platymiscium pinnatum and related species (Leguminosae)

Also called: macacauba preta, macacauba vermelha, macacawood, macacahuba, nambar, vencola, roble colorado. Several species of *Platymiscium* are sold as 'macacauba'

Description
The heartwood ranges from bright red to purplish-red or light reddish-brown, with fine veins of darker variegated red or purple. It has an irregular and interlocked grain with a uniform, medium texture, and a lustrous surface.
Typical dry weight: 60lb/ft³ (960kg/m³)
Specific gravity: .96

Properties
Macacauba is an exceptionally heavy and dense wood, which exhibits medium strength in terms of impact resistance, crushing and bending, and low stiffness. Its steam-bending qualities are rated as poor. The wood generally works well with both machine and hand tools, but when irregular grain is present it can cause difficulty and very sharp cutting edges are required. A reduced cutting angle is recommended for machine planing in order to achieve a clean finish. Macacauba accepts nails, screws, glues and stains well, and can be brought to a smooth polished finish.

Seasoning
The wood requires drying carefully to avoid degrade. It is prone to end splitting and checking while seasoning. There is only small movement in service.

Durability
It is a durable wood and resistant to treatment with preservatives.

Typical uses
Quality furniture and cabinetmaking, quality joinery, musical instruments, flooring, heavy construction and bridges. Macacauba is also sliced to make decorative veneers.

Grows
Brazil, Colombia, Guyana, Nicaragua, Peru, Surinam, Trinidad and Tobago, Venezuela
Typical height: 80ft (24m)
Trunk diameter: 2ft 6in–3ft 6in (0.7–1.1m)

⚠ **Possible health risks**
Not known

POPLAR

Populus spp. (Salicaceae)

P. nigra

P. nigra

Fruit bowl in poplar burr (burl) ▶

Also called: peuplier (French), **Pappel** (German). A large number of species are known as 'poplar'. Amongst them are **European black poplar** (*P. nigra*), **black Italian poplar** (*P. canadensis*), **robusta** (*P. robusta*), **Swedish, Finnish,** etc. **aspen** (*P. tremula*). North American poplars include **Canadian poplar** (*P. balsamifera, P. tacamahaca*), **American whitewood, yellow poplar** or **tulip tree** (*Liriodendron tulipifera*, q.v.), and the **cottonwoods** (*P. tremuloides*, q.v.)

Grows

Europe and North America
Typical height: 100–115ft
(30–35m)
Trunk diameter: 3–4ft
(0.9–1.2m), but varies
according to species

⚠ Possible health risks

Asthma, dermatitis, bronchitis, sneezing and eye irritation

Description

The colour ranges from near-white through creamy-white to grey, and is sometimes pinkish-brown or very pale brown. It is typically straight-grained, with a fine, even texture, but can be woolly.
Typical dry weight: 28lb/ft³
(450kg/m³), with variations dependent on species
Specific gravity: .45

Properties

Poplar has a medium crushing strength, very low stiffness and resistance to shock loads, and a low bending strength, with a poor steam-bending rating. It generally works well with both hand and machine tools. It has a slight blunting effect on cutting edges, which must be kept very sharp to avoid a woolly finish. It glues, nails and screws well, and polishes, paints and varnishes satisfactorily, but staining gives variable results.

Seasoning

It dries fairly rapidly with little degrade, but there can be localized pockets of moisture, and knots are prone to split. There is medium movement in service.

Durability

Poplar is not durable, and is particularly susceptible to insect attack. The sapwood is permeable for preservative treatment, but the heartwood is moderately resistant.

Typical uses

Joinery, light structural work, kitchen utensils, food containers, flooring, boxes and crates, fruit baskets, matches, wood pulp, corestock and plywood. Character logs are sliced for decorative veneer.

COTTONWOOD
Populus deltoides and related species (Salicaceae)

Also called: eastern cottonwood, eastern poplar, poplar

Description
The whitish sapwood merges into the greyish-white to light greyish-brown heartwood. The wood is typically straight-grained, with a uniform coarse texture and a dull lustre. As a true poplar, it has similar qualities to aspen (*P. tremuloides*).
Typical dry weight: 28lb/ft³ (450kg/m³)
Specific gravity: .45

Properties
The wood is soft, low in shock resistance, weak in bending and compression, and has fairly good steam-bending properties. It is generally easy to work, but care needs to be taken to avoid a woolly finish. It nails and screws easily, but does not hold these fixings well. Gluing properties are very good, and the wood can be brought to a satisfactory finish.

Seasoning
Cottonwood can warp severely if drying is not carefully controlled. There can also be problems with honeycombing, water pockets and collapse. There is only slight movement in service.

Durability
Cottonwood has little resistance to decay-causing organisms. It is also moderately resistant to preservative treatment.

Typical uses
Furniture, mouldings, toys, musical instruments, kitchen utensils, venetian blinds, shutters, packing cases, corestock and pulp.

Grows
Canada and USA
Typical height: 100ft (30m)
Trunk diameter: 3–4ft (0.9–1.2m)

⚠ **Possible health risks**
Sawdust may cause dermatitis

CANADIAN ASPEN
Populus tremuloides (Salicaceae)

Also called: trembling aspen (Canada), **quaking aspen** (Canada and USA)

Description
The heartwood, which is not clearly differentiated from the sapwood, is generally creamy-grey to light biscuit-brown in colour. The grain is straight and fine with an even texture, but it can often be woolly. Cut surfaces tend to have a silky lustre. After substantial exposure, the surface weathers to a light grey with a silvery sheen. Canadian aspen is relatively light in weight.
Typical dry weight: 28lb/ft³ (450kg/m³)
Specific gravity: .45

Properties
Aspen is tough, but has a low bending strength and low stiffness, with medium resistance to shock loads. It is easy to work with both hand and powered tools, but has a tendency to bind or tear when being sawn. It can also tear when being planed, so very sharp, thin-edged tools are advisable. The wood can be glued, polished, stained, screwed and nailed well, although there may be some difficulty in obtaining a good finish on woolly surfaces.

Seasoning
Aspen is easy to kiln- or air-dry, but it has to be piled carefully to avoid warping and twisting. There can be problems with honeycombing, water pockets and collapse. There is little movement in service.

Durability
It has negligible resistance to decay fungi and other wood-destroying organisms. Aspen is very resistant to preservative treatment, and is non-durable.

Typical uses
Food containers such as punnets (berry baskets) and cheese boxes, pulp and paper making, vehicle bodies, utility joinery, crates and boxes, plywood, particleboard and chipboard. Highly figured aspen is used for decorative veneers, including marquetry work.

Grows
Northern USA and Canada
Typical height: 50–80ft (15–24m)
Trunk diameter: 16–24in (0.4–0.6m)

⚠ **Possible health risks**
Asthma, dermatitis, bronchitis

MESQUITE

Prosopis juliflora (Mimosaceae)

P. juliflora var. velutina

Also called: honey locust, ironwood, algarroba, honeypod, honey mesquite, Texas ironwood

Description
The heartwood is a rich, deep golden- to reddish-brown with darker wavy lines. It has a fine- to medium-textured open grain, ranging from straight to wavy in form. It often has dramatic figuring and very attractive burrs (burls). The sapwood is a pale yellowish-white and up to 1in (25mm) thick. The variety illustrated is known as **velvet mesquite**.
Typical dry weight: 50lb/ft³ (800kg/m³)
Specific gravity: .80

Properties
Mesquite is a hard, tough and heavy wood that has high crushing and bending strengths. It has medium stiffness and resistance to shock loads, and a moderate steam-bending classification. The wood works easily with both machine and hand tools, with only a slight blunting effect on cutters. Pre-boring is required for nailing. The wood glues well. Mesquite can be brought to a smooth finish, but it is not easy to achieve a good result with stains or polishes.

Seasoning
It dries well, but can develop small checks when air-dried. There is small movement in service.

Durability
Although a durable wood, it is moderately prone to termite attack. The sapwood is permeable for preservative treatment, but the heartwood is resistant.

Typical uses
Mesquite is now gaining commercial importance and has become popular for furniture making, flooring and decorative turnery. It is also used for railway sleepers (railroad ties), poles, piles, vehicle bodies and as a structural timber. Interesting logs are sliced for decorative veneers.

Grows
North and South America
Typical height: 20–40ft (6–13m)
Trunk diameter: up to 20in (0.5m)

⚠ **Possible health risks**
Respiratory irritation, dermatitis

EUROPEAN CHERRY

Prunus avium (Rosaceae)

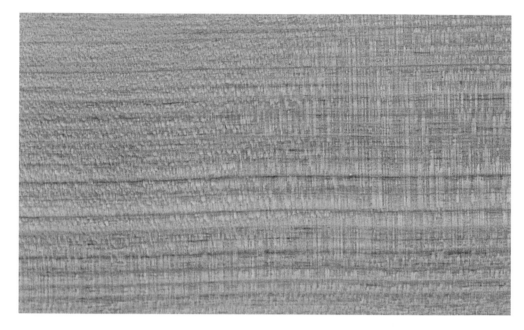

Also called: gean, wild cherry, mazzard, fruit cherry, kers, Kirsche, Vogelkirsche (German), **merisier** (French)

Grows

Europe, western Asia and North Africa

Typical height: 60–80ft (18–24m)

Trunk diameter: 2ft (0.6m)

⚠ **Possible health risks**

Not known

Description

The heartwood is a rich reddish-brown initially, but it ages to a darker colour, losing some of the reddish tint. It is generally straight-grained, with a fairly fine and even texture. The sapwood is clearly differentiated from the heartwood, and is paler.

Typical dry weight: 38lb/ft³ (610kg/m³)

Specific gravity: .61

Properties

European cherry has very good steam-bending characteristics, and has medium properties in terms of resistance to shock loads, bending and crushing. It is low in stiffness, and of a similar strength to oak (*Quercus* spp.). European cherry works well with both hand and machine tools. The wood screws, nails and glues well, but a reduced cutting angle is recommended when machine-planing

Console table ▶

irregular grain. Cherry can be polished to an excellent finish and also stains well, though some prior degreasing may be necessary for best results.

Seasoning

The wood dries rapidly, but can warp and develop end splits if care is not taken. It shows medium movement in service.

Durability

The sapwood is vulnerable to attack by the common furniture beetle, but very resistant to the powder-post beetle. The heartwood shows moderate resistance to decay, and is fairly difficult to treat with preservatives.

Typical uses

European cherry is prized for furniture and cabinetmaking, turnery and carving. It is also used for musical instruments, domestic ware, toys and gunstocks, and is made into decorative veneers.

AMERICAN CHERRY

Prunus serotina (Rosaceae)

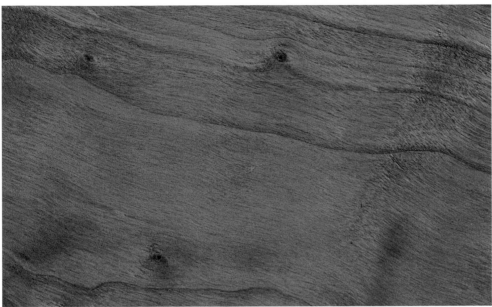

Also called: black cherry, cabinet cherry, choke cherry, Edwards Plateau cherry, wild cherry, wild black cherry, rum cherry, whiskey cherry, New England mahogany

Description

The heartwood can vary in colour from reddish-brown to either deep red or a lighter red-brown. It normally has brown flecks and small gum pockets. There can be marked colour variations between boards. The narrow sapwood is whitish- to reddish-brown, sometimes tending to creamy-pink. American cherry has a fine, straight, close grain, a smooth texture and a rich satiny lustre. It can be found with dark wavy streaks. Quartersawn wood sometimes shows beautiful figure.
Typical dry weight: 36lb/ft³ (580kg/m³)
Specific gravity: .58

Properties

The wood has medium strength and resistance to shock loads, low stiffness and good bending properties. It steam-bends well, and has been compared to beech and ash (*Fagus, Fraxinus* spp.) in this regard. It works well with hand and machine tools, and glues, nails, screws and polishes well. American cherry turns, planes and moulds well, with a moderate blunting effect on tool edges. Exposure to ultraviolet light can change the wood to a mahogany colour.

Seasoning

It dries fairly quickly, but fast drying can cause severe warping. Shrinkage is common, and ring shake can occur. It is dimensionally stable in service.

Durability

The wood is moderately durable and the heartwood is very resistant to decay, though the sapwood is vulnerable to attack from the common furniture beetle. The heartwood is moderately resistant to preservative treatment.

Typical uses

Furniture, cabinetmaking, quality joinery, turnery, carving, musical instruments including pianos and violin bows, decorative veneers.

Grows
Canada and USA
Typical height: 80ft (24m)
Trunk diameter: 2ft (0.6m)

⚠ **Possible health risks**
Wheezing and giddiness

▼ Writing desk

DOUGLAS FIR
Pseudotsuga menziesii (Pinaceae)

Also called: Oregon pine (USA)**, British Columbian pine, Columbian pine, blue Douglas fir.** Also distinguished by origin: **Colorado, Oregon, Rocky Mountain Douglas fir**

Grows
Canada and USA; also introduced in UK, Ireland, New Zealand, Australia, France and Belgium
Typical height: 80–200ft (24–60m), but can reach 300ft (90m) in North America
Trunk diameter: 2–5ft (0.6–1.5m)

⚠ Possible health risks
Dermatitis, nasal cancer, rhinitis, respiratory problems; splinters are liable to become septic

Description
The sapwood can be whitish to pale yellow or reddish-white, and varies in thickness. The heartwood is variable in colour, with a very marked contrast between earlywood and latewood. The summerwood is harder and red-brown, whereas the springwood is softer and a paler pinkish-yellow. The grain is normally straight, and can be even or uneven; sometimes it is wavy or curly. Wood with narrow rings has a more uniform texture than that with wider rings, which are often uneven.
Typical dry weight: 33lb/ft³ (530kg/m³)
Specific gravity: .53

Properties
It has high crushing and stiffness strength, high bending strength and medium resistance to shock loads. Wood from the Pacific coast is tougher, harder and stronger than that from other areas. It works very well with hand and machine tools, but does have a blunting effect on cutters. It planes, nails, screws, turns and glues very well. It has poor painting and varnishing qualities, but stains satisfactorily.

Seasoning
Due to the low moisture content of the heartwood, the wood dries quickly and readily. There can be problems with staining from extractives, and occasionally with honeycombing and ring failure.

Durability
Douglas fir has little resistance to decay, and is vulnerable to attack from longhorn and jewel beetles. The heartwood is resistant to preservative treatment, and the sapwood has adequate absorption.

Typical uses
It produces more plywood than any other timber, and vast quantities of veneer. It is also used for structural beams, building, domestic and factory flooring, formwork, packing cases, marine piling, interior and exterior joinery, cabins, vats and railway sleepers (railroad ties).

◀ 'Waves' carving

MUNINGA

Pterocarpus angolensis (Leguminosae)

Also called: mninga, bloodwood, brown African padauk, mukwa, kiaat, kajat, ambila

Description

The sapwood, which is clearly defined from the heartwood, is grey or yellow. The heartwood can have a wide range of colours, from golden-brown through chocolate-brown to purple-brown, with darker irregular reddish streaks. The grain can range from straight to interlocked, with a medium to coarse texture. It can have attractive striped, wavy or mottled figure, but lacks lustre. Small white spots sometimes occur in the wood.
Typical dry weight: 39lb/ft³ (620kg/m³)
Specific gravity: .62

Properties

This is a heavy, dense wood which resists wear. It has very low stiffness, low resistance to shock loads, high crushing strength and medium bending strength. Steam-bending qualities are rated as moderate. Muninga works well with hand and machine tools, but does have a moderate blunting effect on cutting edges. A reduced planing angle is advised for stock with interlocked grain, and pre-boring is recommended for nailing. The wood turns, moulds, carves, glues and sands well, and responds well to stains and polishes.

Seasoning

The wood is easy to dry, and shows very little degrade. It has exceptional stability in service.

Durability

The heartwood is highly durable, is resistant to decay, and has a moderate to high resistance to attack by termites and marine borers. The sapwood is vulnerable to the powder-post beetle. The heartwood is resistant to preservative treatment, but the sapwood is adequately permeable.

Typical uses

Furniture including office furniture, quality joinery and turnery, boatbuilding, domestic flooring and parquet. Choice logs are sliced for decorative and architectural veneers.

Grows

Angola, Botswana, Congo, Namibia, South Africa, Tanzania, Zambia, Zimbabwe
Typical height: 40–60ft (12–18m)
Trunk diameter: 1ft 4in–2ft 6in (0.4–0.75m)

⚠ Possible health risks

The sawdust can cause dermatitis, nasal irritation and bronchial asthma

ANDAMAN PADAUK
Pterocarpus dalbergioides (Leguminosae)

Also called: Andaman redwood, padauk, East Indian mahogany, Indian redwood, vermilion wood

Description
The heartwood can vary in colour from a rich crimson through shades of red to brown, often with darker streaks of red, purple or black. On exposure the wood darkens to a deep reddish-brown. It has a rather coarse texture, a high lustre, and an irregular and interlocked grain that can produce a variety of interesting figure, including roe, curly and ribbon.
Typical dry weight: 48lb/ft³ (770kg/m³)
Specific gravity: .77

Properties
The wood is heavy, dense and resistant to wear. It has a high crushing strength, low stiffness and resistance to shock loads, and medium bending strength. It is not suitable for steam bending. It works well with hand tools, but the interlocking grain has a moderate blunting effect. When planing quartersawn stock, a reduced cutting angle is advised; moulding can be difficult. Pre-boring

is recommended for nailing. The wood saws, turns, glues, screws and sands well, and can be brought to a good polish.

Seasoning
It dries well and rapidly with little degrade, especially if standing trees are girdled and allowed to dry before felling. The wood has very good dimensional stability.

Durability
The heartwood is very durable and moderately resistant to termites and other insects; it can last up to 25 years in contact with the ground. The sapwood is vulnerable to pinhole borers, and is permeable for preservative treatment, but the heartwood is fairly resistant.

Typical uses
Office and domestic furniture, quality joinery, exterior joinery, billiard or pool tables, bank counters, decks, parquet flooring, shingles, shipbuilding and vehicle bodies. It is also sliced for decorative veneer and plywood.

Grows
Andaman Islands
Typical height: 80–120ft (24–37m)
Trunk diameter: 2–4ft (0.6–1.2m)

⚠ **Possible health risks**
The sawdust can cause itching, swollen eyelids, nasal irritation and vomiting

Curved cabinet ▶

AMBOYNA

Pterocarpus indicus (Leguminosae)

Also called: Philippines or Solomons padauk, Papua New Guinea rosewood, yaya sa, narra; red narra, yellow narra (USA), **sena, angsena**

Description

The light straw-coloured sapwood contrasts with the heartwood, which varies from light yellow to golden-yellow to brick-red. Amboyna from Cagayan in the Philippines is usually somewhat heavier and harder, and blood-red in colour. The colour darkens on exposure to air and light. The figure can be mottled, fiddleback, ripple or curly due to wavy, crossed and irregular grain. Flatsawn surfaces can have a flame figure, and quartersawn surfaces may show ribbon figure. Amboyna has a moderately fine to moderately coarse texture and is fairly lustrous.

Typical dry weight: 41lb/ft³ (660kg/m³)
Specific gravity: .66

Properties

Amboyna has medium strength in all categories, with moderate steam-bending properties. It works well with hand tools, and is good for carving and turning; the dulling effect on cutters is only slight. It can be nailed and glued satisfactorily, and screwed easily; it stains and polishes well. Curiously enough, amboyna shavings are said to turn water fluorescent blue.

Seasoning

It dries fairly slowly but with little degrade; the red wood takes longer to season than the yellow. It is very stable in use.

Durability

The wood is highly durable and very resistant to termites and other insects. It resists preservative treatment.

Typical uses

Furniture; high-quality joinery and flooring, including parquet; interior trim, carving, turnery; parts of musical instruments, including pianos and violin bows; rustic furniture and sports goods. The wood is also sliced to make decorative veneers. Amboyna burr (burl) is particularly valued for a range of decorative uses.

▲ Amboyna burr (burl)

Grows
East Indies, the Philippines
Typical height: 130ft (40m)
Trunk diameter: 3ft (1m)

⚠ **Possible health risks**
Dermatitis, asthma, nausea

◀ Natural-edged vessel

BURMA PADAUK

Pterocarpus macrocarpus (Leguminosae)

Also called: mai pradoo, pradoo, pterocarpus

Grows
Burma (Myanmar), Laos,
Philippines, Thailand,
Vietnam
Typical height: 80ft (24m)
Trunk diameter: 2–3ft
(0.6–0.9m)

⚠ **Possible health risks**
Dermatitis, asthma and nasal
irritation

Description
The heartwood of Burma padauk is
yellowish-red to brick-red, with occasional
darker lines. On exposure it turns to a
golden-brown and loses its initial lustre.
The sapwood is narrow and greyish-white.
Typically, the grain is interlocked, with a
moderately coarse or medium texture and
a medium to high lustre. Quartersawn
stock sometimes shows a handsome
ribbon-striped figure.
Typical dry weight: 53lb/ft³ (850kg/m³)
Specific gravity: .85

Properties
Burma padauk is a hard, heavy, dense and
strong wood with very high bending and
crushing strengths, and is much stronger
than Andaman padauk (*P. dalbergioides*).
It is hard to work with hand tools, and
sawing dry stock is difficult. The wood has
a moderate blunting effect on cutting
edges, and pre-boring is required for
nailing and screwing. Machine-planing
requires a reduced cutting angle, and
carving, moulding and boring qualities
are poor. It glues and sands well, and can
be brought to a high natural polish.
Despite its difficult working properties in
other operations, it turns excellently.

Seasoning
The wood generally dries well with little
degrade, but does tend to suffer from
surface checking. It is very stable in use.

Durability
The heartwood is highly durable, and
extremely resistant to preservative
treatment, which is not really necessary
in any case. The sapwood is vulnerable to
the powder-post beetle, and is moderately
resistant to preservative treatment.

Typical uses
Furniture and cabinetmaking, flooring,
bank and shop fittings, boat frames,
billiard or pool tables and cues, oil
presses and tool handles. Burma padauk
is also sliced for decorative veneers.

AFRICAN PADAUK

Pterocarpus soyauxii (Leguminosae)

Also called: barwood, bosulu, camwood, corail, mbe, mututi, ngula

Description

The heartwood is a vivid reddish-orange when freshly cut, but changes over time to bright red, red or coral-pink with dark streaks. It can darken further to a reddish or purplish brown or black. The colour fades with age. The grain can range from straight to interlocked, with a fine to medium texture and a natural sheen. When newly cut, the sapwood, which is clearly demarcated from the heartwood, is white, but it turns to grey or brownish-yellow when exposed to light.

Typical dry weight: 45lb/ft³ (720kg/m³)
Specific gravity: .72

Properties

A heavy and dense wood, it has high bending and crushing strengths, with medium stiffness and resistance to shock loads, and high resistance to abrasion. It is not suitable for steam bending. African padauk works well despite its density, with only a slight blunting effect on cutting edges. It planes, moulds, turns, bores, sands and carves well. Small stock is liable to split when nailing or screwing, so pre-boring is advisable. It glues very well and can be brought to an excellent polished finish. It also weathers very well.

Seasoning

It dries with almost no degrade and shows negligible movement in service.

Durability

The heartwood is highly durable. It is resistant to termite attack and can last over 25 years in contact with the ground, even without any protective treatment. The heartwood is quite resistant to preservative treatment, and the sapwood is moderately resistant.

Typical uses

Quality furniture and joinery, cabinetmaking, office furniture, heavy-duty and parquet flooring, tool and knife handles, shuttles and sporting goods. It is also sliced for decorative veneers.

Grows

Tropical West and Central Africa
Typical height: 100–130ft (30–40m)
Trunk diameter: 2–4ft (0.6–1.2m) or wider

⚠ Possible health risks

Sawdust can cause skin and respiratory problems, swelling of the eyelids, itching and vomiting

Hollow form ▶

AFRICAN PTERYGOTA

Pterygota bequaertii and *P. macrocarpa* (Sterculiaceae)

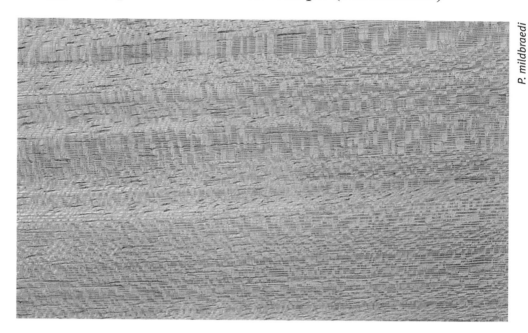

P. mildbraedi

Also called: ake, anatolia, awari, efok, impa, kefe, koto, poroposo

Description

The pale yellow sapwood is not clearly demarcated from the heartwood, which is creamy-white to pale yellow with a greyish tinge. The wood is usually straight-grained or shallowly interlocked, and sometimes includes small knot clusters. It is typically fairly coarse-textured and lustrous. Quartersawn surfaces show a marked fleck figure produced by the strong medullary rays.

Typical dry weight: *P. bequaertii* 41lb/ft³ (650kg/m³), *P. macrocarpa* 35lb/ft³ (560kg/m³)

Specific gravity: .65 and .56 respectively

Properties

Pterygota is heavy and dense. It has low stiffness, medium to low resistance to shock loads, medium crushing and bending strength, and a poor rating for steam bending. The wood works fairly well with hand tools and is easy to work with machine tools, but blades must be kept sharp. A reduced cutting angle is advised when planing irregular-grained stock, and it has only a slight blunting effect on cutting edges. It glues, nails, sands and polishes well, and turns, moulds, mortises and routs fairly well.

Seasoning

The wood dries easily and fairly rapidly. It may surface-check, distort and cup moderately. It exhibits medium movement in use.

Durability

It is not durable, with little natural resistance to decay. The sapwood is vulnerable to attack from termites, marine borers and powder-post beetles. The sapwood is permeable for preservative treatment, and the heartwood is moderately so.

Typical uses

Furniture and cabinetmaking, furniture components, kitchen cabinets, interior joinery, boxes and crates, corestock and plywood. Character logs are sliced for decorative veneer.

Grows
Tropical West Africa
Typical height: 120–135ft (37–40m)
Trunk diameter: 2–4ft (0.6–1.2m)

⚠ **Possible health risks**
Not known

PEAR

Pyrus communis (Rosaceae)

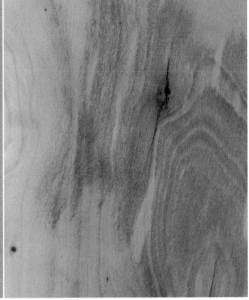

Also called: pearwood, common pear, peartree, wild pear, choke pear, poirier (French), **Birnbaum** (German)

Description

The heartwood ranges from pale flesh tones to a light pinkish-brown (which may be enhanced by steaming), and has fine pores and rays. The grain is usually straight and the wood has a characteristically fine, even and smooth texture. A mottled figure may sometimes be present on quartersawn surfaces.

Typical dry weight: 44lb/ft³ (700kg/m³)
Specific gravity: .70

Properties

Pear is tough and stable, but, since it is normally available only in small sections, structural strength categories are not of great relevance. The wood is not used for steam bending. It works well overall, but has a moderate blunting effect on cutting edges, and sawing can be difficult. It plancs, sands, nails and screws well, has very good turning qualities and carves excellently. It can be polished to a very good finish, and has excellent staining properties. Because of it smooth surface it makes a convincing ebony substitute when dyed black. It also peels well for veneer.

Seasoning

It is a slow-drying wood and will warp and distort if the stacks are not weighted down. Mild kiln-drying is more satisfactory than air-drying. There is very little movement in service.

Durability

It is not durable and has almost no resistance to decay and insect attack, but it is permeable for treatment with preservatives.

Typical uses

Veneers for marquetry, inlay and cabinetmaking; recorders, brush backs, engraving, carving; drawing instruments such as rulers, set squares (triangles) and French curves; tool handles, turnery. It is also dyed black for fingerboards of stringed instruments and for piano keys.

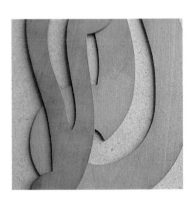

▲ French curves

◄ Carving of edible crab

Grows
Europe, Western Asia and USA
Typical height: 30–40ft (9–12m)
Trunk diameter: 1–2ft (0.3–0.6m)

⚠ **Possible health risks**
Not known

The genus *Quercus*
Oaks

There are in excess of 600 species in the northern hemisphere that come under the genus *Quercus*, including American white oak (*Q. alba* and others), American red oak (*Q. rubra* and others), and those common in northern Europe: common, English or pedunculate oak (*Q. robur*) and sessile or durmast oak (*Q. petraea*).

Of all the woods grown in northern Europe, oak probably has the most historical, architectural and cultural interest – especially, perhaps, in Britain, where it is said to be the most common broadleaved woodland tree. There are ancient oak trees that could be up to 800 years old, and it is quite common for oaks to live 300 years. Acorns are not normally produced until the tree is over 40 years old, with maximum output between 80 and 120 years.

There is evidence that oak was used for building as much as 9,000 years ago in Germany and 7,000 years ago in Ireland. Since medieval times oak has had a great impact on building in much of Europe, with timber-framed construction dominant until the late seventeenth century. Oak was the principal material used for furniture in many homes at that time, and has remained a key joinery, cabinetmaking and building material ever since. Today green oak is used for exposed timber framing on specialist new housing, and seasoned oak for furniture making and cooperage.

Oak was prized for shipbuilding, and was the foundation of most navies until the introduction of iron ships in the nineteenth century. It is said that over 2,000 oak trees were used in the construction of HMS *Victory*, the flagship of British admiral Horatio Nelson at the Battle of Trafalgar in 1805 – which means that something like 54,000 oak trees were used to make the 27 British ships that took part in the battle, and well over 100,000 trees if you include the opposing French and

▲ *Top:* Carved fragment in European oak, provenance unknown

▲ *Above:* Of the two species native to northern Europe, the English or pedunculate oak (*Q. robur*) tends to have the more gnarled and meandering appearance

▶ *Right:* Suspended cabinet in plain and brown oak

Spanish fleets. HMS *Victory* still exists today, and can be visited at Portsmouth Historic Dockyard on the south coast of England.

It is estimated that 90,000 tons of oak bark a year, which required the felling of 500,000 tons of oak, were used for tanning in the second decade of the nineteenth century. This was a far greater amount than was used in both naval and mercantile shipping at the time.

▲ *Above:* A new oak-framed house under construction using traditional methods

▲ *Above right:* Carving dated 1596 on Harvard House, Stratford-upon-Avon, England

▶ *Right:* In much of northern Europe, oak is the preferred material for church fittings. This bench-end has the type of Gothic finial known as a 'poppyhead'

AMERICAN WHITE OAK

Quercus alba and related species (Fagaceae)

Also called: Arizona oak, stave oak, roble. 'White oak' includes many species with similar characteristics, such as **Q. prinus, Q. lobata** and **Q. michauxii**

▲ Drawer: side in white oak, front in Brazilian mahogany (*Swietenia macrophylla*)

Grows

Eastern Canada and USA
Typical height: 80–100ft (25–30m)
Trunk diameter: 3–4ft (0.9–1.2m)

⚠ **Possible health risks**

Asthma, sneezing and irritation to nose and eyes; nasal cancer

Description

The heartwood can vary in colour from light tan or pale yellow-brown to dark or pale brown, and can have a pinkish tint. The wood usually has a straight, open grain, and is medium to coarse in texture. It has longer rays than red oak (*Q. rubra* and related species), and therefore displays more figure, which can include swirls, crotch pattern, burrs (burls) and a tiger-ray flake pattern. The sapwood is whitish to light brown, and varies in width.
Typical dry weight: 47lb/ft³ (760kg/m³)
Specific gravity: .76

Properties

White oak is a hard and heavy wood. It has medium crushing and bending strength, and low stiffness. The wood has excellent steam-bending properties, is almost waterproof, and has exceptional resistance to wear. It has a moderate blunting effect on cutting edges, but generally works well, though this depends on the precise species used. The wood planes, turns, bores, sands, mortises, stains and polishes well. Pre-boring is advised for nailing and screwing, and it glues satisfactorily. The tannin content can react with ferrous metals to cause iron staining.

Seasoning

It is slow-drying and difficult to season. End and surface checks, honeycombing, collapse, ring failure and iron staining can occur whilst drying. The wood displays medium movement in service.

Durability

The heartwood is resistant to decay, but the wood can be attacked by ambrosia beetles and other insects. The heartwood is resistant to preservative treatment, and the sapwood moderately so.

Typical uses

Furniture and cabinetmaking, joinery, office furniture, boatbuilding, trim, panelling, flooring, cooperage for wine and whisky, coffins, shingles, sleepers (railroad ties); also sliced for figured veneers and rotary-cut for plywood.

JAPANESE OAK

Quercus mongolica and related species (Fagaceae)

Q. mongolica var. grosseserrata

Also called: Manchurian oak, Mongolian oak, ohnara; also closely related species: **konara, kashiwa, shira-kashi, aka-gashi, ichii-gashi**

Description

Japanese oak is typically paler than European and American oaks. The heartwood is a pale biscuit colour, and the wood from Honshu has a pinkish hue. It is typically straight-grained, knot-free, and with a coarse texture. When quartersawn, the medullary rays produce an attractive figure. Trees from Hokkaido are reputed to produce a better quality of timber than those from Honshu, as they grow more slowly and evenly.

Typical dry weight: 41lb/ft³ (660kg/m³)
Specific gravity: .66

Properties

Japanese oak is of medium strength for bending and crushing, with low resistance to shock loads and low stiffness. It has very good steam-bending characteristics. It is easier to work by hand than other white oaks, and has only a slight dulling effect on cutting edges. It glues, planes, nails and screws well, has very good staining qualities, and can be brought to an excellent polished finish.

Seasoning

It dries slowly with little degrade, and shows medium movement in service.

Durability

The heartwood is naturally resistant to attack by decay-causing fungi, but the sapwood is susceptible to attack from beetles. The sapwood is permeable for preservative treatment.

Typical uses

Furniture and cabinetmaking, joinery, interior construction, boatbuilding, flooring blocks, panelling and charcoal. It is rotary-cut for plywood and sliced for decorative veneer.

Grows

Japan
Typical height: 100ft (30m)
Trunk diameter: 3ft (1m)

⚠ Possible health risks

Dermatitis, sneezing, nasal cancer

EUROPEAN OAK

Quercus robur and *Q. petraea* (Fagaceae)

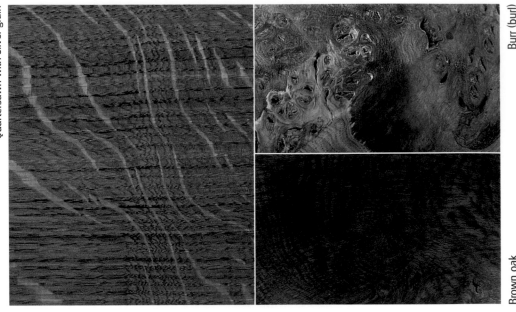

Quartersawn with silver grain

Burr (burl)

Brown oak

Syn. for *Q. robur*: *Q. pedunculata*; for *Q. petraea*: *Q. sessiliflora*
Also called: English oak, common oak, pendunculate oak (*Q. robur*); sessile oak, durmast oak (*Q. petraea*); chêne (French), Eiche, Stieleiche (German). Also by place of origin: English, French, Baltic, Slavonian, etc.

▲ Mule chest detail

Grows
Europe, Turkey, North Africa; also south-eastern Canada and north-eastern USA
Typical height: 60–100ft (18–30m)
Trunk diameter: 4–6ft (1.2–1.8m)

⚠ Possible health risks
Sneezing, dermatitis and nasal cancer

Description
Depending on origin, the heartwood varies from light tan to biscuit or deep brown, with distinct bands of earlywood and latewood. The grain is usually straight, but irregular or cross grain can occur. The texture is coarse, and rays and growth rings show an attractive figure ('silver grain') when quartersawn. Fungal attack in the growing tree results in **brown oak**.
Typical dry weight: 45lb/ft³ (720kg/m³), varying with species
Specific gravity: .72

Properties
The wood is fairly hard, heavy and dense, with high crushing and bending strength, low stiffness and resistance to shock loads. It is very good for steam-bending. It is fairly hard to work with hand tools, with a moderate to severe blunting effect. Pre-boring is advised for nailing and screwing, and a reduced planing angle for irregular or cross-grained stock. It turns satisfactorily, is good for gluing, painting,

sanding, staining and varnishing, and will take a high polish. It can be darkened by fuming with ammonia. The tannin content may corrode ferrous metals.

Seasoning
Drying is slow, with a tendency to check, split, warp and honeycomb; shrinkage is high. Movement in service is medium.

Durability
The heartwood is durable and highly resistant to preservatives. The sapwood is permeable, and vulnerable to powder-post and common furniture beetles.

Typical uses
Furniture and cabinetmaking, quality joinery including church pews and pulpits, office furniture, kitchen cabinets, flooring including parquet, coffins, boats and harbour work, truck bodies. Also cooperage for wines, cognac and beer. Oak is sliced for decorative veneers, and rotary-cut for plywood.

AMERICAN RED OAK

Quercus rubra and related species (Fagaceae)

Also called: northern red oak, red oak, Canadian red oak, grey oak; also sold with **southern red oak** or **Spanish oak (*Q. falcata*)** as 'red oak'

Description

The heartwood has a biscuit to pinkish- or reddish-brown colour. Red oak is similar in appearance to white oak, but has smaller rays, which results in a less pronounced figure. The grain is usually straight and open, but can vary. It generally has a coarse texture, but this can also vary depending on the origin of the tree. Quartersawn stock can have a flake pattern that is sometimes referred to as 'butterflies' or 'tiger rays'. The sapwood is white to light brown.
Typical dry weight: 48lb/ft³ (770kg/m³)
Specific gravity: .77

Properties

It is heavy and hard, with medium stiffness and bending strength and a high crushing strength. It steam-bends very well, and is very hard-wearing. The wood works well with sharp hand and machine tools. It has a moderate blunting effect on cutting edges, but can be planed, sawn, turned, bored and sanded well. Pre-boring is advised for screwing and nailing, and it glues satisfactorily. Red oak takes stain and polishes well, and can be limed to good effect.

Seasoning

The wood dries slowly and is fairly difficult to season. There can be problems with end-grain checking, ring failure, honeycombing and iron stains. It is moderately stable in service.

Durability

Red oak has little resistance to attack from decay-causing organisms and insects. The heartwood has moderate resistance to preservative treatment, whereas the sapwood is permeable.

Typical uses

Furniture and cabinetmaking, interior joinery, boatbuilding, domestic flooring including parquet, organ pipes, dry cooperage, railway sleepers (railroad ties) and vehicle construction. American red oak is sliced for decorative veneers and rotary-cut for plywood.

Grows
Eastern Canada and USA; also grown in Iran, Europe and UK
Typical height: 60–90ft (18–27m)
Trunk diameter: 3ft (1m)

⚠ **Possible health risks**
Asthma, sneezing, irritation to eyes and nose, nasal cancer

ROBINIA

Robinia pseudoacacia (Leguminosae)

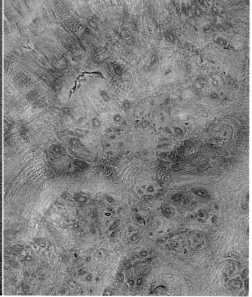

Burr (burl)

Also called: black locust, false acacia, locust, yellow locust; robinier, faux acacia (French); **Akazie, Robinie** (German); **valse acacia** (Dutch)

Hollow form in robinia burr (burl) ▶

Description
The heartwood ranges
from greenish-yellow
to dark or golden
brown, sometimes
with a green tinge. It
darkens on exposure
to a golden-brown or
russet. The wood has a
prominent straight grain
and a coarse texture, with
marked contrast between the dense
latewood and large-pored earlywood.
The narrow sapwood is yellow.
Typical dry weight: 45lb/ft³ (720kg/m³),
but varies markedly
Specific gravity: .72

Properties
It is a tough and durable wood with
medium crushing and bending strength,
low stiffness and resistance to shock
loads, and very good steam-bending
qualities. The wood is fairly difficult to
work with both hand and machine tools,
and has a moderate blunting effect on
cutting edges, but a clean finish can be
achieved. Pre-boring is advised for nailing,
and screwing properties are
poor. It glues easily, stains
satisfactorily, and can be
polished to a high finish.

Seasoning
Robinia is slow-drying
and prone to warp or
distort badly; there can be
both end and surface checking.
The wood shows medium
movement in use.

Durability
The heartwood has natural resistance to
decay, but the sapwood is vulnerable to
the common furniture and powder-post
beetles. The heartwood is extremely
resistant to preservative treatment.

Typical uses
Quality stock is used for cabinetmaking
and joinery, and sliced for decorative
veneer. Other uses include boat planking,
woodenware, gates, stakes, posts, casks,
propellers, bearings and bushings,
weatherboards, fencing, boxes, skids,
pulleys and vehicle bodies.

WILLOW

Salix spp. (Salicaceae)

Also called: white willow, common willow (*S. alba*); cricket-bat or close-bark willow (*S. alba* var. *coerulea*); crack willow (*S. fragilis*); black willow, Gooding willow, Dudley willow (*S. nigra*), saule (French), **Weide** (German). There are about 350 species

S. alba

Description

Willow has a whitish sapwood of variable thickness, and a white to pinkish heartwood. It is usually straight-grained, with a fine and even texture. Black willow (*S. nigra*) has heartwood ranging from pale reddish-brown to greyish-brown, with an interlocked grain.
Typical dry weight: 28lb/ft³ (450kg/m³), but can be lighter.
Specific gravity: .45

Properties

Willow is light, but flexible and resilient. Its strength properties are low and it has a poor steam-bending rating. It works easily by hand or machine, with only a slight blunting effect on cutting edges. When planing, a reduced angle and very sharp blades are advised to avoid a woolly finish. Willow turns, moulds, bores, routs, carves and sands well, provided sharp cutters are used. It nails and screws very well, has excellent gluing qualities, and can be brought to a high finish.

Seasoning

The wood dries fairly quickly with minimal degrade, but it can retain pockets of moisture. Crack willow (*S. fragilis*) can split badly when drying. There is small movement in use.

Durability

Willow is not durable, and has very little resistance to either decay or insect attack. The sapwood is vulnerable to both the common furniture and powder-post beetles. The sapwood is permeable for preservative treatment, but the heartwood is resistant.

Typical uses

Cricket bats from selected cricket-bat willow; artificial limbs, flooring, sieve frames, trugs (gardeners' baskets), boxes and crates, dry cooperage and corestock. It is also sliced for decorative veneer, as it can have a mottled or moiré figure. Willow osiers (pliable branches) are used for baskets and wickerwork.

Grows
Europe, western and central Asia, North Africa and North America
Typical height: 70–90ft (21–27m)
Trunk diameter: 3–4ft (0.9–1.2m)

⚠ **Possible health risks**
Sensitizer. Those who are allergic to aspirin could also be allergic to willow

SASSAFRAS

Sassafras officinale and *S. albidum* (Lauraceae)

Also called: cinnamon wood, red sassafras, black ash, golden elm, saxifrax tree, aguetree

S. albidum

Grows
USA
Typical height: 40–90ft
(12–27m)
Trunk diameter: 2–5ft
(0.6–1.5m)

⚠ **Possible health risks**
Sensitizer; irritation of skin and
respiratory system; suspected
carcinogen

Description
The heartwood is pale brown, but on
exposure darkens to a dull orange-brown;
the sapwood is light yellow and gradually
merges into the heartwood. It is typically
straight-grained, with a coarse texture and
a medium lustre. It has an interesting
grain pattern and is sometimes compared
with ash or chestnut (*Fraxinus*, *Castanea*
spp.), but is softer.
Typical dry weight: 28lb/ft³ (450kg/m³)
Specific gravity: .45

Properties
Sassafras is rated medium in all categories
apart from stiffness, for which it is rated
low; it is suitable for steam bending. It
works well with both hand and machine
tools, and can be planed to a good clean
surface. Pre-boring is advised for nailing,
but it screws, glues and finishes well.

Seasoning
It seasons without difficulty, but can be
subject to slight checking. There is small
movement in use.

Durability
It is moderately durable, has a high
natural resistance to decay, and is
moderately resistant to preservative
treatment. The sapwood is vulnerable to
attack by the powder-post beetle, and is
permeable for preservative treatment.

Typical uses
Furniture, window frames, doors,
mouldings, boatbuilding, kitchen
cabinets, boxes and crates, millwork,
posts, fencing and dry cooperage. Choice
logs are sliced for decorative veneer.

QUEBRACHO

Schinopsis spp. (Anacardiaceae)

S. haenkeana

Also called: quebracho macho, quebracho hembra, quebracho moro, quebracho colorado, quebracho chaqueno, quebracho santiagueno, brauna, baruana

Description

The heartwood is light red when first cut, but deepens to a uniform brick-red on exposure to light and air; it sometimes has black streaks. Quebracho has an irregular grain with a fine, uniform texture and a low lustre. The heartwood has a high tannin content. The sapwood is yellowish and is not sharply demarcated from the heartwood.

Typical dry weight: 62lb/ft^3 (1000kg/m^3)
Specific gravity: 1.00

Properties

Quebracho is extremely hard and heavy; its name derives from 'break axe' in Spanish. The wood is very hard to work when dry, since it tends to split, and is difficult to work in most machining operations. It can, however, be brought to a very highly polished finish.

Seasoning

It is a very difficult wood to dry, with severe checking and warping, especially on the thinner boards.

Durability

The wood is highly durable when dry, with a high natural resistance to attack from wood-destroying insects and decay. However, the bark must be removed immediately after felling, or beetles may deposit their eggs in it, which leads to destruction of the log.

Typical uses

Previously used for tannin extraction, the wood is now used in South America for construction, posts, railway sleepers (railroad ties), wood-block paving and fuel. It is also hand-carved into small decorative items, which are sold as typical Argentine craft.

◀ Anonymous carving from Argentina: heads in quebracho, bodies palo santo (*Bulnesia sarmientoi*)

Grows

Argentina, Bolivia, Brazil, Paraguay
Typical height: 30–50ft (9–15m)
Trunk diameter: 1–2ft (0.3–0.6m)

⚠ Possible health risks

Dermatitis, respiratory and nasal irritation, nausea, malaise; a possible carcinogen

SEQUOIA (REDWOOD)
Sequoia sempervirens (Taxodiaceae)

Also called: Californian redwood, redwood, coast redwood; burrs (burls) are marketed as **vavona burr (burl).** This is not the giant redwood or wellingtonia (*Sequoiadendron giganteum*, syn. *Sequoia gigantica*), which is not usually used for commercial timber

Description
The heartwood ranges from light cherry-red to dark reddish-brown; the sapwood is near-white or pale yellow. Sequoia is straight-grained with a fine to coarse texture, and the contrasting earlywood and latewood form a clear growth-ring figure. Interesting burrs (burls) up to 6ft (1.8m) in diameter are fairly common.
Typical dry weight: 26lb/ft³ (420kg/m³)
Specific gravity: .42

Hollow form in sequoia burr (burl) ▶

Properties
Sequoia can vary widely in its strength properties. Typically, it has at best very low stiffness and low strength for resistance to shock loads, bending and crushing. Steam-bending is poor. It works easily with both machine and hand tools, and has little blunting effect on cutters. Very sharp cutters are advised when machining, to reduce splintering and chip bruising. It does not hold nails and screws well, but planes, mortises, turns, bores and moulds well. The wood glues very well, but alkaline adhesives may cause staining. Sequoia takes paint very well and can be brought to a good finish.

Seasoning
Although the tree holds a lot of water when felled, the wood dries quickly and easily with minimal degrade. It exhibits small movement in use.

Durability
The wood is durable and very resistant to most insects and fungi. The heartwood is notably durable in moist conditions, and takes preservative treatment fairly well.

Typical uses
Rustic furniture and flooring, exterior joinery, cladding (siding), shingles, vats, coffins, posts, wine casks, fencing and decking. The bark is used for particleboard. The wood is rotary-cut for plywood, and select logs are sliced for veneers. Vavona burr (burl) is prized for its decorative qualities.

Grows
California and Oregon, USA
Typical height: 200–325ft (60–100m)
Trunk diameter: 10–15ft (3–4.6m). A typical lifespan can be 800 years or more

---

⚠ Possible health risks
Asthma, wheezing, dermatitis, nasal cancer and hypersensitivity pneumonia; the dust is a respiratory irritant

WHITE LAUAN ✍

Shorea contorta (Dipterocarpaceae)

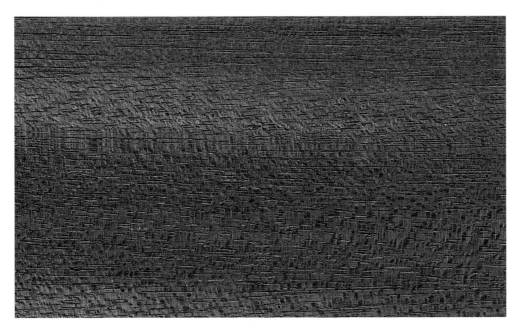

Syn.: *Pentacme contorta*
Also called: light red lauan, meranti bunga, perawan, light red meranti. Lauan is one of a group that includes **light and dark red meranti** and **seraya,** all within the extensive genus *Shorea*

Description

The heartwood can be grey with a pinkish tinge, or pale pink to red. The grain is normally interlocked or crossed, and has a moderately coarse texture. It ranges from slightly lustrous to lustrous in appearance, and usually contains resin streaks and oil.
Typical dry weight: 33lb/ft³ (540kg/m³)
Specific gravity: .54

Properties

White lauan has medium crushing and bending strength, combined with low shock resistance and low stiffness.
It has a good steam-bending classification. The wood generally works well, but a reduced cutting angle is recommended when machine-planing specimens with interlocked grain. There is only a slight blunting effect on cutting edges. White lauan is usually easy to turn, bore and carve. It glues and polishes well, and is rated as satisfactory for screwing, nailing and staining.

Seasoning

Lauan generally dries easily with little degrade. Thin stock can, however, warp, and thick material may suffer surface checking. There is only small movement in service.

Durability

The wood has poor to moderate resistance to decay, and the sapwood is vulnerable to attack from the common furniture beetle. The heartwood can be resistant to preservative treatment, but the sapwood is fairly permeable.

Typical uses

Furniture and cabinetmaking, joinery, kitchen cabinets, office furniture, domestic flooring, boat planking, rough construction, veneer and plywood.

Grows
Philippines, Malaysia, Indonesia, Thailand
Typical height: 150–200ft (45–60m)
Trunk diameter: 3–6ft (0.9–1.8m)

⚠ **Possible health risks**
Dermatitis and irritation to the nose, throat and eyes

TAMBOTI

Spirostachys africana (Euphorbiaceae)

Syn.: *Excoecaria africana*
Also called: tambotie, thombothi, tomboti, sandalo, sandalo africano, zunvorre.
Not to be confused by name with Indian and Australian sandalwoods (*Santalum album*, *S. spicatum*)

Grows
Eastern Africa and
Mozambique
Typical height: 60ft (18m)
Trunk diameter: 1ft (0.3m)

⚠ Possible health risks

The bark – removed during dimensioning – exudes a sticky latex sap, which is highly irritant to skin and eyes, and is said to cause blisters and blindness. The sawdust can be harmful to the eyes and may apparently cause blindness. Meat cooked over a fire made from tamboti causes severe diarrhoea with a risk to life

Description

This beautiful wood is richly coloured. The heartwood is dark brown with darker streaks or with bands of light and dark reddish honey-browns. The figure can also be mottled and banded, sometimes exhibiting visible growth rings. The narrow sapwood has a light, creamy butter colour, making a fine contrast with the heartwood. The grain is generally straight, but can be interlocked or wavy. Tamboti is lustrous and has a powerful scent that persists a long time after the wood is cut. An item of furniture made from tamboti can scent a room for quite a long time.
Typical dry weight: 65lb/ft³ (1041kg/m³)
Specific gravity: 1.04

Properties

This is a heavy, strong and dense wood. When dry it is easy to saw, and planes well if care is taken. It requires pre-boring for nailing and screwing, and generally glues slowly. Tamboti's oily nature makes sanding difficult, but it does take a high polish and can be varnished. The wood turns very well, and is very suitable for decorative items.

Seasoning

Tamboti dries very slowly without distortion.

Durability

Tamboti is highly durable and resistant to fungal and insect attack. The heartwood is resistant to impregnation.

Typical uses

Being quite a rare wood, it is used for decorative items, high-quality furniture and turnery. Traditionally it is also used for hut rafters, fencing, walking sticks and necklaces.

NIOVÉ

Staudtia stipitata (Myristicaceae)

Syn.: *S. gabonensis*
Also called: African cherry, kamashi, oropa, ekop, m'bonda, m'boun, nikafi. The name
'African cherry' is also applied to makoré (*Tieghemella heckelii*) and to *Prunus africanus*,
a non-commercial wood

Description
The heartwood is red-brown to yellow-brown and can have darker streaks. The sapwood is quite wide and is typically pale yellow to orange-brown. Niové has a very fine, straight grain that is slightly lustrous. It can be oily. The wood has a peppery scent. With the appropriate finish it closely resembles American or black cherry (*Prunus serotina*).
Typical dry weight: 51lb/ft³ (830kg/m³)
Specific Gravity: .83

Properties
Although a hard, dense wood, it is fairly easy to work with both hand and machine tools. To avoid splitting, pre-boring is advised for nailing and screwing. It glues satisfactorily, but its natural oil content can cause problems unless the surface is properly prepared. Niové sands to a clean, smooth finish and polishes well, especially with wax. Quartersawing is recommended.

Seasoning
The wood seasons slowly with little warping, but care is required to avoid end-checking and shakes; very slow kiln-drying is advised. Niové exhibits only small movement in service.

Durability
It has excellent durability and is resistant to insect attack, including termites, and to decay. Niové is extremely resistant to preservative treatment. Its durability makes it very good for external joinery and structural work.

Typical uses
Cabinetmaking, external and internal joinery, turnery, heavy-duty flooring and decorative veneers. Used as a substitute for American cherry (*Prunus serotina*).

Grows
Central West Africa, particularly Gabon, Cameroon and Congo region
Typical height: 70–100ft (22–30m), sometimes taller.
Trunk diameter: 3ft (0.9m)

⚠ **Possible health risks**
Not known

AMERICAN MAHOGANY
Swietenia macrophylla and *S. mahagoni* (Meliaceae)

Also called: zopilote gateado, acahou, mogno, big-leaf mahogany, caoba, aguano, baywood; also often distinguished by country of origin: **Central American, Brazilian, Honduras, Cuban, Costa Rican** etc.

▲ Breakfront bookcase detail

Grows
Central America and northern South America
Typical height: 150ft (45m)
Trunk diameter: 6ft (1.8m)

⚠ Possible health risks
Dermatitis, respiratory problems, irritation, giddiness, vomiting and furunculosis

Description
The wood can vary considerably in colour. When freshly cut it may be yellowish, reddish, pinkish or salmon-pink. It matures to a deep rich red or brown with time. The grain ranges from straight to roey, curly or wavy. Grain irregularities produce very attractive figure such as mottle, stripe or roe, blister and fiddleback. It has a fine or medium to coarse uniform texture, and white deposits or dark gum may show in the pores. American mahogany is highly lustrous and golden.
Typical dry weight: 36lb/ft³ (590kg/m³), but with wide variation
Specific gravity: .59

Properties
American mahogany has very low stiffness and resistance to shock loads, and medium crushing strength. Although it has a low bending strength, it steam-bends moderately well. Provided sharp tools are used, it works easily with both hand and machine tools. It screws, nails, glues and stains well, and can be brought to an excellent polished finish.

Seasoning
It dries easily, with minimal degrade in the form of checking or distortion. It is very stable in service.

Durability
The heartwood is very durable and resistant to both white-rot fungi and brown rot. The sapwood is vulnerable to attack from the powder-post and common furniture beetles. The sapwood is resistant to preservative treatment, and the heartwood highly resistant.

Typical uses
High-quality furniture and cabinetmaking, turnery, reproduction furniture, boat interiors, interior joinery and panelling, musical instruments including pianos, canoes and shipbuilding. Very decorative veneers may be obtained.

TURPENTINE

Syncarpia glomulifera (Myrtaceae)

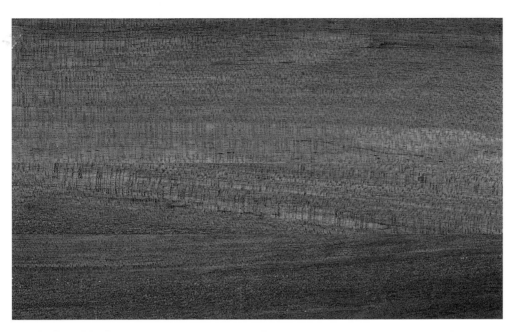

Syn.: *S. laurifolia*
Also called: luster, red luster

Description

The heartwood varies from deep red to deep brown, and the sapwood, which is distinct, is paler. It has a uniform fine- to medium-textured grain, which is often wavy and also frequently interlocked. Turpentine is free from gum veins.
Typical dry weight: 61lb/ft³ (995kg/m³)
Specific Gravity: .99

Properties

Turpentine is a very hard, tough wood, and due to its high silica content it can have a marked blunting effect on cutting edges. Its high density makes it hard to work with hand tools. It will take fittings and fixings with no problem, and will accept paint, stain and polish readily. Gluing can be problematic and is best done immediately after surface preparation.

Seasoning

Turpentine has a tendency to collapse and distort during drying, so particular care has to be taken.

Durability

The wood is highly resistant to decay in persistently damp or poorly ventilated areas and when in the ground. It has outstanding resistance to marine borers due to its high silica content and the extractives in the wood. Its sapwood is not vulnerable to lyctid borer attack. The sapwood will readily accept preservative treatment, but penetration of the heartwood is negligible. It is one of the world's most resistant timbers to fire damage.

Typical uses

Turpentine is highly valued for marine piling because of its durability. It is also used for joinery, internal, external and parquet flooring, laminated beams, bench tops, boatbuilding, wine casks, house framing, lining, cladding (siding), wharf and bridge construction, mining timbers, railway sleepers (railroad ties) and plywood.

Grows
New South Wales and Queensland, Australia. Also plantation-grown in Hawaii and South Africa
Typical height: 125–160ft (40–50m)
Trunk diameter: 3–4ft (1–1.3m)

⚠ **Possible health risks**
Irritation to mucous membranes

PRIMAVERA

Tabebuia donnell-smithii (Bignoniaceae)

Syn.: *Cybistax donnell-smithii*
Also called: duranga, San Juan, palo blanco, cortez, cortez blanco, roble

Description

Newly cut wood is cream or pale yellow, and darkens on exposure to a yellowish-rose with red, brown and orange stripes. It has a straight, interlocked or wavy grain that can produce interesting ribbon, mottle, raindrop, roey and narrow fiddleback figure. Primavera is fairly lustrous and has a medium to somewhat coarse texture. It can resemble Ceylon satinwood (*Chloroxylon swietenia*).
Typical dry weight: 28lb/ft³ (450kg/m³)
Specific gravity: .45

Properties

The wood has low stiffness, medium strength in resistance to shock loads, bending and crushing, and steam-bends well. Primavera works readily with both machine and hand tools, and has a medium blunting effect on cutting edges. A reduced cutting angle is advised when planing wood with an irregular or interlocked grain. It moulds, bores, mortises, carves, glues, nails, screws, sands, varnishes and stains well, and can be brought to a highly polished finish.

Seasoning

It dries easily with little degrade, but there can be slight warping and checking. There is only small movement in use.

Durability

The wood is not durable, and is vulnerable to decay and to attack by pinhole borers and the common furniture beetle. The sapwood is adequately permeable for preservative treatment, whereas the heartwood is moderately difficult to treat.

Typical uses

Quality furniture and cabinetmaking, office furniture, interior joinery and panelling. Interesting logs are sliced into highly decorative veneers for cabinetwork and panelling.

Grows
Central America
Typical height: 75–100ft
(23–30m)
Trunk diameter: 2–3ft
(0.6–0.9m)

⚠ **Possible health risks**
Not known

IPÊ

Tabebuia serratifolia and *T. ipê* (Bignoniaceae)

Also called: amapa prieta, bastard lignum vitae, bethabara, pau d'arco, ipê tabaco, wassiba, ébano verde, ironwood, Surinam greenheart, lapacho

Description

The sapwood is clearly distinct from the heartwood, and is yellowish-white or white. The heartwood is generally olive-brown, but can be darker, and has darker or lighter streaks. The pores frequently appear as fine yellow dots or lines; this is lapachol powder, which turns deep red in alkaline solutions. The grain is straight to very irregular, with a fine to medium texture and a low to medium lustre.
Typical dry weight: 67lb/ft³ (1080kg/m³), but with wide variation
Specific gravity: 1.08

Properties

Ipê is a strong, dense and heavy wood. It is rated high in all the strength categories except bending, in which it is rated as moderate, and steam bending, which is rated as difficult. It is not easy to work with hand tools, is difficult to saw and requires a very low blade angle for planing. The wood has a moderate blunting effect on cutting edges. Surface preparation is required for gluing, and pre-boring for nailing. It stains, holds screws, sands and polishes well, provided the lapachol powder is removed first.

Seasoning

Despite its high density, it dries without difficulty. There can be slight cupping, twisting and end checking during drying. There is only small movement in service.

Durability

The heartwood is highly resistant to decay and termite attack, and resistant to other dry-wood insects, but can be affected by marine borer attack. It is highly impermeable for preservative treatment.

Typical uses

Cabinetmaking, turnery, tool handles, archery bows, walking sticks, factory and parquet flooring, truck bodies, naval architecture, bridge building, railway sleepers (railroad ties), marine construction, exterior construction, domestic exterior decking. The wood is also cut into decorative veneers.

Grows
South America and Caribbean
Typical height: 65–85ft (20–25m)
Trunk diameter: 2ft 6in (0.75m)

⚠ Possible health risks

The yellow dust can cause skin and eye irritation. May also cause shortness of breath, headache and visual disturbance

BALD CYPRESS

Taxodium distichum (Taxodiaceae)

Also called: cypress, red cypress, yellow cypress, southern cypress, gulf cypress, cow cypress, swamp cypress

Description

The pale yellowish-white sapwood merges into the heartwood, which ranges from yellowish to light or dark brown, on to reddish-brown and almost black. The darker varieties tend to be found in swamplands of the southern USA. It normally has straight grain, which may be even or uneven, and a coarse texture. The oil content gives it a greasy feel.
Typical dry weight: 29lb/ft³ (460kg/m³)
Specific gravity: .46

Properties

It is soft to moderately hard, with moderate strength and stiffness. It has medium crushing and bending strength. The wood works easily with hand and machine tools, holds screws and nails well, glues satisfactorily, sands easily and readily accepts finishes.

Seasoning

As the green wood has a high moisture content, extra time and care are required for kiln-drying. Problems may include brown chemical stains, water pockets and end checks. Once dried, the wood has good dimensional stability.

Durability

The oils in the heartwood make it very durable when exposed to moist conditions. The heartwood is moderately resistant to preservative treatment.

Typical uses

The wood is used for furniture, boatbuilding, flooring, shutters, shingles, fence posts, panelling, cooperage, food containers, corestock, and plain and figured veneers. The 'knees' which grow upwards from the tree's roots are used for artistic or whimsical carvings.

Grows

Eastern USA
Typical height: 100–120ft (30–37m)
Trunk diameter: 3–5ft (0.9–1.5m

⚠ **Possible health risks**
Respiratory problems; sensitizer

EUROPEAN YEW
Taxus baccata (Taxaceae)

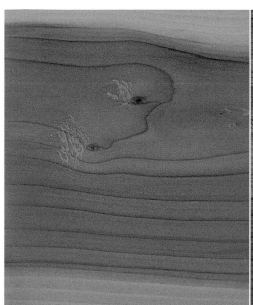

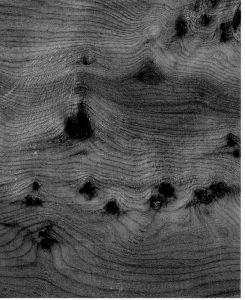

Knotty sample

Also called: yew, yewtree, if (French), **Eibe** (German), **venijnboom** (Dutch), **iubhar** (Gaelic), **ibar** (Old Irish), **iur** (Irish), **ywen** (Welsh)

Description
The near-white sapwood is distinct from the heartwood, which is usually golden orange-brown and is often streaked with mauve and darker brown, with patches of dark purple. Clusters of ingrown bark and tiny knots are frequent. Though typically straight-grained, yew is very often wavy, curly and irregular, with a medium, even texture. All these features make it a very attractive wood.
Typical dry weight: 42lb/ft³ (670kg/m³)
Specific gravity: .67

Properties
Yew is a hard, elastic wood, with medium crushing and bending strength, low resistance to shock loads, low stiffness, and a good steam-bending rating when air-dried and straight-grained. It is fairly difficult to work by hand. Straight-grained wood planes well, but irregular grain is prone to tear-out, and other machining qualities depend on grain direction. Yew splits easily. Gluing can be tricky due to the oily nature of the wood. Pre-boring is advised for nailing and screwing. Yew turns very well indeed, stains well, and can be polished to an excellent finish.

Seasoning
Yew dries quickly and well, with little degrade if care is taken. It can distort slightly, and new shakes can form or existing ones open up. It exhibits small movement in use.

Durability
Yew is durable and has a high natural resistance to decay fungi, but is vulnerable to the common furniture beetle. It resists preservative treatment.

Typical uses
Yew is the famed wood from which English longbows were once made. It is now also used for furniture, decorative turnery, interior and exterior joinery, rustic furniture and the bent parts of Windsor chairs. Its attractive qualities, including magnificent burrs (burls), make it highly sought-after in veneer form for cabinetwork, marquetry and panelling.

Grows
Europe, Turkey, northern Iran, North Africa, the Caucasus, the Himalayas and Burma (Myanmar)
Typical height: 50ft (15m)
Trunk diameter: 1–3ft (0.3–0.9m)

⚠ Possible health risks
Headaches, nausea, fainting, intestinal irritation, visual disturbances, lung congestion, reduced blood pressure; highly toxic to humans and cattle; sensitizer

◄ Hollow form in burr (burl) yew

The genus *Taxus*
Yews

In many ways the yew is an unusual tree. Although it is a hard, dense wood to work, it is classified as a softwood. Its great weight and elasticity made it very much prized in the past for the making of spears and longbows. Spears were made from yew many thousands of years ago, and yew longbows were used in neolithic times. In England in the Middle Ages the military use of yew to make longbows was of key importance, and the growth of yew was very much encouraged. King Edward IV (reigned 1461–83) gave a proclamation that every Englishman should have a longbow made of yew, ash or laburnum. Richard III (reigned 1483–5) issued a decree for the general planting of yew and for the importation of yew staves from abroad. At that time longbows were often the key to success in battle, as they could be reloaded very much faster than the crossbows used by England's great enemy of the time, the French.

▲ Coffee table with drawers

▲ Writing slope, showing both heartwood and sapwood

Yew was also used for making pegs or 'treenails' in Viking ships, and later for furniture, including the bent parts of Windsor chairs, for mill-wheel cogs, axles, wheels and the pins in pulleys.

The yew is one of the longest-lived trees on earth. There are many yew trees that are several hundred years old, and it is thought that some ancient yews still growing are up to 4,000 years old. Venerable yews can be found in many English churchyards, and various reasons have been suggested. One is that they were planted in medieval times to ensure a ready supply of wood for bow making. However, there is clear evidence that yew has had religious associations for a much longer period, going back to pre-Christian times. Possibly because of their longevity, yew trees have been seen as symbols of immortality, but also as omens of impending doom. The Druids of pre-Christian times regarded the yew as sacred, perhaps because of its properties of regeneration – the drooping branches of old yews can root if they touch the ground, thus forming a circle of new trunks around the original tree. Later the yew came to symbolize death and resurrection in Celtic culture. In Christian times there was a custom of burying yew shoots with the dead, and carrying boughs of yew on Palm Sunday and at funerals. In the English county of Kent, the yew can also be referred to as a 'palm'. The leaves (or needles), bark and seeds are toxic. Eating these parts has been known to kill horses, cattle, deer, sheep and humans – though apparently some domestic animals can gain immunity by a regular intake of small amounts of the leaves. The Roman historian Pliny the Elder, writing around AD 60, described a case of four soldiers dying after drinking wine from hip flasks made of yew. There may even be a connection between the word *toxic* and the Latin name for yew, *taxus*.

Like so many toxic plants, it also provides valuable medicines. The bark of the Pacific yew (*T. brevifolia*) provides a drug called Taxol® or paclitaxel, used for treating ovarian and breast cancer. A similar substance has since been found in the leaves of the European yew (*T. baccata*), and this is now used for the production of the drug. Taking the required extract from the leaves rather than the bark is of course preferable if we wish to preserve our yew trees. In the past yew has been used as a cardiac stimulant, and the sickly-sweet berries, which are the only non-toxic part of the tree, are a laxative and diuretic. However, to avoid the risk of poisoning no part of a yew tree should ever be used as a food.

Even though it can be unpredictable in its grain and figure, yew is one of the woods I really enjoy working on the lathe. It is invariably full of surprises, but can give very pleasing results that are enhanced by the sharp contrast between the creamy-white sapwood and the beautiful orange-red heartwood.

▲ The characteristically fluted trunk of a mature yew. Very large, old specimens are usually hollow

▶ 'Blondel' clock in burr (burl) yew, bog oak (*Quercus* sp.) and patinated cast bronze

▼ 'Streptohedron' boxes with interchangeable lids

PACIFIC YEW
Taxus brevifolia (Taxaceae)

Also called: American yew, Californian yew, Oregon yew, yew, western yew

Description
Pacific yew has a thin light tan sapwood, with a brown to bright orange heartwood. It has a very fine, close and straight grain with a fine texture. The wood has a high lustre and no characteristic odour.
Typical dry weight: 42lb/ft³ (670kg/m³)
Specific gravity: .67

Properties
The wood is dense, very hard, elastic and strong. It has good shock resistance and steam-bending properties. It usually works well, but pre-drilling is advised for screwing and nailing, as the wood has a tendency to split. Pacific yew turns very well, and can be brought to a good smooth finish.

Seasoning
Pacific yew seasons well, but there can be some distortion and appearance of new shakes. It is stable in use.

Durability
Pacific yew is highly resistant to heartwood decay, and can be used outdoors without preservative treatment.

Typical uses
Cabinetmaking, furniture, veneer, marquetry, panelling, archery bows, rustic furniture, carvings, canoe paddles. Much valued in Asia for making ceremonial items. The bark has been used for making the anti-cancer drug paclitaxel (Taxol ®).

Grows
Western Canada, western USA
Typical height: up to 50ft (15m)
Trunk diameter: 2ft (0.6m)

⚠ **Possible health risks**
All parts of the tree are highly toxic to humans, with the exception of the fleshy part of the aril (fruit), but the seed within it is toxic. Do not ingest any part of this tree. Also irritant, can cause dermatitis

TEAK

Tectona grandis (Verbenaceae)

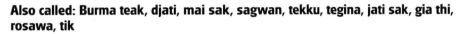

Also called: Burma teak, djati, mai sak, sagwan, tekku, tegina, jati sak, gia thi, rosawa, tik

Description

True Burma teak has a uniform dark golden-brown heartwood, which is free of markings and darkens to a mid- or dark brown on exposure. Most teak is a dark golden-yellow that turns to a rich brown with darker, deep brown markings. The distinct narrow to medium-width sapwood is white to pale yellow. The grain is typically straight but sometimes wavy, with a coarse, uneven texture and an oily feel.

Typical dry weight: 40lb/ft³ (650kg/m³)
Specific gravity: .65

Properties

Teak is a hard, medium-density wood, strong and durable. It has low stiffness and resistance to shock loads, with high crushing strength, medium bending strength and moderate steam-bending qualities. It is acid- and fire-resistant. The wood is relatively easy to work with both hand and machine tools, but does have a severe blunting effect on cutting edges due to its silica content, so tungsten-carbide-tipped (TCT) blades are advisable. Pre-boring is advised for nails and screws. Provided cutters are kept sharp, it bores, routs, carves, turns and moulds fairly well; newly finished surfaces glue well. It can be brought to a satisfactory finish, and paints, varnishes and stains fairly well.

Seasoning

The wood dries slowly but well, though there can be large variations in drying rates. There is small movement in use.

Durability

It is very durable and resistant to termites and fungi. The sapwood is vulnerable to the powder-post beetle. The heartwood is highly resistant to preservative treatment, the sapwood moderately so.

Typical uses

Domestic, outdoor and office furniture, joinery, flooring, kitchen cabinets, harbour work, boat and ship building, oars, decking, laboratory benches, vats, plywood and decorative veneers.

Grows

Burma (Myanmar), India, Indonesia, Thailand and Java; also Malaysia, Borneo, Philippines, Central America and tropical Africa

Typical height: 130–150ft (39–45m)

Trunk diameter: 3–5ft (0.9–1.5m)

⚠ **Possible health risks**

Dermatitis, conjunctivitis, irritation to the nose and throat, swelling of the scrotum, nausea and oversensitivity to light

INDIAN LAUREL

Terminalia alata, T. coriacea, T. crenulata (Combretaceae)

Also called: taukkyan, asna, cay, hatna, neang, mutti, sain

Description

The sapwood, which is very clearly demarcated from the heartwood, is a reddish-white colour. The heartwood ranges from light brown with few fine streaks to dark brown with darker bands or streaks. The wood is reasonably straight-grained, but often interlocked or irregular, with a coarse to medium texture and a dull to medium lustre. Quartersawn surfaces can show an attractive figure.
Typical dry weight: 53lb/ft³ (860kg/m³)
Specific gravity: .86

Properties

Indian laurel is an elastic, dense and heavy wood. It has high crushing strength, medium bending strength and stiffness, and a poor steam-bending rating. It is not easy to work with hand tools, and is fairly difficult to work with machine tools also. Pre-boring is advised for nailing and screwing; it bores and mortises well, and turns very well. Indian laurel glues well. It needs filling if a good finish is to be obtained, wax or oil being the most effective finishes.

Seasoning

The wood is difficult to season, and is liable to surface check, split and warp. Slow drying is recommended to reduce degrade. There is medium movement in use.

Durability

It is moderately durable, but can be subject to insect and fungal attack. The sapwood is permeable for preservative treatment, and the heartwood is resistant.

Typical uses

Furniture and cabinetmaking, joinery, turnery, boatbuilding, tool handles, police truncheons, gunstocks and decorative veneer. The wood is also used locally for marine structures, piling and railway sleepers (railroad ties).

Grows
India, Burma (Myanmar),
Bangladesh and Pakistan
Typical height: 100ft (30m)
Trunk diameter: 3ft (1m)

⚠ **Possible health risks**
The dust can be an irritant

IDIGBO

Terminalia ivorensis (Combretaceae)

Also called: framiré, emeri, black afara, bajee, bajii

Description

The sapwood is yellow-brown or light pinkish-brown and not clearly demarcated from the heartwood. The latter is a pale yellow-brown, and can have a light pinkish cast. The wood is normally straight-grained, but sometimes the grain is interlocked, creating a ribbon-stripe figure on quartersawn surfaces. It has a fairly coarse and moderately open, uneven texture, with a medium to high lustre. There can be lightweight brittleheart in the inner core.

Typical dry weight: 35lb/ft³ (560kg/m³)
Specific gravity: .56

Properties

It has generally low strength properties, which can be even lower if brittleheart is present. Steam-bending properties are rated as very poor. The wood works well with hand and machine tools, but the slightly interlocked grain can pick up on planing. There is a slight blunting effect on cutting edges. The wood has satisfactory nailing qualities, and carves, glues, screws, stains and polishes well. The acid in the wood can cause corrosion in ferrous metals, and textiles can be stained by yellow dye.

Seasoning

Idigbo dries rapidly with little distortion or checking, but knots can sometimes split. Movement in service is small.

Durability

The heartwood is usually durable, but the sapwood can be vulnerable to attack from powder-post and longhorn beetles. The heartwood is very resistant to preservative treatment, whereas the sapwood has medium permeability.

Typical uses

Furniture, interior and exterior joinery, domestic flooring including parquet, construction work, roofing shingles and turnery. Logs can be rotary-cut for plywood, and selected wood is sliced for decorative veneers.

> **Grows**
> West Africa
> **Typical height:** 150ft (46m)
> **Trunk diameter:** 3–5ft
> (0.9–1.5m)

⚠ Possible health risks

The sawdust can cause skin and respiratory problems

AFARA

Terminalia superba (Combretaceae)

Also called: limba, light limba, limba clair, limba blanc, korina (USA), **akom** (Cameroon), **ofram** (Ghana), **fraké.** Varieties with darker heartwood are known as **limba bariolé, dark afara, dark limba, limba noir**

Grows
West Africa
Typical height: 150ft (45m)
Trunk diameter: 5ft (1.5m)

⚠ Possible health risks
Splinters become septic; nettle rash, nose and gum bleeding, and decrease in lung function

Description
Afara is pale yellow-brown to straw-coloured, and the heartwood may have grey-black streaks. The sapwood and heartwood are not clearly differentiated. The wood is straight and close-grained, with a moderately coarse texture. It can sometimes have wavy or interlocked grain, giving interesting figure.
Typical dry weight: 34lb/ft³ (550kg/m³)
Specific gravity: .55

Properties
It has low bending strength with low stiffness and medium crushing strength. The light-coloured wood is resistant to shock, but the heartwood can be brittle. Afara can be easily worked with both machine and hand tools, with only a slight blunting effect on cutters. Irregular grain can tear if a low cutter angle is not used, and it is necessary to pre-bore for nailing and screwing. Gluing is satisfactory, and it stains well. It will take an excellent finish provided filler is used.

Seasoning
Afara kiln-dries well with little movement, and air-dries rapidly but with a tendency to shake or split.

Durability
It is liable to attack by pinhole borers, is non-durable and not resistant to decay. The sapwood can be vulnerable to powder-post beetle. It is liable to blue sap stain and is moderately resistant to preservative treatment.

Typical uses
Furniture, interior joinery, turnery, shop fittings (store fixtures), coffins and light construction. The black heartwood is made into decorative veneers for marquetry and panelling.

THUYA BURR

Tetraclinis articulata (Cupressaceae)

Also called: thuya, thyine wood, citron burl, sandarac tree, thuyawood

Description

The part of the tree of interest to woodworkers is actually a root burr (burl), and is created by the repeated removal of the coppice growth, which stimulates increased growth underground. The burrs are a rich golden-brown to orange-red or even darker. The wood is very knotty and contorted, with an interlocked, fine-textured grain. The figuring is usually bird's-eye or mottled, and very attractive. The strong, resinous scent is distinctive and long-lasting.

Typical dry weight: 42lb/ft³ (670kg/m³)
Specific gravity: .67

Properties

Since this is a burr with contorted and interlocked grain, very sharp tools are required. It can be turned, planed and sliced, but this requires a lot of skill. It glues well if the joints are first wiped with solvent to reduce the oil content. Surfaces can be finished with cabinet scrapers, and the wood can be brought to a very high finish if sanded down to 1200 grit.

Seasoning

The oil content helps the wood to season well, as it slows the loss of moisture. Slow kilning is advised.

Durability

Since the wood is used only decoratively, durability is of relatively low importance.

Typical uses

Cabinetmaking, decorative veneer, marquetry, panelling, jewellery boxes, small turned boxes and trinkets.

Grows
North Africa and southern Spain; also East Africa, Cyprus and Malta
Typical height: 50ft (15m)

⚠ **Possible health risks**
Not known

◀ Box in thuya burr veneer

WESTERN RED CEDAR
Thuja plicata (Cupressaceae)

Also called: red cedar (Canada), **British Columbia red cedar** (UK), **giant arborvitae** (USA); also **canoe cedar, shinglewood, Pacific red cedar, giant cedar**

Grows
Canada and USA; also New Zealand and UK
Typical height: 100–175ft (30–53m)
Trunk diameter: 2–8ft (0.6–2.4m)

⚠ Possible health risks
Asthma, rhinitis, dermatitis, mucous membrane irritation, nosebleeds, stomach pains, nausea, giddiness and disturbance of the central nervous system

Description
When newly cut, the heartwood can vary from salmon-pink to dark chocolate-brown. It ages to a reddish-brown and eventually to a silver-grey, which makes it much prized for its weathered appearance. The sapwood is whitish and clearly differentiated from the heartwood. Western red cedar has a straight and even grain with a coarse texture. It is non-resinous, and has a cedar-like smell, but is not a true cedar.
Typical dry weight: 23lb/ft³ (370kg/m³)
Specific gravity: .37

Properties
Western red cedar has very low resistance to shock loads and very low stiffness. Its bending and crushing strength are low, and its steam-bending classification very poor. It works well with hand and machine tools. It nails well without splitting, and glues and screws well. The wood planes well and has only a minor blunting effect on cutting edges. Its straight grain allows it to be split easily for roof shingles. Its acid properties can corrode iron, so copper or galvanized nails should be used.

Seasoning
Thicker stock must be dried with care to avoid honeycombing and collapse. Thinner stock dries without problems and with minimum degrade.

Durability
This is a durable wood that weathers very well. It can, however, suffer from attack from the western cedar borer when growing, and the common furniture beetle when seasoned. It is difficult to treat with preservatives.

Typical uses
Guitar parts, ship and boat building, roofing shingles, exterior cladding (siding), beehives, sheds and greenhouses, and decorative veneer.

MAKORÉ

Tieghemella heckelii and *T. africana* (Sapotaceae)

Syn.: *Mimusops heckelii*
Also called: African cherry, abacu, agamokwe, baku, douka, okolla. Not to be confused with *Prunus africana* or with niové (*Staudtia stipitata*), both also known as African cherry

Description
The heartwood can vary from pink to rich red-brown, or from pinkish-red to blood-red. It is generally straight-grained, but can be interlocked, which produces a decorative mottled figure that sometimes has darker streaks. Figured wood can show a watered-silk pattern. The texture is normally uniform and ranges from medium to very fine. Makoré has a fine natural lustre.
Typical dry weight: 39lb/ft³ (620kg/m³)
Specific gravity: .62

Properties
Makoré has low stiffness and resistance to shock loads, with medium bending and crushing strengths. The heartwood has good steam-bending qualities. The wood has a high silica content, which can exert a severe blunting effect on cutting edges, consequently making the wood difficult to work. Tungsten-carbide-tipped (TCT) saw blades are recommended. The wood planes, glues, sands, turns, moulds and mortises reasonably well, and requires pre-boring for nails and screws. Makoré

stains well, and can be brought to an excellent finish, provided filler is used. Ferrous fastenings should be avoided, as they are liable to stain the wood blue.

Seasoning
The wood dries at a slow to moderate rate, with little degrade. There might be slight twisting and minimal splitting around knots while drying. Makoré is stable in service.

Durability
The heartwood is very durable and resistant to preservative treatment. The sapwood is vulnerable to attack from powder-post beetle and is moderately resistant to preservative treatment.

Typical uses
Furniture and cabinetmaking, quality joinery, boatbuilding, laboratory benches, domestic flooring including parquet, and marine plywood. It is also sliced into decorative veneers for panelling and cabinetmaking.

▲ Desk detail

> **Grows**
> West Africa
> **Typical height:** 120–150ft
> (36–45m)
> **Trunk diameter:** 4ft (1.2m)

⚠ Possible health risks
Dust from machining can cause dermatitis, nose and throat irritation, nosebleeds, nausea, headaches and giddiness. It can affect the blood and the central nervous system

BASSWOOD
Tilia americana and related species (Tiliaceae)

Also called: American lime (UK), **American whitewood, lime tree, whitewood, American linden** (USA); **Florida basswood, Florida linden, Carolina linden**

Description
Basswood sapwood is creamy-white to pale pinkish-brown in colour and gradually merges with the heartwood. The wood will darken to pale brown on drying. It has a fine, straight grain, which is uniform in texture. The sapwood is sometimes sold as **white basswood**.
Typical dry weight: 26lb/ft³ (410kg/m³)
Specific gravity: .41

Water-poppy carving ▶

Properties
Basswood is a light, soft and weak wood. It is low in strength and has a poor steam-bending classification. This wood works very easily, and has a low resistance to cutting. Sharp, thin tools are required to obtain a clean finish. It can take stain and polish without difficulty; planes, glues, screws and nails well; and has good carving properties.

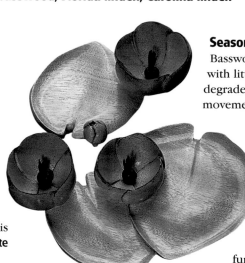

Seasoning
Basswood dries fairly quickly with little distortion or degrade. There is minimal movement in service.

Durability
It is non-durable, and permeable for preservation treatment. The sapwood is vulnerable to attack from the common furniture beetle and, when in log form, from the longhorn beetle.

Typical uses
Since it is odour-free, basswood is used for food containers; other uses include hand carving, patternmaking, furniture, quality joinery, cooperage, mallet heads, beehives, toys, picture framing and piano keys. It is also used for plywood, corestock and veneers.

Grows
Eastern Canada and USA, Great Lakes region
Typical height: 65–100ft (20–30m)
Trunk diameter: 4ft (1.2m) max.

⚠ Possible health risks
Not known

EUROPEAN LIME

Tilia vulgaris and related species (Tiliaceae)

Syn.: *T. x vulgaris, T. x europaea*
Also called: linden; tilleul (French), **Linde** (German)

Description

European lime is initially pale yellow or uniform white, and ages to pale brown after extended exposure. The grain is usually straight and has a fine and uniform texture, generally with little or no figure. The sapwood is usually not distinct from the heartwood.
Typical dry weight: 34lb/ft³ (540kg/m³)
Specific gravity: .54

Properties

European lime is rated as medium in bending and crushing strength, and low in resistance to shock loads and in stiffness. The wood can be steam-bent to a moderate radius. It is dense and resistant to splitting. Lime is easy to work with both hand and machine tools. It is, however, inclined to be woolly in its finish, so sharp, thin-edged tools are advised. It has only a slight dulling effect on cutters. The wood turns, bores, glues and stains well, and is rated satisfactory for polishing, bandsawing and nailing. Lime carves very well, as it resists splitting in any cutting plane.

Seasoning

The wood dries at a pretty rapid rate and is prone to distortion. Slow kilning is advised to minimize degrade. There is medium movement in service.

Durability

The heartwood has little resistance to decay, and the sapwood is vulnerable to attack from the common furniture beetle. Both heartwood and sapwood are permeable for preservative treatment.

Typical uses

Lime is particularly valued for carving, and is also used for musical instruments including harps and piano keys, bobbins, toys, turnery, and working surfaces for leatherwork. Selected logs are sliced for decorative veneers.

▲ Carved figure

> **Grows**
> Europe, including UK
> **Typical height:** 80–100ft
> (25–30m)
> **Trunk diameter:** up to 4ft
> (1.2m)

⚠ **Possible health risks**

Not known

AUSTRALIAN RED CEDAR

Toona ciliata (Meliaceae)

T. ciliata var. australis

Syn.: *T. australis*
Also called: Indian cedar, Moulmein cedar, Queensland red cedar, red cedar

Grows
Eastern Australia, Papua New Guinea, Philippines and India. Plantation-grown in Hawaii and Tonga
Typical height: 130ft (40m)
Trunk diameter: 3–6ft (1–2m), sometimes greater

⚠ Possible health risks
Dermatitis, violent headache, giddiness, stomach cramps, asthma, bronchitis. The dust can be an irritant to nose and throat

Description
The heartwood ranges from pink to deep red-brown, often with darker streaks, and the sapwood is normally yellowish-white to light grey. Australian red cedar has a coarse, open and usually straight grain. It can sometimes be wavy and interlocked, which creates an attractive fiddleback figure. The growth rings and vessel lines are clear when the wood is backsawn. The heartwood has a pleasant spicy aroma. It is not related to the true cedars, and is so called only because of the colour and scent of its wood.
Typical dry weight: 28lb/ft³ (450kg/m³)
Specific gravity: .45

Properties
The wood can be woolly, but works easily. However, when quartersawn it is difficult to obtain a good finish unless the cutters are extremely sharp. It is a relatively soft, weak wood and exhibits very poor steam-bending properties. It glues, nails and screws satisfactorily, and takes paint, polish and stain easily, but may require filling due to the coarse grain. The wood can be brought to a good finish with care.

Seasoning
Australian red cedar can be dried satisfactorily by air or kiln, but care must be taken to avoid surface checking and collapse on thicker stock, and warping and cupping of thinner boards. The wood is stable in service.

Durability
Above ground, Australian red cedar is highly resistant to decay even when fully exposed to the weather. The sapwood readily accepts preservative treatment, but penetration of the heartwood is negligible. Untreated sapwood can be susceptible to attack from lyctid borers.

Typical uses
Furniture, quality joinery, musical instruments, turnery, picture frames and inlay work; also light boatbuilding, venetian blinds, patternmaking, gunstocks and plywood.

OBECHE

Triplochiton scleroxylon (Sterculiaceae)

Also called: wawa, arere, ayous, samba, okpo, m'bado

Description

Obeche is creamy-white to pale yellow. There is no clear differentiation between the sapwood, which can be up to 6in (150mm) thick, and the heartwood. The grain is usually interlocked, and can show a faint stripe on quartersawn surfaces. The texture can be coarse or moderately fine and even, with a natural sheen.
Typical dry weight: 24lb/ft³ (380kg/m³)
Specific gravity: .38

Properties

It is not a strong wood. It has low crushing and bending strengths, with very low stiffness and resistance to shock loads. It has moderate steam-bending qualities. Obeche is very easy to work with both hand and machine tools, and has only a slight blunting effect on cutting edges. A reduced cutting angle and sharp blades are advised for planing, moulding and routing. It carves, glues and sands well, and filling is required before staining and polishing to obtain a good finish. It is too soft for hand turning, and although it nails easily, its holding properties are only fair.

Seasoning

Obeche dries rapidly and readily, with little degrade. Knot splits and distortion can occur during drying. There is minimal movement in service.

Durability

It is not durable, and is vulnerable to attack from termites, pinhole borers, longhorn beetles and sap-stain fungi. The sapwood can be attacked by the powder-post beetle. The sapwood is permeable, but the heartwood is resistant to preservative treatment.

Typical uses

Furniture and furniture components, office furniture, interior trim and joinery, cabinet framing, model making, marquetry. It is also used to make particleboard, blockboard, plywood corestock and figured veneer.

Grows
West Africa
Typical height: 150–180ft (45–55m)
Trunk diameter: 3–5ft (0.9–1.5m)

⚠ Possible health risks

Dust from sawing can cause dermatitis, nettle rash, asthma, lung congestion, sneezing and wheezing

WESTERN HEMLOCK
Tsuga heterophylla (Pinaceae)

Also called: Pacific hemlock, Alaska pine, hemlock spruce, British Columbian hemlock, west coast hemlock

Grows
Western Canada and USA;
also UK, China and Japan
Typical height: 100–150ft
(30–46m)
Trunk diameter: 3–4ft
(0.9–1.2m)

⚠ **Possible health risks**
Bronchial problems, rhinitis,
dermatitis, eczema and possibly
nasal cancer

Description
The sapwood is typically 3–5in
(75–125mm) thick and difficult to
differentiate from the heartwood, which is
creamy-brown to pale yellowish-brown.
Latewood areas are darker and frequently
tinged with a roseate, purplish or red-
brown colour, producing a well-defined
growth-ring figure on plainsawn surfaces.
Dark streaks, known as 'bird pecks' but
caused by maggots, are frequently present.
The grain is usually straight and even,
with a medium to fine texture. Western
hemlock can be confused with **amabilis fir**
(*Abies amabilis*), which is very similar.
Typical dry weight: 31lb/ft³ (500kg/m³)
Specific gravity: .50

Properties
It has low hardness and stiffness, and
medium bending and compressive
strength. The wood has similar mechanical
qualities to Scots pine (*Pinus sylvestris*).
It works readily with both machine and
hand tools. Western hemlock planes,
turns, screws, glues, stains and varnishes
well. There is little dulling effect on
cutting edges. Pre-boring is advised for
nailing near the ends of boards.

Seasoning
The wood dries slowly, but seasons well.
Shakes, uneven moisture content, iron
stains and warping can occur. There can
be fine surface checking when it is kiln-
dried. There is little movement in service.

Durability
The heartwood has little natural
resistance to decay and insects, and is
moderately difficult to treat with
preservatives. The sapwood is permeable.

Typical uses
It is used worldwide for construction,
joinery, turnery, flooring, boxes and
crates, pulp for quality newsprint, pallets,
formwork, joists, framing, decks, vehicle
bodies, railway sleepers (railroad ties) and
decorative and utility plywood. It is also
used as a source of cellulose for making
rayon, cellophane and plastics.

AVODIRÉ

Turraeanthus africanus (Meliaceae)

Also called: apeya, apapaye, engan, agbe, esu, m'fube, wansenwa, African satinwood

Description
There is little or no distinction between sapwood and heartwood. The wood is typically creamy-white to pale yellow, but darkens on exposure to a golden yellow. It has a good natural lustre and a fine, uniform texture. Avodiré has a wavy or irregularly interlocked grain, which can produce very pleasing figure, either striped, mottled or curled.
Typical dry weight: 34lb/ft³ (550kg/m³)
Specific gravity: .55

Properties
The wood is of medium density and has generally poor steam-bending qualities. It has very low stiffness and low resistance to shock loads. It works well with both machine and hand tools, with only a slight blunting effect on cutting tools. Interlocked grain can pick up on planing, so a reduced cutting angle is advised. It has good gluing and screwing properties, but pre-boring is advisable for nailing. It stains and finishes well, giving a good lustrous finish, though staining may be uneven on quartersawn stock.

Seasoning
The wood must be dried carefully, otherwise it can warp, twist and cup. It does, however, dry rapidly. Shakes may lengthen on drying, and some splitting can occur around knots.

Durability
Avodiré is very resistant to preservative treatment. The heartwood can be vulnerable to attack from fungi, termites, pinhole and marine borers. The wood is non-durable.

Typical uses
Cabinetmaking, quality joinery, shop and office fittings, organ pipes and xylophones. High-quality veneers are produced from well-figured wood.

Grows
Tropical West Africa
Typical height: 115ft (35m)
Trunk diameter: 2–3ft (0.6–0.9m)

⚠ **Possible health risks**
Dermatitis, nosebleeds, possible internal bleeding, respiratory irritation

The genus *Ulmus*
Elms

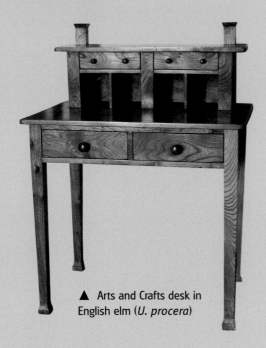

▲ Arts and Crafts desk in
English elm (*U. procera*)

▲ Elms in Brighton, England

The *Ulmus* genus contains up to 60 species, native to Asia, Europe, the Mediterranean, South, Central and North America. Sadly, the world population of elms has been devastated by the relentless spread of Dutch elm disease. This disease, which affects many elm species and is almost invariably fatal, is caused by the fungi *Ophiostoma ulmi* (syn. *Ceratocystis ulmi*) and the more virulent *O. novo-ulmi*, both spread by elm-bark beetles. The disease is so called because early research on it was carried out in the Netherlands; it is not specific to the Dutch elm (*U. hollandica*). One place where mature elms can still be seen is Brighton, on the south coast of England, where the disease has been arrested by prompt felling of infected trees, and a number of experimental disease-resistant hybrids have been planted.

Elm is virtually imperishable when under water, so in the past it was used for piles, water pipes, ships' pumps and keels. However, when alternately wet and dry it can be prone to rapid rot and decay, which makes it an ideal timber for coffins (caskets) to return us to the dust from which we came. It is also used for the seats of Windsor chairs, and other furniture of a rural origin.

I am lucky enough to have quite a stock of burr (burl) elm that I acquired before the major British outbreak of Dutch elm disease in the 1970s, and find it a lovely wood to turn as it has such a fine-quality figuring supplemented by interesting burr clusters.

◄ Elms in early spring; the right-hand one is in flower

AMERICAN ELM

Ulmus americana and related species (Ulmaceae)

Also called: American white elm, elm, Florida elm, soft elm, white elm, water elm.
There are six species of elm in North America, all with similar characteristics

Description
The heartwood is light brown to mid-brown, often with a reddish tinge. The grain is generally straight but sometimes interlocked. Its texture is coarse and rather woolly. The sapwood is greyish-white to light brown.
Typical dry weight: 35lb/ft³ (560kg/m³)
Specific gravity: .56

Properties
It has medium crushing and bending strengths, a high resistance to shock loads, very low stiffness and good steam-bending properties. Provided cutting edges are kept sharp, the wood works well with hand and machine tools. It has good nailing, screwing and gluing properties. When planing, sharp and thin cutting edges are required to avoid a woolly finish. It takes stain well and can be polished to a high finish.

Seasoning
It dries well, but care should be taken to prevent warping. Ring failure can occur.

Durability
The heartwood is vulnerable to decay and is susceptible to attack from wood borers. Dutch elm disease continues to pose a risk to growing trees. The sapwood is permeable for preservative treatment, and the heartwood moderately resistant.

Typical uses
Furniture, boat and ship building, boxes and crates, pallets, skids, rocking-chair rockers, sleigh runners, coffins and gymnasium equipment. It is also rotary-cut for plywood and sliced to make decorative veneers.

Grows
Canada and USA
Typical height: 100ft (30m)
Trunk diameter: 2–4ft
(0.6–1.2m)

⚠ **Possible health risks**
Dermatitis; dust is an irritant to nose and eyes

WYCH ELM
Ulmus glabra (Ulmaceae)

Also called: Scots elm, Scotch elm, Irish leamhan, elm, mountain elm, white elm, alm, orme blanc (French), **Bergulme** (German)

Grows
North and west UK, Ireland, Europe, western Asia
Typical height: up to 130ft (40m)
Trunk diameter: 5ft (1.5m)

⚠ Possible health risks
Dermatitis, nasal cancer; dust can be an irritant

◄ Low-back Windsor chair: seat in wych elm, other parts oak (*Quercus petraea* or *Q. robur*)

Description
The heartwood is light brown, sometimes with a green hue, or green streaks. The sapwood is paler and clearly defined from the heartwood when newly cut. Wych elm is generally straight-grained, with a medium texture; the grain is usually straighter and finer than in English or Dutch elm (*U. procera, U. hollandica*). The wood can be attractively figured.
Typical dry weight: 42lb/ft³ (670kg/m³)
Specific gravity: .67

Properties
Wych elm is quite heavy and dense, with a fairly high bending and crushing strength and medium hardness. Air-dried wood is very suitable for steam bending, but it will fracture or buckle if too green; it must be knot-free for good bending

results. Wych elm has a moderate blunting effect on cutting edges, machines satisfactorily, and generally works well with hand tools. It also nails and glues well, and is rated as satisfactory for screwing, staining and sanding. Polishing is only fair.

Seasoning
It dries fairly rapidly and well, but can be prone to distortion. Closely spaced sticking is advised when drying. There is medium movement in service.

Durability
The heartwood has low resistance to decay, and the sapwood is susceptible to attack from common furniture and powder-post beetles. The sapwood is permeable for preservative treatment, but the heartwood is resistant to it. It does not decay when immersed in water, and has therefore often been used for piling.

Typical uses
Furniture including chests, turnery, boatbuilding, coffins and piling. Used in the past for wheel hubs, water pipes, troughs and sea defences.

DUTCH ELM
Ulmus hollandica (Ulmaceae)

Also called: cork-bark elm, orme hollandais (French), **hollandische Ulme** (German), **Hollandse bastaardiep** (Dutch)

Description
When newly cut, the sapwood of Dutch elm is clearly distinct from the heartwood. After seasoning, the wood is a dull brown. It usually has straight grain, but cross grain can occur. The annual rings are very conspicuous, because of the large pores in the earlywood, and form an attractive figure in this coarse-textured wood.
Typical dry weight: 34lb/ft³ (550kg/m³)
Specific gravity: .55

Properties
It has low bending and crushing strengths, and very low stiffness and resistance to shock loads. Dutch elm is much tougher than English elm (*U. procera*), and has very good steam-bending qualities. The wood can be difficult to work if it contains irregular grain. It has a moderate blunting effect on cutting edges, and is liable to tear during planing and to bind when being sawn. It accepts glues, stains, nails and screws well, and a good finish can be obtained by polishing or waxing.

Seasoning
Dutch elm dries rapidly, and can experience distortion along with checking and slight splitting, unless care is taken.

Durability
The sapwood is vulnerable to attack from the common furniture beetle and the powder-post beetle. It takes preservative treatment well, whereas the heartwood is moderately difficult to treat.

Typical uses
Cabinetmaking, chairs, turnery, domestic flooring; also a source of decorative burrs (burls) and veneers.

Grows
Netherlands, France, Germany, Poland, Denmark, Norway and UK
Typical height: 120–150ft (38–45m)
Trunk diameter: 3–5ft (1–1.5m)

⚠ **Possible health risks**
Dermatitis, irritation to nose and throat, and nasal cancer

ENGLISH ELM

Ulmus procera (Ulmaceae)

Syn.: *U. minor* var. *vulgaris*, *U. campestris*
Also called: elm, nave elm, red elm, vanlig alm, orme d'Angleterre (French), **Feldulme,
Englische Ulme** (German), **Engelse veldiep** (Dutch)

▲ Pedestal desk detail: American
walnut (*Juglans nigra*) with burr
(burl) elm panels

Grows
UK, northern Europe (range
greatly reduced by Dutch elm
disease since the 1970s)
Typical height: 80ft (24m)
Trunk diameter: 3ft (0.9m)

⚠ **Possible health risks**
Dermatitis, irritation to eyes, nose
and throat, nasal cancer

Description
The heartwood of English elm is a dull
reddish-brown, and is clearly
differentiated from the sapwood when
freshly cut. It has cross and irregular
grain, which results in an attractive figure.
The wood is coarse-textured, with
prominent annual rings.
Typical dry weight: 34lb/ft³ (550kg/m³)
Specific gravity: .55

Properties
English elm has very low resistance to
shock loads, very low stiffness and low
bending and crushing strengths, but is
notably resistant to splitting. Steam-
bending properties are poor, because the
wood tends to distort while setting. Very
sharp cutting edges are required, and the
wood has a medium blunting effect on
tool cutters. The surface tends to pick up
during planing, and the irregular grain
can result in a woolly finish. It takes glues
and stains well, screws and nails without
splitting, and can be polished to a high
finish. It is not an easy wood to work with
hand tools.

Seasoning
It dries fairly rapidly, but has a strong
tendency to distort unless closely
stickered and well weighted. It can suffer
checks, splits and sometimes collapse.
There is medium movement in service.

Durability
The heartwood is susceptible to decay
and insect attack, and is moderately
resistant to preservative treatment. The
sapwood is permeable.

Typical uses
Cabinetmaking, chairs including Windsor
chairs, bent components, coffins, dock
and harbour work, flooring including
parquet, decorative veneers and
weatherboarding. It was formerly the
wood of choice for wheel hubs, water
pipes and pumps.

ROCK ELM

Ulmus thomasii (Ulmaceae)

Also called: Canadian cork elm, Canadian rock elm, cork elm, hickory elm

Description

The wood is light brown, and there is no clear distinction between heartwood and sapwood. It normally has straight grain, which is sometimes interlocked. Rock elm has a moderately fine texture, which is the finest texture amongst the elms.
Typical dry weight: 43lb/ft³ (700kg/m³)
Specific gravity: .70

Properties

Rock elm has a high resistance to shock loads, low stiffness, medium bending and crushing qualities, and is classified as very good for steam bending. It is highly resistant to wear and tear. Because of its high density it is fairly difficult to saw, rather difficult to plane, and has a moderate blunting effect on cutters. Rock elm glues and stains well, nails and screws satisfactorily, and polishes to a smooth finish.

Seasoning

Drying must be carried out carefully; otherwise the wood is liable to check, warp and shrink.

Durability

The wood is not durable, with little natural resistance to decay, and the sapwood is vulnerable to attack by the powder-post beetle. The heartwood is resistant to preservative treatment.

Typical uses

Ribs and framing in boatbuilding, rubbing strips, boxes and crates, food containers, chair rockers, gymnasium equipment, sleigh runners, underwater elements for docks, plywood and decorative veneer.

Grows
Eastern Canada and USA
Typical height: 15–30m
(50–100ft)
Trunk diameter: 0.5–0.9m
(1ft 6in–3ft)

⚠ **Possible health risks**

Skin irritation, dermatitis

MYRTLE
Umbellularia californica (Myrtaceae)

Also called: acacia, baytree, bay laurel, California laurel, mountain laurel, Oregon myrtle, Pacific myrtle, Californian olive, pepperwood, spice tree

Description
The pale brown sapwood is thick and not clearly demarcated from the heartwood, which is a rich golden-brown to yellowish-green. The grain is usually straight but frequently wavy or irregular, and is close, compact and smooth. The wood has a medium and firm texture, conspicuous medullary rays and a medium lustre. It sometimes displays interesting and attractive figure.
Typical dry weight: 53lb/ft³ (850kg/ft³)
Specific gravity: .85

Properties
Myrtle is heavy, hard-wearing and resilient. Strength ratings are not really relevant for the uses to which the wood is put. It can be a difficult wood to work, and has a rapid blunting effect on cutting edges. A reduced cutting angle is recommended for planing and moulding.

However, it glues, bores, nails and screws well, and polishes very well. Myrtle is prized by woodturners for its excellent turning properties.

Seasoning
If great care is not taken, the wood will check and warp during drying. Myrtle is sometimes submerged in water to effect colour changes in the drying process. The wood is relatively stable in use.

Durability
It is not very durable, with a low natural resistance to decay, and is attacked by powder-post beetles. Sap-stain infestation can also be a problem.

Typical uses
Furniture, cabinetmaking, flooring, turned bowls, novelties, wall panelling, figured veneer, marquetry and woodenware.

Grows
Oregon and California, USA
Typical height: 40–80ft (12–24m)
Trunk diameter: 1ft 6in–2ft 6in (0.5–0.8m)

⚠ Possible health risks
Sensitizer; dust, leaves and bark can cause respiratory problems

▶ Turned vase

LIGHT VIROLA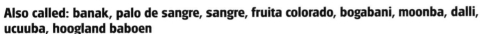

Virola spp., incl. *V. koschnyi* and *V. surinamensis* (Myristicaceae)

V. koschnyi

V. surinamensis

Also called: banak, palo de sangre, sangre, fruita colorado, bogabani, moonba, dalli, ucuuba, hoogland baboen

Description

The sapwood of light virola is not clearly differentiated from the heartwood, which ranges from pinkish to golden-brown in colour when freshly cut, and darkens to a deep reddish-brown on exposure. Virola is typically straight-grained, with a medium to coarse texture, and has a low to medium lustre.

Typical dry weight: 33lb/ft³ (530kg/ft³)
Specific gravity: .53

Properties

It has medium crushing strength, low bending and stiffness strengths, very low resistance to shock loads, and a poor steam-bending classification. Virola can be worked readily with both machine and hand tools, and exerts only a minimal blunting effect on cutting edges. The wood saws, planes, bores, mortises and routs well, and readily accepts nails, screws and glue. It is fairly easy to carve and sand. Light virola takes stain well and has satisfactory characteristics for turning and polishing.

Seasoning

Virola dries slowly, and if care is not taken it is prone to honeycomb, collapse, check and warp. It exhibits medium movement in service.

Durability

The wood is not at all durable, and is vulnerable to attack by decay fungi, termites and other insects. Both sapwood and heartwood are permeable for preservative treatment.

Typical uses

Domestic, office and rustic furniture, light joinery, framing, kitchen cabinets, boxes and crates, matches, casks, coffins, cigar boxes, corestock and plywood. It is also sliced for decorative veneers.

Grows
Central and tropical South America
Typical height: 140ft (43m)
Trunk diameter: 2–3ft (0.6–0.9m), but sometimes broader

⚠ **Possible health risks**
Not known

WEST INDIAN SATINWOOD
Zanthoxylum flavum (Rutaceae)

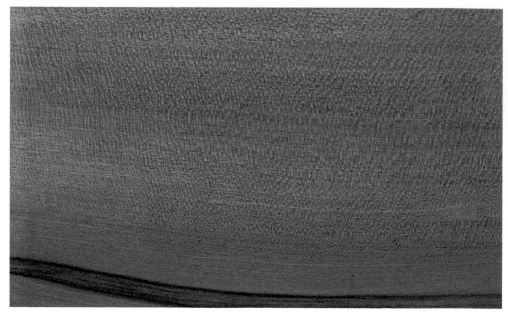

Syn.: *Fagara flava*
Also called: aceitillo, espinillo, Jamaican satinwood, yellow sanders (cf. *Buchenavia capitata*, page 271), **yellow wood, yellowheart; noyer** (French)

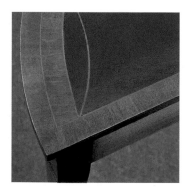

▲ Table in Brazilian mahogany (*Swietenia macrophylla*) with satinwood crossbanding

Description
The sapwood darkens progressively from the bark until it merges into the heartwood. The heartwood is a creamy colour at first, and darkens to a light orange or golden-tan. It has an interlocked or irregular grain, with a fine, even texture and a high lustre. Roey and mottle figure are often present.
Typical dry weight: 45lb/ft³ (730kg/m³)
Specific gravity: .73

Properties
West Indian satinwood is very dense, strong and heavy. It works well with hand tools, though it does have a moderate blunting effect on cutting edges. Machine-planing can be difficult, as the wood is prone to riding on the cutters. It turns excellently, carves very well and can take a very high polish.

Seasoning
It is slow-drying; no further information is available.

Durability
It is generally not durable, but is resistant to dry-wood termite attack. Its typical uses do not require preservative treatment.

Typical uses
High-quality furniture, turnery, carving, inlays and premium-quality veneers.

Grows
Caribbean and southern Florida, USA
Typical height: 40ft (12m)
Trunk diameter: 15–20in (0.4–0.5m)

⚠ **Possible health risks**
Dermatitis, giddiness, nausea, lethargy, visual disturbances

ADDITIONAL WOODS IN BRIEF

Name	Grows	Specific gravity	Properties
Subalpine fir *Abies casiocarpa*	Canada and USA	.32	Works fairly well
Californian red fir *Abies magnifica*	USA	.38	Works well
Japanese fir *Abies mariesii*	Japan	.42	Works easily
Raspberry jam wood *Acacia acuminata*	Australia	1.04	Works to a high finish
Mulga *Acacia aneura*	Australia	1.10	Reasonably easy to work
Black wattle *Acacia auriculiformis*	Australia, Papua New Guinea, Indonesia	.67	Works reasonably easily
Gidgee *Acacia cambagei*	Australia	1.20	Hard, but works to a good finish
Brigalow *Acacia harpophylla*	Australia	1.00	Moderately difficult to work
Sen *Acanthopanax ricinofolius*	China, Japan, Sri Lanka	.56	Works easily
Vanuatu blackwood *Adenanthera pavonia*	Vanuatu	.86	Works fairly easily
East Indian kauri *Agathis dammara*	South-East Asia, Philippines	.55	Works easily
West African albizia *Albizia ferruginea*	Tropical West Africa	.64	Works very well
Yellow siris *Albizia xanthoxylon*	Queensland, Australia	.41	Works easily
Haiari *Alexa imperatricis*	Brazil, Guyana, Surinam and Venezuela	.44	Works well
Forest oak *Allocasuarina torulosa* (syn. *Casuarina torulosa*)	Australia	.96	Works relatively easily Not a true oak
Espavé *Anacardium excelsum*	Latin America	.45	Works reasonably well
Curupay *Anadenanthera macrocarpa* (syn. *Piptadenia macrocarpa*)	Brazil	1.05	Works well
Aningeria *Aningeria* spp.	West and East Africa	.54	Works fairly well
Kaatoan bangkal *Anthocephalus chinensis*	Philippines, Indonesia, India	.40	Works relatively easily
Antiaris *Antiaris toxicaria*	West, Central and East Africa	.43	Works easily
Duru *Apeiba aspera*	Latin America	.25	Fairly difficult to work
Red lancewood *Archidendropsis basaltica*	Queensland, Australia	1.20	Fairly difficult to work
Pawpaw *Asimina triloba*	Canada and USA	.43	Works well
Araracanga *Aspidosperma desmanthum*	Latin America	.80	Works easily
Blackheart sassafras *Atherospermum moschatum*	Australia	.65	Works easily

Name	Grows	Specific gravity	Properties
Moabi *Baillonella toxisperma*	Nigeria and Gabon	.80	Works fairly easily
Tawa *Beilschmiedia tawa*	New Zealand	.73	Works moderately well
Berlinia *Berlinia* spp.	Tropical West Africa	.72	Works moderately well
Brazilnut *Bertholletia excelsa*	Amazon	.59	Works well
Sweet birch *Betula lenta*	Canada and USA	.60	Works well
Japanese birch *Betula maximowicziana*	China and Japan	.67	Works well
Bishopwood *Bischofia javanica*	Oceania and South-East Asia	.56	Works well
Pochote *Bombacopsis quinata*	Latin America	.50	Works well
Alone *Bombax brevicuspe*	West Africa, South America, southern Asia	.55	Works easily
Okwen *Brachystegia* spp.	West Africa	.62	Difficult to work
Capomo *Brosimum alicastrum*	Central and South America	.85	Works well
Satiné *Brosimum rubescens*	Brazil, Peru, Venezuela	1.01	Works fairly easily
Cocuswood *Brya ebenus*	Cuba and Jamaica	.90	Works well
Yellow sanders *Buchenavia capitata*	Latin America	.66	Works reasonably well
Jucaro *Bucida buceras*	Caribbean	1.00	Difficult to work
Verawood (Maracaibo lignum vitae) *Bulnesia arborea*	Colombia and Venezuela	1.00	Works like soft metal
Palo santo *Bulnesia sarmientoi*	Argentina and Paraguay	1.10	Works satisfactorily
Serrette *Byrsonima coriacea*	Latin America	.76	Works moderately well
Cangerana *Cabralea cangerana*	Argentina, Brazil, Paraguay, Uruguay	.55	Works well
Rose alder *Caldcluvia australiensis*	Australia	.60	Works moderately easily
White cypress pine *Callitris glauca*	Australia	.68	Moderately hard to work
Genero lemonwood *Calycophyllum multiflorum*	Central and South America	.86	Works well
Sajo *Campnosperma panamensis*	Latin America	.38	Works easily
Cananga *Canangium odoratum*	Oceania and South-East Asia	.30	Works well
Crabwood (Andiroba) *Carapa guianensis*	Central and South America	.64	Works moderately well
Jequitibá *Cariniana pyriformis*	Brazil, Colombia, Venezuela	.58	Works well

Name	Grows	Specific gravity	Properties
American hornbeam *Carpinus caroliniana*	Canada and USA	.58	Works moderately well
Piqui *Caryocar villosum*	Latin America	.84.	Moderately difficult to work
Giant chinkapin *Castanopsis chrysophylla*	North America	.48	Works well
Northern catalpa *Catalpa speciosa*	Canada and USA	.38	Works easily
Trumpetwood *Cecropia peltata*	South America	.30	Works reasonably well
Acajou rouge *Cedrela huberi*	Latin America	.41	Works easily
Spanish cedar *Cedrela odorata*	Central and South America	.40	Works easily
Canarywood *Centrolobium* spp. (many species)	Central and northern South America	.65	Works easily
Arariba *Centrolobium ochroxylon*	Brazil	.85	Works easily
Katsura *Cercidiphyllum japonicum*	Japan	.47	Works very easily
Fustic *Chlorophora tinctoria*	West Indies and South America	.92	Works well
Camphor laurel *Cinnamomum camphora*	Australia, South-East Asia, Japan	.64	Works well
Coconut *Cocos nucifera*	Tropics worldwide	.56	Works satisfactorily
Esia *Combretodendron macrocarpum*	Tropical West Africa	.80	Difficult to work
Etimoé *Copaifera salikounda*	West Africa	.77	Works fairly easily
West African cordia *Cordia abyssinica*	Nigeria, Kenya, Tanzania	.43	Works easily
Light American cordia *Cordia alliodora*	West Indies, tropical South America	.55	Works easily
Cow tree *Couma macrocarpa*	South America	.61	Works well
Capa de tabaco *Couratari guianensis*	South America	.70	Works fairly well
Bolly silkwood *Cryptocarya oblata*	Queensland, Australia	.56	Works easily
Sugi *Cryptomeria japonica*	Japan and Taiwan	.40	Works moderately well
Muhimbi *Cynometra alexandri*	Central and East Africa	.90	Difficult to work
Kahikatea *Dacrycarpus dacrydioides* (syn. *Podocarpus dacrydioides*)	New Zealand	.46	Works easily
Flamewood *Dalbergia cochinchinensis*	South-East Asia	.82	Works moderately well
Ogea *Daniellia ogea*	West Africa	.50	Works easily
Northern sassafras *Daphnandra dielsii*	Queensland, Australia	.60	Works fairly easily

Name	Grows	Specific gravity	Properties
Angelica tree *Dendropanax arboreus*	Central and South America	.50	Works easily
Morototo *Didymopanax morototoni*	Central and South America	.55	Works moderately well
Gabon ebony *Diospyros dendo*	West Africa	.82	Hard, but works well
Kaki *Diospyros kaki*	China and Japan	.83	Works moderately well
Marblewood *Diospyros marmorata*	Andaman Islands	1.03	Difficult to work
Keruing *Dipterocarpus* spp. (many species)	South-East Asia, Philippines, Malaysia, India	.82	Works satisfactorily
Tonka *Dipteryx odorata*	Northern South America	.90	Difficult to work
Paldao *Dracontomelum dao*	Philippines	.74	Works easily
Kapur *Dryobalanops* spp.	Indonesia, Malaysia, South-East Asia	.77	Works well
Lampati *Duabanga sonneratioides*	Burma (Myanmar), India, Indonesia	.41	Works easily
New South Wales scented rosewood *Dysoxylum fraseranum*	New South Wales, Australia	.72	Works easily. Also known as NSW rose mahogany
Miva mahogany *Dysoxylum muelleri*	Australia	.67	Works easily
Brown quangdong *Elaeocarpus coorangooloo*	Queensland, Australia	.60	Works fairly easily
White quangdong *Elaeocarpus grandis*	Queensland, Australia	.50	Works easily
Kauvula *Endospermum medullosum*	Papua New Guinea	.44	Works easily
Omu *Entandrophragma candollei*	West Africa	.64	Works well
Timbauba *Enterolobium schomburgkii*	South America	1.00	Fairly difficult to work
Jaboty *Erisma uncinatum*	Northern South America	.55	Works well
Poplar gum *Eucalyptus alba*	Oceania and South-East Asia	.91	Fairly difficult to work
Australian white ash *Eucalyptus fraxinoides*	New South Wales	.69	Works well. Not a true ash
Blue gum *Eucalyptus globulus*	Australia and Hawaii	.80	Works moderately well
White-topped box *Eucalyptus quadrangulata*	Western Australia	.99	Fairly difficult to work. Not a true boxwood
Ulmo *Eucryphia cordifolia*	Argentina and Chile	.48	Works well
Water gum *Eugenia* spp.	Malaysia and Papua New Guinea	.77	Works fairly easily
Pau amarello *Euxylophora paraensis*	Brazil	.80	Works well
Japanese beech *Fagus crenata*	Japan	.62	Works satisfactorily

Name	Grows	Specific gravity	Properties
Fitzroy cypress *Fitzroya cupressoides*	Argentina, Chile	.48	Works easily
Jagua *Genipa americana*	Central and South America	.66	Works well
Ginkgo *Ginkgo biloba*	China	.40	Works well
Mutenye *Guibourtia arnoldiana*	Tropical West and Central Africa	.88	Works well
Copaiba *Guibourtia langsdorfii*	Brazil	.80	Works well
Red chacate *Guibourtia schliebenii*	Brazil	1.15	Works well
Oysterwood *Gymnanthes lucida*	Caribbean and Brazil	.88	Works well
Leche perra *Helicostylis tomentosa*	Brazil	.68	Fair to good
Rubbertree (rubberwood) *Hevea brasiliensis*	Amazon, South-East Asia, West Africa	.49	Works easily
Blue mahoe *Hibiscus elatus*	Caribbean, Peru, Brazil	.62	Works easily
Hura possumwood *Hura crepitans*	Latin America	.35	Quite difficult to work
Kirikawa (marakaipo) *Iryanthera* spp.	Brazil, Colombia	.35–.57	Works well
South American walnut *Juglans neotropica*	Argentina, Colombia, Mexico, Peru, Venezuela	.65	Works easily
Ashe juniper *Juniperus ashei*	USA and Mexico	.65	Works fairly easily
Kempas *Koompassia malaccensis*	Indonesia and Malaysia	.88	Works reasonably well
Tea tree *Leptospermum scoparium*	Australia and New Zealand	.83	Fairly difficult to work
Bombanga *Macrolobium coeruleoides*	Tropical West Africa	.61	Works easily
Cucumber tree *Magnolia acuminata*	Eastern USA	.44	Works well
Oboto *Mammea africana*	West Africa	.62	Works moderately well
Mango *Mangifera indica*	Many tropical areas	.52	Works moderately well
Massaranduba (bulletwood) *Manilkara bidentata*	West Indies and Central America	.85	Moderately difficult to work. NB: Many other species are known as 'bulletwood'
Sapodilla *Manilkara zapota*	Caribbean	.84	Difficult to work
Carne d'anta *Maytenus* spp.	Tropical America	.70	Works satisfactorily
Rengas *Melanorrhoea curtisii*	Malaysia, Philippines, Papua New Guinea	.83	Works moderately well
Breadtree *Melia azedarach*	Oceania and South-East Asia	.55	Works well, but surface can be woolly

Name	Grows	Specific gravity	Properties
Chechem *Metopium brownei*	Caribbean	.68	Hard but workable
Grumixava *Micropholis guianensis*	Latin America	.75	Hard; rated as easy to moderately difficult to work
Manwood *Minquartia guianensis*	Central and South America	.91	Very hard
Balsamo *Myroxylon balsamum*	Central and South America	.78	Moderately difficult to work
Louro preto *Nectandra mollis*	Brazil	.70	Works well
Danta *Nesogordonia papaverifera*	West Africa	.74	Works moderately well
Coigue *Nothofagus dombeyi*	Chile and Argentina	.49	Works fairly easily
Antarctic beech *Nothofagus moorei*	Australia	.77	Moderately difficult to work
Rauli *Nothofagus procera*	Chile	.54	Works well
Water tupelo *Nyssa aquatica*	USA	.50	Fairly difficult to work
East African camphorwood *Ocotea usambarensis*	Kenya and Tanzania	.59	Works easily
Lancewood *Oxandra lanceolata*	Caribbean	.81	Hard but works well
Tchitola *Oxystigma oxyphyllum*	West Africa	.61	Works satisfactorily
Nyatoh *Palaquium* spp.	Malaysia and South-East Asia	.67	Works moderately well
Beli *Paraberlinia bifoliolata*	Tropical West Africa	.80	Works fairly well
Angico *Parapiptadenia rigida*	Brazil	.95	Works well
Red siris *Paraserianthes toona* (syn. *Albizia toona*)	Australia	.72	Works easily
Japanese spruce *Picea jezoensis*	Japan	.43	Works easily
Black spruce *Picea mariana*	Canada and USA	.38	Works well
Red spruce *Picea rubens*	Canada and USA	.37	Works easily
Bristlecone pine *Pinus aristata*	USA	.46	Works moderately easily
Caribbean pine *Pinus caribaea*	Caribbean	.50	Works easily
Japanese red pine *Pinus densiflora*	Japan	.40	Works easily
Table Mountain pine *Pinus pungens*	Eastern USA	.49	Fairly difficult to work
Siberian yellow pine *Pinus sibirica*	Siberia and Manchuria	.42	Works easily

Name	Grows	Specific gravity	Properties
Dahoma *Piptadeniastrum africanum*	Tropical West, Central and East Africa	.69	Works moderately well
Podo *Podocarpus* spp.	South and East Africa	.51	Works easily
Amunu *Podocarpus neriifolia*	Oceania and South-East Asia	.51	Works well
Totara *Podocarpus totara*	New Zealand	.43	Works easily
Taun *Pometia pinnata*	South Pacific	.70	Works well
Cativo *Prioria copaifera*	Jamaica and Central America	.40	Fairly difficult to work
Carbonero *Pseudopiptadenia pittieri* (syn. *Piptadenia pittieri*)	Venezuela, Colombia	.62	Fair to good
Amendoim *Pterogyne nitens*	Argentina, Brazil, Paraguay	.80	Works well
Arkansas oak *Quercus arkansana*	South-eastern USA	.55	Works well
Swamp white oak *Quercus bicolor*	Canada and USA	.71	Works well
Scarlet oak *Quercus coccinea*	Canada and USA	.61	Works well
Oregon white oak *Quercus garryanna*	Canada and USA	.72	Works well
Live oak *Quercus virginiana*	Eastern USA	.80	Very hard to work
Mangrove *Rhizophora mangle*	South-eastern USA, Latin America	.89	Difficult to work
Sandalwood *Santalum album*	India	.75	Works very well
Australian white birch *Schizomeria ovata*	Australia, Papua New Guinea	.61	Works easily. Not a true birch
Odoko *Scottellia* spp.	West Africa	.62	Works fairly easily
Akossika *Scottellia chevalieri*	Tropical West Africa	.62	Works well
Giant sequoia *Sequoiadendron giganteum*	California	.29	Works easily
Balau *Shorea* spp.	Malaysia	.93	Moderately difficult to work
Meranti *Shorea* spp. (many species)	Malaysia, Sarawak, Brunei, Philippines	.67	Works well
Sepetir *Sindora* spp.	South-East Asia	.67	Fairly difficult to work
Yellow carabeen *Sloanea woollsii*	Australia	.45–.72	Works relatively easily
Sophora *Sophora japonica*, *S. tetraptera*	China, Japan, New Zealand	.68	Works easily
Hoeboe *Spondias mombin*	Latin America and Africa	.48	Works well
Brown sterculia *Sterculia rhinopetala*	West Africa	.82	Works moderately well

Name	Grows	Specific gravity	Properties
Chewstick *Symphonia globulifera*	Africa, Central and South America	.68	Works well
White hazelwood *Symplocos stawellii*	Australia	.60	Works easily
Tamarind *Tamarindus indica*	Many tropical areas	.90	Difficult to work
Red tulip oak *Tarrietia argyrodendron*	Queensland, Australia	.85	Works satisfactorily
Niangon *Tarrietia utilis*	West Africa	.56	Fairly difficult to work
Nargusta *Terminalia amazonia*	Central and South America	.80	Fairly difficult to work
Indian silver greywood *Terminalia bialata*	Andaman Islands	.67	Works easily
Indian almond *Terminalia catappa*	India	.65	Fairly difficult to work
Izombe *Testulea gabonensis*	Gabon	.80	Works easily
Calantas *Toona calantas*	Philippines	.44	Works well
Long John *Triplaris surinamensis*	Latin America	.70	Works well
Brush box *Tristania conferta*	Australia	.9	Difficult to work
Japanese hemlock *Tsuga sieboldii*	Japan	.47	Works well
Smooth-leaved elm *Ulmus carpinifolia*	Europe	.58	Works reasonably easily
Cedar elm *Ulmus crassifolia*	Southern USA	.59	Difficult to work
Wacapou *Vouacapoua americana*	Brazil, Guyana, Peru	.93	Difficult to work
New Guinea boxwood *Xanthophyllum papuanum*	Oceania and South-East Asia	.75	Difficult to work due to high silica content. Not a true boxwood
Keyaki *Zelkova serrata, Z. carpinifolia*	China, Japan, Iran	.62	Works well
Ébano *Ziziphus thyrsiflora*	Ecuador and Peru	.78	Works well

About the author

Terry Porter was born and raised in Cambridge, England. His lifelong interest in wood, and working with wood, was instilled in him from an early age by his father. Terry spent many years as a teacher and examiner in English as a Foreign Language, both in Britain and abroad. During this period he took up woodturning, which furthered his interest in wood, and particularly in the many different species suitable for turning. Combining his skills in woodwork, photography and writing, he went on to write many articles on woodwork. His period as editor of GMC's *Woodturning* magazine gave him a deeper interest in 'woody' matters and the world of woodworking. He now works as a freelance writer, and is a regular contributor to woodworking magazines.

Acknowledgements

I would like to thank my editor, Stephen Haynes, who was so helpful, supportive, knowledgeable and good-humoured at all times during the writing of this book. The publishers and I would also like to thank all those who kindly made wood samples available for photography, or assisted in tracking down the species required. Several members of the International Wood Collectors Society (www.woodcollectors.org) gave invaluable help, notably Ken Southall (first and foremost), Alan Curtis, Gary Green, Ed Carter and Ernie Ives. Thanks also to Windsor-chair maker James Mursell; to Mark Baker, former editor of *Woodturning* magazine; to Paul Richardson, formerly publisher at GMC Publications; and to Covers of Lewes. Special thanks are due to Ann Biggs for her splendid botanical illustrations.

The editor and author extend a general 'thank you' to all those who expressed a willingness to help, though in the event not all these offers could be taken up. We are grateful also to those who kindly gave permission for photographs of their work to be included. A final note of thanks should go to Professor John MacLeod, Royal Horticultural Society Professor of Horticulture, for his advice on plant physiology and taxonomy.

Illustrators
Pages 7-32 Simon Rodway
Botanical illustrations Ann Biggs

Makers
David Allaway (pp. 103, 226), Mark Baker (4 L, 18 R, 39, 41, 47, 68 R, 85, 88, 124, 170, 185 btm, 207 btm, 210, 230, 234, 243), Arthur & Rachel Cadman (214, 224 R), Seamus Cassidy (52), Robert Chapman (143), Nigel Churchouse (105), Jane Cleal (108), John Cousen (185 R), Colin Eden-Eadon (253), Adrian Foote (des. John Makepeace) (245 top L), Frank Fox-Wilson (5, 136, 151 R, 155, 174, 216), Catherine Haynes (designer) (112), Stephen Haynes (58, 112, 129 top mid, 183, 194), John Hunnex (44, 106, 120, 134 R, 221), Robert Ingham (38 mid, 60, 101, 113, 175 R), Richard Jones (207 R), Brian Jordan (71), Richard Kennedy (260), Philip Koomen (38 R), James Krenov (218), Andrew Lawton (191, 215), Kevin Ley (135, 150 L, 264), Peter Lloyd (4 R, 43, 68 btm, 131 btm, 150 btm, 244 btm), John Makepeace (designer) (245 top L), Bert Marsh (46, 96, 104, 118 btm, 175 btm, 219, 266), James Mursell (262), Rupert Newman/Westwind Oak Buildings (225 top L), Tim O'Rourke (129 top R), Wayne Petrie (118 top R), Terry Porter (21 L, 75 btm, 225 top R, 233), Paul Richardson (228, 238, 268), Mark Ripley (18 L, 134 btm), Cynthia Rogers (254), Andrew Skelton (24 R), David Springett (245 btm), Richard Stevenson (244 R), Chris Stott (1, 61, 62, 67, 76, 102, 121, 147 btm, 153, 168, 173, 190, 192), Ian Thompson (251), Andrew Varah (147 R), Alison Ward (119 R), Gordon Wight (45), Frederick Wilbur (98), Sara Wilkinson (223 btm, 255), Richard Williams (107), Alex Willis (23 L).

Photographic credits
All photographs of wood samples except p. 83 are by Anthony Bailey, © GMC Publications Ltd 2006. Other photographs are by Anthony Bailey with the following exceptions:

David Allaway (pp. 103, 226), American Hardwood Export Council (83 top L), Craig Brown (107), Arthur Cadman (214, 224 R), Manny Cefai (18 L), Robert Chapman (143), Nigel Churchouse (105), Jane Cleal (108), Martin Fisher (253), Stephen Haynes (10, 16 top R, 19, 23 R, 25 L, 38 L, 58, 68 L, 75 R, 98, 109, 112, 119 top, 129 top L, top mid and btm, 131 R, 134 L, 141, 183, 185 R, 194, 196 btm L and R, 197, 223 R, 224 mid L and btm L, 225 btm, 245 top R and btm, 260 trees), Stephen Hepworth (24 R), Alan Holtham (17 top L), John Hunnex (44, 106, 120, 134 R, 221), Robert Ingham (38 mid, 60, 101, 113, 175 R), Richard Jones (207 R), Brian Jordan (71), Richard Kennedy (260 desk), Andrew Lawton (191, 215), Kevin Ley (135, 150 L, 214, 224 R, 264), Phil Morash (9), Francis Morrin (52), Rebecca Mothersole (196 mid), Mike Murless (245 top L), Tim O'Rourke (129 top R), Gilda Pacitti (leaves, pp. 38, 68, 118, 129, 134, 196, 224, 244, 260), Terry Porter (13, 21 L, 75 btm), Edward Reeves (278), Paul Richardson (268), Steven Russell (83 btm L and R), David Smith (38 R, 134 btm), Sterling Publishing (218), Richard Stevenson (244 R), Andrew Varah (147), Rod & Alison Wales (118 top R, 119 R), Gordon Wight (45).

Index of common names

Index of botanical names

To request a full catalogue of GMC titles, please contact:

GMC Publications, Castle Place, 166 High Street, Lewes, East Sussex BN7 1XU, United Kingdom
Tel: 01273 488005 Fax: 01273 402866
www.gmcbooks.com